WRITTEN BY: ROBIN ROTH

Illustrated By: Aimee Goren

Copyright © 2022 by Robin Roth
All rights reserved.

Robinrothreporter.com
Robinrothentertainer.net

ISBN: 979-8-9854012-0-2 (hardback)
      979-8-9854012-1-9 (paperback)
      979-8-9854012-2-6 (ebook)

Illustrations by Aimee Goren
Book Design by TeaBerryCreative.com

IMPORTANT DISCLAIMER, WAIVER AND RELEASE OF RIGHTS

Disclaimer

The Expressed views, opinions, suggestions and advice written in "HEART TO BUMP CONVERSATIONS" were generated purely and solely for entertainment value and should not be relied upon at all. NEITHER Robin Roth, the Author, Publisher, Distributor(s), Retailer(s), nor anyone else involved with the writing, preparation, dissemination or sale or otherwise of this Book is responsible for any negative consequences of any kind whatsoever in the event anyone relies on any opinions or advice set out in the Book. ABSOLUTELY NONE of the advice or opinions has been subject to any kind of scientific, professional, federal, state or local governmental or agency review, of any kind whatsoever and has not been approved by any person or entity. It is not even known whether any professional, medical, financial or even competent person has read the Book.

Waiver

Anyone who takes any action based on any opinion, suggestion, thought or any statement of any kind in this Book does so entirely "AT YOUR OWN RISK".

This Book is first and foremost written for entertainment, not to provide any actual advice whether medical, financial, health or otherwise. The Book is simply the experience of the Author written for entertainment purposes and NOT to be taken as a serious, proven basis for any action by the Reader.

Neither Robin Roth (the Author), Publisher, Distributor(s), Retailer(s), nor anyone else involved with the writing, preparation, dissemination or sale or otherwise of this Book (collectively, the "Book Originators") will be held liable or responsible for any actual or perceived loss or damage of any kind whatsoever caused or alleged to have been caused Directly or Indirectly by anything in this Book, including, without limitation, actual, compensatory, incidental, consequential, nominal. punitive or any other kind of damage whatsoever. THE READER AND ON BEHALF OF ITS HEIRS, SUCCESSORS AND ASSIGNS SPECIFICALLY WAIVES ANY AND ALL RIGHTS OF EVERY NATURE AND SORT WHATSOEVER TO ASSERT ANY CLAIM AGAINST ANY OF THE FOREGOING PERSONS OR ENTITIES IN ALL RESPECTS WHETHER SUCH CLAIM ARISES NOW OR HEREAFTER OR IS NOW KNOWN OR IS UNKNOWN.

Release In Full Of Rights

In consideration of the writing, preparation costs arising from the Publishing. Disseminating and other related costs of the Book and other good and valuable consideration, the Reader and any heirs, successors and assigns irrevocably and unconditionally, fully and forever, release discharge and relinquish and agree to hold harmless the Book Originators, collectively and individually, each of their predecessors and their respective officers, directors, employees, agents, representatives, successors and assigns (hereinafter collectively referred to as the "Releasees") from all actions, claims, causes of action, suits, liabilities or obligations of any kind whatsoever in law or in equity, that now exist or may hereafter accrue based on matters now unknown as well as known, and matters unanticipated as well as anticipated, which the Reader and its heirs successors and assigns can, shall or may have against the Releasees, upon or by reason of any matter or thing set out in the Book occurring from the beginning of time up to the date of this Release.

Each Reader and each of its heirs successors and assigns expressly waives the benefit of any statute or rule of law, which, if applied to this Release, would otherwise exclude from its binding effect any claim not known by such Reader on the date of reading any portion, or being informed by third parties, of any portion of this Book.

The Reader and each of its heirs, successors or assigns further agree not to bring, continue or maintain any claim or legal proceeding against the Releasees before any court, administrative agency or other forum by reason of any matters hereby released.

Each Reader confirms that it (i) understands all aspects of this Disclaimer, Waiver and Release, (ii) has had sufficient time to review it (and with its attorney), (iii) voluntarily agrees to all the terms in this Disclaimer, Waiver and Release; and (iv) voluntarily agrees to be bound by all of the terms of this Disclaimer, Waiver and Release.

This Disclaimer, Waiver and Release shall be binding upon the undersigned and its successors and assigns and shall inure to the benefit of each of the Releasees and their respective successors and assigns. This Release is made and entered into in the State of Nevada and shall be in all respects governed under the laws of said state.

THINK BEFORE YOU BUY.

If you don't accept this DISCLAIMER, WAIVER AND RELEASE IN ALL RESPECTS, THEN PLEASE DO NOT PURCHASE OR READ THIS BOOK.

All Fictional Characters

Any and all Characters referenced in this Book are fictional and do not reference anyone living or deceased. Any similarity of any Character in this Book to any living or deceased Person is purely coincidental.

Author's Dedication...

I dedicate "Heart to Bump Conversations" to my extraordinary daughters, Jennifer and Chloe, who inspired every word. Our special bond created and enhanced all the feelings of love and emotions written in each chapter. My beautiful, talented, hilarious, intelligent girls, you are the center, heart, and soul of my universe. You are the very best part of my life and the most miraculous accomplishment I could ever hope to achieve. I am immensely grateful for the supreme joy, privilege, and honor of being your mom.

I'm exceptionally proud of the spectacular, unique women you have become. Thank you for showing me what it truly means to be a mommy and for literally teaching me how to be one. I appreciate the adorable way you both cleverly taught me to laugh at myself, while you stood firm, giggling directly at me. Your humor is one of my favorite things about you girls. You've filled the places in my heart I didn't even realize were empty before you both came to me. I treasure every single memory, all our happy times, lessons learned, tears, dramas, failures, triumphs, and the tons of endless laughter we have shared throughout the years. You have overflowed my soul with beautiful emotions of heavenly love. The pure love I never understood before you were born. You're the loves of my life and the miracles I had always dreamed of and prayed for. You girls have made my world joyful, blissful, and complete.

My precious Jennifer and Chloe, I also, dedicate this book to your awesome, fantastical children, Jacob and Hadley Devorah, Chaya, Levi, and to all of your children yet to be born, as well as all of their children, and children's children to follow.

I devote this book to my beloved parents, the greatest *mom and dad* who ever lived. You far and away surpassed the parental bar of excellence. My remarkable parents, you will always remain a constant source of guidance and support for me. You are *my forever north,* and I miss you eternally each and every day. You're remembered and cherished more than you'll ever know. I feel incredibly blessed and fortunate to have been raised by such tremendous people. You showed me daily that I was deeply loved, and I am grateful for your luminous gift of devotion. I will love you beyond any words can express, forevermore. Thank you for being the magical, steadfast miracle in my life.

And to Shara, my Best Friend Forever, and Godmother, to my girls…

I thank you for *always* being there for me with your love, wisdom, humor, sarcasm, and guidance. There could never be a more unbelievable, perfect friend than you are to me. You are the sister I chose. Although you hate to hear it, "I love you!" Deal with it!

I also thank the brilliant Aimee Goren for her spectacular works of art. For her endless hours of devotion, vision, spirituality, and support that made this book come to life. Lastly, I dedicate "Heart To Bump Conversations" to all pregnant women, moms, and women hoping for the dream of becoming a mommy. Go for it! You are not alone…

Illustrator's Dedication...

I dedicate this work to my beloved husband, who tirelessly supported me through this journey with immense love. Barry, thank you for all you have done to make our house a home. You have created and brought love, warmth, and happiness to our family. You have overflowed our lives with pure joy.

I also dedicate this work to my brilliant mom, who has always given me her unconditional love and support throughout all my endeavors in life. I will forever love you Mami, unconditionally, and with all my heart.

I am very grateful to have had the opportunity to work with Robin Roth, who is such an extraordinary woman. Thank you, Robin!

AimeeGoren.Author@gmail.com

Table of Contents

1. The Results 1
2. The First Trimester: The Realization 5
3. Panic 9
4. I'm Pregnant? 13
5. Telling Daddy 19
6. Can We Talk? Can You Hear Me? 25
7. Oh No, Wait... Can I Really Do This? 29
8. "Sweetheart, are we Allowed to Have Sex?" 35
9. What, Me? Bitchy? 39
10. The Purest Sounds of Love 45
11. I Very Often Wonder 51
12. I'm Not Emotional...Well, I'm Not! 59
13. On Being a Mommy 63
14. The Second Trimester...We're Showing! 73
15. Ya Just Can't Win! 81
16. You Kicked! 87
17. What Do You Look Like? 91
18. Growing Up Baby 97
19. Gaining Weight... WTF ? 103
20. I'm Not Jealous! Well, I'm Not! 109
21. Maternal Feelings 115
22. Lunch With Colette 121
23. The Rollercoaster of Worries 129
24. A Call From Mommy's Mommy 135

25.	A Call From Daddy's Mommy... 141
26.	About Babies 147
27.	Women Always Know 153
28.	Now I'm the Mommy and You are the Baby 161
29.	Sex… And Pregnancy? 171
30.	Goin' With The Flow 179
31.	Bored? 185
32.	Spoiling a baby? Can That Even Happen? 193
33.	God's Splendid Creation… Grandparents! 199
34.	About Maternity Clothes 205
35.	Just so you know little one, a Mother is: 215
36.	Things I Promise to try, "Never to Say to You!" 225
37.	A Lesson from a Very Bad Dream 231
38.	Whoo-Hoo… The Third Trimester 237
39.	I Mean, Like, How Can a Teeny-Weeny Little Baby Need So Much Stuff Anyway? 245
40.	I Swear To God, I Feel Like a Frickin' Farmer! 251
41.	I Promise I Will Never… 257
42.	All of Your Monumental Milestones and Firsts 265
43.	Natural Childbirth And Other Classes 281
44.	About Daddies 287
45.	Let's Talk Cravings 297
46.	What's in a Name? 303
47.	Selecting the Perfect Pediatrician? 309
48.	There is So Much I Want to Teach You 315
49.	Another one of God's Miracles… Friends! 321
50.	I'm Overdue! Hello? I Said, I am Overdue! 327
51.	The Biggest Challenge of All… 335
52.	A Huge Thank You to Daddy! 343

53. What Mommy for Sure, Knows for Sure!	349
54. Another Call from Daddy's Mommy...	371
55. Another Call from Mommy's Mommy...	375
56. OMG... OMG... Are We in Labor?	379
57. It's Time!!!!	385
58. Our Very Last Conversation Till We Meet	391
59. Labor	397
60. I Made a Wish... and You Were Born!	409

Introduction...

I wrote this book with love, compassion, understanding, and humor for every pregnant woman and all women who have had, or hope to have, a baby. Ladies, you are all extraordinary heroes and God's amazing angelic helpers. Without each one of you, the entire human race would literally not exist. Hence, "You Go Girls!"

Through my writing, I hope to provide women with an outlet to feel safe, normal, and excited about having a baby. My desire was to blend all things concerning pregnancy with sensitivity, fun, and giggles. I wanted to illustrate most of what you are feeling in your own personal universe of pregnancy is common and natural. While you may become lonely or feel as though you're the only woman in the world who ever had a baby, that's very understandable and pretty typical. Pregnancy can bring out many emotions and insecurities, proving, "It's no bed of roses!" This journey you are on can sometimes make any mom-to-be feel pretty isolated. Allow me to say, *"You, are not alone!"* Every woman who ever had a baby has gone through precisely what you are experiencing. While reading "Heart to Bump Conversations," your thoughts, fears, reactions, concerns, worries, doubts, and uncertainties are all revealed, noted, and validated.

Appreciate *you are special, powerful, bold, and astonishingly strong.* You are an amazing superwoman, and all you are enduring makes you spectacular. You must understand this is one of the most unbelievable accomplishments you'll ever fulfill in this life. Hopefully, my book will give you a humorous heads-up on what to expect while expecting, whilst helping you to embrace and enjoy this astounding experience. You just can't compare your pregnancy to anything else you'll ever do or achieve in your lifetime.

Having a baby, bringing life into this world is dazzling and far beyond incredible. FYI, it will help you greatly to be *"in a zone"* where you can appreciate and love every second with happiness and elation. To be honest, this entire process is spiritual, God-like, and divine. Relish each moment, for your energy and spirit lights up the soul of the baby within you. The day your child is born is also the day you'll be reborn. The first time you hold that precious baby in your arms, you'll grasp that you've created a genuine miracle.

If you reflect, as I did, you'll wonder what your existence was really all about before you had a child. A baby, no matter what you did previously, creates purpose, fulfillment, and true meaning to your world. The eternal blessings and joy a child brings are unimaginable. I hope my book fully expresses all the bliss and wonder of giving birth.

Time passes ever so quickly when you have a baby. Therefore, I hope you will cherish every single second your baby is growing inside you and after, being a mom. Don't waste a minute on things that don't matter or aren't important enough to spend precious time on. Trust me, these moments can never be replaced, so treasure them. Enjoy this divine miracle and spectacular journey. Congrats, I wish you the best pregnancy and birth ever!

CHAPTER 1

My heart was pounding out of my chest, and I could hardly breathe. Appreciating I was currently way too hyper to wait a microsecond longer, I nervously telephoned the seven numbers, now etched indelibly in my overly angst-ridden brain...

"Good morning, Dr. Myer's office!"

"Yes, good morning, this is Leona Robins. I'm calling regarding my, my a... Ah! (Breathe, Leona.) I'm calling to find out the results of my, umm, my pregnancy test?"

"Hold please!"

Hold please? Hold Please? Is she kidding me? How the hell could she say that to me? Could she not recognize the immense anxiousness in my trembling, quivering voice? While still holding, I thought, if I could hear the "thump, thump, thump, of my heart," she clearly had to, as well. How casual and uncaring could this woman at my gynecologist's office be? Seriously, lady, I'm about to fall over and faint, so how can I, "Hold Please?" Are you for real? What gall. And, if that weren't enough to make my nerves unravel, I suddenly heard elevator music from the 30s blasting in my ears. Dated, elevator music! *"Back in the saddle again?"* Just great, that's exactly how I got here, to begin with.

With my blood pressure pounding and most likely reaching 190/120 mm Hg, I could barely hear the voice now talking to me on the other end of my cell phone.

"Dr. Myers, speaking. How are you today, Leona? I suppose you are calling about the results of your pregnancy test? Oh darn. Wait a brief moment for me. Hold Please!"

Again? Hold Please? What is wrong with these people? Aren't they embarrassed? Have they no compassion? Are they that desensitized, reporting pregnancy results to frantic, wanna-be moms? And why was he speaking in slow motion like a Kung Fu film?

"Okey dokey, I'm back. Let me see here now. Let's take a look-see, shall we? Ok. Ah-ha, all right then. As I see it... Oh, gee, wait just a moment, I'll be right back to you!"

THE RESULTS

Really? Wait a moment? I felt myself fuming like an enraged cartoon character.

One more "*Wait a moment,*" this office makes me wait, and this might turn into a crime scene. Roped off barricades, yellow tape and all. Let's just say it won't end well.

"Ok Leona, I'm back now. So sorry about all that, it's such a busy day here."

I wanted to scream, but instead questioned firmly, "Dr. Myers, and? And? And?"

"And... I'm happy to inform you, Leona, that your test is, *Positive! Indeed, you are pregnant!* How exciting. Congratulations to you both! Can you hold, please?"

"CLICK!"

CHAPTER 2

The First Trimester: The Realization

Pregnant! I'm pregnant? With child, expecting, mother-to-be, in the family way, a bun in the oven, knocked-up, and preggers, Oh, My, God, I'm childing?

Gosh, I thought I wanted to be pregnant? I emphatically hoped to be pregnant. But do I really want a baby? Disturbingly, I don't know? I'm not sure now. Maybe I ought to pass? Oh Lord, but it's irreversible. Not the best time, *not* to be sure, I'm thinking. My head was dizzy with insecure emotions. Because I've prayed endlessly for a baby, I was perplexed and shocked that this enormous news seemed to be throwing me for a loop. A big loop, with lots of knots, twists, and spirals. It all seemed entirely surreal and very strange, "You are pregnant!" Perhaps they should have made me "Hold Please," a while longer? Goodness, how is it even possible I'm unsure how I feel? It's insane and hard to fathom. After all, we've been trying to have a baby for so long! Breathe, Leona, breathe.

Ok, for real, who am I kidding? I am sure. Certainly, I'm sure. I am absolutely, surely, sure. But am I ready? Does it even matter if I'm not? Ugh, it sounds so utterly definite and terrifying. "You're pregnant, Ta-Da!" I mean, do I even have the potential to be a good mom? Abruptly, total confusion and chilling doubts came crashing in on me.

Trying to calm down, I quickly remembered as a child, I knew I'd hear those words one day. Now, hearing them in real-time made me grasp, "Girrrl, you are all grown-up now." I was no longer that little *girl*, for I had become a woman. This is the benchmark, making one realize you've become an adult. Talk about scary realizations.

"I'm pregnant. I am pregnant. I am going to have a baby!" As the shock of the news began to wear off, I relaxed, giggled, and could barely contain the glowing smile stretching across my face. This is the coolest thing I'll ever do. I'm bringing life into the world and I'm going to be a mommy. It's unbelievable. I was suddenly excited, coming to terms with the news. Actually, I could hardly wait to tell the world, "I am pregnant!"

THE FIRST TRIMESTER: THE REALIZATION

Sitting at the kitchen table with a half-eaten iced pumpkin scone and a cappuccino (double espresso), I started to baby-dream. Then, the first worry hit me. "Oh no, should I drink this coffee?" Silly, of course, but I felt like the only woman in the entire universe to learn such breaking news, "You're pregnant!" Wow, I am going to be a mommy."

And for the rest of my life, I will always remember those two little words... ... ...

"Hold, Please!"

CHAPTER 3

Panic

Could the test be wrong? It's natural to question? Wait! Perhaps it's a false positive? This sort of thing happens all the time. I most definitely should take it again. Maybe all that *"Hold, Please"* crap was them stalling because they screwed up the test?

Ok yes, true, I am 4 weeks late and I have never been late before in my whole life. Still, it might be wrong? Maybe 4 weeks late is entirely common? Well, theoretically, I could be 6 weeks late. Hmm, possibly even 7? Holy crap! But, I'm not even nauseous? Besides, if I am pregnant, shouldn't I already have a huge, ginormous baby-bump by now? Honestly, it's only a test. I shouldn't be so gullible. Surely, anyone can go from a "B" cup bra to a "double C" overnight. So, I'm swollen? It happens after eating shellfish.

Big deal, what if my nails are long and hard for the first time, ever? So what if my eyes are twinkling, my hair is shiny, and my face is glowing? Big whoop and whatever!

About the 6 pounds I've gained recently? Nothing concrete there either. We've been doing a great deal of socializing and eating out this month. I'll lose it this week.

To be frank, which I always hate being, (don't even like the guy) I don't feel pregnant at all. Not one bit. Perhaps the test was unequivocally wrong. Yes, indeed, it's completely wrong. This is all so ridiculously unnerving. I seriously need to day-drink. I'm opening up a bottle of Riesling and pouring a giant glass at once. Huh, I probably shouldn't? What if the test is accurate? Perfect, I'm entering full terror, panic mode.

As I think about it, my best friend Shara recently took a pregnancy test. It came out positive, and she wasn't even pregnant. In other breaking news, when my friend Zoey took some kind of test, it came out negative when, in fact, she was positive. Oh, wait, that was actually a herpes test. Never mind. My point is, tests are virtually wrong all the time.

If we are going with the science, false positives can occur when one has blood or protein in their urine. Certain drugs, such as tranquilizers, anticonvulsants, hypnotics, and fertility drugs, could cause false-positive results. Granted, I didn't have any of that going on. And anyway, just because I had lots of sex when I was ovulating, also means nothing!

Holy Moly, anxiety, alarm, and fear are seeping and oozing in quickly! "WTF?"

I think the test might be right. Gosh, if that's true, and the test is correct, I have to stop cursing right away. They say the baby can hear everything in the womb. I don't want my baby's first word to be, "F@%^$." Shit! Oops, I mean *shoot*! Chillingly, not cursing will be as hard as giving up wine. On second thought, it's kind of a toss-up. OK, Leona relax. The test *is* correct and it's gonna be great. I'm pregnant. Panic be-gone. Now ooze on out.

Seriously, still, the test could be wrong? But then, why are my boobs this sore? Of course, my period is coming. For sure, I'm just late. Late, just like I said to begin with!

CHAPTER 4

OK... So, it appears I'm a little (a lot) nauseous. And where on earth did this huge, ugly pimple come from? Yikes, all kidding aside, I am terribly nauseous. OOOOH damn, where are the Saltines? More to the point, I need a toilet, and fast!

Wow, so that was totally gross. *I'm clearly pregnant.* Hurray! I think? No, I mean hurray, undoubtedly! In the corners of my mind, I thought about my dad, who is such an amazing, wonderful, naïve man. To this day, he's in major denial and still believes I'm a virgin, even though I'm married. It's magic daddy "Bibbidi-Bobbidi-Boo, I'm pregnant!"

Since I've accepted that I'm indisputably expecting, there are an infinite number of goals I'll soon have to accomplish. There is much to do, and an unlimited amount of decisions to decide upon. Wouldn't you just know it? Right when I finally settled in, able to enjoy my ideal, skinny-jeans weight, and ultimately developed those perfectly toned abs and arm muscles (that everyone seems to envy), I get pregnant. I suppose I'll have to give up my high-impact aerobics, too. Funny, to me, exercising during pregnancy feels like eating kale on my designated cheat day! After training strenuously, forever, perhaps losing my impeccable body won't really be such a big deal? Maybe it won't bother daddy either?

Evidently, that's my anxiety showing its ugly, sarcastic head. Forget all of that nonsense. What about my baby? Will it be normal and healthy? I pray all the antibiotics, wine, antihistamines, and occasional sleeping pills I took don't affect the baby? It's all so troubling. Gosh, what if I accidentally hurt my baby? I must stop all of this negativity at once. Surely, it's not good for the baby. Everything's fine. It's all good, no more worries.

Oh Lord, *"I'm Pregnant!"* As I ponder, being *with child*, I'll need to give up a lot of things, activities, foods, and bad habits. I'll have endless investigating to do. It's like going back to college. I gather this ends any notion of taking up parachuting, kickboxing, or

I'M PREGNANT?

enrolling in X-ray machine or toxic chemicals 101-classes. Science will have to wait.

"I'm Pregnant!" Oh My Gosh, Hamilton... *"This is the womb where it happens!"*

Goodbye wine with dinner. Hello, Perrier with lime. I won't mind at all talking politics and religion with the 75-year-old couple at the next booth while everyone's having fun, drinking, eating, and dancing on tables. I see my "Girls Gone Wild Days" are clearly a thing of the past! Fun is not as important or satisfying as bridging the gap between the generations. I can't believe I'm saying this shit. Oops, stuff. Yep, I'm definitely pregnant.

The worst part of all... It was only 10 months ago I was ecstatic being hired for an extremely terrific, high-profile reporter position. Justifiably, my producer/boss made me vow and promise I wasn't starting a family anytime soon. He needed to rely on me. He also expected and trusted that I would stay with the job for the foreseeable future. To which I assured him completely, "Mr. Reynolds, I promise, nothing like that will happen. Being a journalist is the most important thing in my life and starting a family is not in the cards for a very long time. I am a serious, devoted team player. I will never let you down, Sir. It is truly an honor and privilege to be offered this position at such an esteemed Cable News Network, working by your side, and with this awesome team of professionals."

He replied, "All right then and with that promise, Leona Robins, you are hired! Welcome to the network. You'll be a tremendous asset, as you are a brilliant journalist."

I'm predicting Mr. Reynolds won't find any humor in my exciting news? How will I explain to him, "Sir, I'm pregnant, (10 months into the job) and I'm so sorry for the broken promise about the family that was not in the cards?" Ugh! Could I possibly expect a smile, congrats, or even a maternity leave with pay? Or should I just shrewdly pack my things right away and leave a Post-It on his desk? A few days later, when I explained my situation to Mr. Reynolds, as expected, I was fired. Naturally, he had to be quick on his toes, creating another excuse for canning me. Getting fired for being pregnant wouldn't be socially or ethically correct. The network could be sued for this action. Yet, I did fail him, so I accepted it like a lady. I moved on, knowing something far better was coming.

"I'm Pregnant!"

Massive changes will occur in the *preggo months ahead,* and after birth as well...

No more horseback riding, no more go-cart lessons, or the Indianapolis car racing classes. No more tightrope walking as they did in the circus, rugby, or even mountain climbing. No more zip-lining, bull riding, hell skiing, or having fun diving from the highest board. I mean, I don't do any of that, anyway! It's just nice to know the options were out there.

"I'm Pregnant!"

What about all the birth-plan decisions? I would very much like to try natural childbirth? Sure, I can handle massive pain, using only breathing techniques, along with a designated object to concentrate on, warm caring smiles, and people screaming at me in 4 languages, "You can do this!" No problem, not having any drugs to help me through the long hours of agonizing labor. Heck, if I can handle the pain of family holidays, I most certainly can handle natural childbirth? No biggie, it will be a breeze, a walk in the park? Yet thinking logically, I'm not sure I'm game for the 20-hour-back-labor,

I'M PREGNANT?

natural childbirth, and pain thing? Why? All that screaming, yelling, crying, and for what? And all that is just, daddy!

After the baby is born, I absolutely agree with demand feeding and a demand schedule. I unquestionably feel a mother has every right to demand that her own child eat and sleep when she wants her baby to! After all she went through, she should demand whatever she wants, dammit! Oh, darn it. This no cursing thing may take a while to kick.

Breastfeeding? Well, because it's the thing to do and politically correct (though I'm thinking politics should have no place near my boobs), I assume I'll give that a try. It sounds ideal. It's a natural source of nutrition and a special time for love to be exchanged through a tender bonding experience between mother and child. Not to mention, I hear it helps to lose weight and promotes the uterus to go down quicker. Moreover, let's not forget the lovely perk of enjoying the chance to have huge breasts for another full year.

"I'm Pregnant!" I'm actually, Pregnant! Oh, *but* I'm nauseous, so very nauseous. Where the hell did I put those damn Saltines, which seriously don't work at all? And where is your daddy, little Jake or Beth? I have to tell him already. He doesn't even know that our lives will soon change in every way imaginable. He is going to be so ecstatically excited. *I hope!* I'll know because he scrunches up his nose when he's excited. So cute...

CHAPTER 5

Telling Daddy...

Telling your daddy we are expecting you, little one, will be the most extraordinary memory mommy and daddy will ever know and forever cherish. I decided it would be best to ease into my wonderful news carefully, rather than blurting it all out abruptly. After all, no matter how fabulous the newsflash is, one needs a moment to process *Breaking News*. A brilliant reporter (even one who has been fired) knows about these things. *All right, here goes. Wish me luck, little angel.* "3-2-1... And, We're Live!"

"Muah, kiss. Hug, muah! How was your day, Asherkins, my luv, my *BABY*?"

"Great, but I'm exhausted. We were unusually busy at the hospital the entire day."

"Sorry sweetheart. Anyway, I have something very important to share with you."

"I know about it, honey. The stock market went up, 300 points and the Boston Red Sox won today as well. It's a win-win, wouldn't you say?"

"For sure and yes, very critical news. However, *Baby-cakes*, this is way more important than money or even the Red Sox leading the World Series, winning the game 7 to 6, bottom of the 9th with 2 men out, for the win over The Dodgers."

"Kidding, right? *More Important?* How aloof can you be, my wife, who I adore*!*"

"Come on, Asher sweetheart, please! I'm trying to be serious here for a second."

"All right, I'm sorry. Go ahead. But really L, what's with all the *babykins lingo*?"

"Let it go. Anyway, remember how much we've been making love this month?"

TELLING DADDY...

"I know, right? It's been totally awesome. Care to go again? Sorry, babe! Go on."

"Yes, it's been totally great. However, haven't you noticed anything irregular?"

"No, not really Leona. What do you mean? Honey, what are you talking about?"

"Well, didn't you notice *babykins,* that I haven't asked you to pick up a box of Tampax Pearl extra-strength tampons this month, because I forgot to get them, as usual?"

"Yea? So? You remembered them yourself. And what's with all the *babykins?*"

"Oh come on Asher, don't you notice something different about me? Anything?"

"You cut your hair? Changed your nail polish? New shoes! Wait, are you sick?"

"No, obviously I'm not sick. I'm something else. Seriously Ash, look at me! I've gained weight recently and I'm bloated and tired all the time. There's a reason for this!"

"Of course Leona, we've been overly pigging out and partying this month. You'll lose it. Who cares? I love you just the way you are. You're probably just PMS-ing."

I thought to myself, never a good thing to say to a woman, let alone a hormonal pregnant one. "No, no, I'm not just PMS-ing. Quite far from it, *baby!* Dude, come on? Ok, here's a hint. It begins with the letter 'P,' has 2 syllables with the accent on the first."

"You are playful and perfect. You're my princess? Am I getting close? Leona, spill the beans, already. I'm too tired for games. What the heck are you trying to tell me?"

"I'm... I'm, a... I am... Oh, Ash, I am pregnant! We are going to have a baby! Isn't it fantastic? Together we made a miracle that will soon make us a mommy and daddy."

Judging by the glazed-over, distant, blank look on your daddy's face, little baby, I didn't know whether to be overjoyed or cry. He looked like he was about to faint. I could not detect any emotion whatsoever upon his handsome face. Yes, daddy is totally dreamy looking and impossibly hot. I'll explain more about that to you later on in about 18 years.

"Asher, hello? I'm pregnant! Are you happy? Are you thrilled? Asher, talk to me! What are you thinking? You will love the pitter-patter of little feet around the house. You loved that about dogs, right? Please, say something, anything. I'm freakin' out here."

After seeing tears raining down from your daddy's blue eyes, a crushing bear hug, and a long passionate kiss, he simply walked away? Oh-Ma-God, he hates kids? Not the best time to learn that fact. He's leaving me. It's over. I am now yet another divorce statistic. All righty then, it'll just be you and me kid, all alone. My heart exploded and crashed. No, it'll be fine, little one. I can do this. I'll love you enough for the both of us. I can be your mommy and daddy. Other women do it all the time. I won't disappoint you.

As my terror mounted, I had no other choice but to run after your father, who has let us down so horribly. Hey, he can't do this to us! I won't allow it! No way, no how... My insides were screaming, "Why I oughta!" I flew down the hall to our bedroom and slammed open the door with my fierce, pregnant anger and fury, which in-and-of-itself is something to be reckoned with. Standing there with disappointment mud, dripping down my face, I found your adorable daddy on the phone, calling his parents with our

TELLING DADDY...

exciting, blissful news. He was beaming with unparalleled, wild delight and elation over becoming a dad. "I'm going to be a father. Leona is pregnant! We are having a baby," he bellowed into his cell, with his nose scrunched up. Before I could even sit down, he pulled me onto his lap with effortless love and euphoria, holding me affectionately with glowing pride, jubilation, and happiness. We sat together tickled pink and blue, only calling close family for now. All the while my little sweet baby, your soon-to-be daddy, never stopped crying.

After the calls, we cuddled on our bed for hours. Daddy, the most sensitive, loving man, held me tenderly all night long as if I were a fragile, porcelain china doll.

"Leona, this is the greatest gift imaginable. Can you even visualize holding our baby for the first time? The first hug, the first kiss, the first smile. I don't have the words to express, my luv, just how much I wanted us to have a baby. This is way too exciting to even believe. A baby, our baby, I am beside myself. Sweetheart, I don't care if it's a boy or a girl, and I don't think I really want to know until the day our child is born."

"I think for now I agree with you, honey. Let's see how we feel as we go along."

That is your fantastical daddy, Jason or Andrea. Did you hear how thrilled he was at the thought of you? He is over-the-moon, excited. I knew he would be. But still, Phew!

Since my life-changing Headline *News*, every time I talk about you, daddy's face lights up with a warm, beaming smile as he listens intently. His love and longing for your arrival will grow deeper and stronger with each day that passes. I thought it would be difficult enough for me, but I personally don't know how he is going to last 7

½ more months. Oh, and by the way, Chet or Ada, in other Breaking News... The Boston Red Sox won the baseball World Series and the stock market was down by month's end.

CHAPTER 6

Can We Talk? Can You Hear Me?

Big ask? Who am I talking to? Does this happen to all pregnant women?

I am literally talking out loud to myself? Hmm, this is something I've never done before! What's even scarier? I hear responses! See, this is exactly why I don't like scary movies!

Introspectively, I can't imagine I've been talking to myself, because I definitely sensed and heard answers. If I'm not talking to myself, than who am I talking to out there in the mysterious unknown? Oh, My, Gosh. *It's you!* My sweet baby, I'm speaking to *you!* I've been talking in my outside voice, hoping you heard me. And you did. It's you!

What a charming, lovely notion to be chatting with my unborn child, who I already love so dearly. It's uncanny, for in the solitude of my awareness, I knew with total certainty you heard me. Baby Copperfield, I'm actually aware of your thoughts. I'm convinced you could also feel and catch mine using, I guess, telepathic communication?

Since the day I first found out about you (The "Hold Please," day), I have felt and sensed all of your thoughts. And now, since you've communicated this to me, I know at last with reassurance that you can hear me, too. I love this so much! What an awesome, mind-blowing phenomenon. So cool, being able to share my personal, cozy, special conversations with my unborn child. It is unbelievably miraculous? We can talk, connect, and bond together. It's amazing that we can mentally express everything during the endless months ahead as you grow within me. Our private tête-à-têtes will absolutely help us get through the long months of waiting until the day we finally get to meet each other.

The past few weeks, I thought I was going crazy, only imagining I was picking up on your thoughts. Yoda, I haven't even told daddy yet! How astonishing, not to mention I am quite relieved.

CAN WE TALK? CAN YOU HEAR ME?

Baby Samantha, Endora, Harry Potter, or Houdini, it's clear we have superpowers going on between us. Does this make us clairvoyant or psychic? Are we mind reading? How spiritual and mystical this gift we're secretly experiencing is. Baby Glinda or Merlin, I trust we're sharing what they call extra-sensory-perception (ESP). Or, perhaps it's simply biology, connecting us as one person, as we are sharing one body right now. I hope this marvel-thing will last through our entire pregnancy. And, I whole-heartedly pray I'll get this back, (whatever this is) when you are a typical teenager. That's when you won't share anything with *mom or dad.* So, this secret, clandestine, spying-ish ability would come in handy. I wonder, do all moms-to-be acquire magical superpowers?

Baby Salem or Essex, let's keep our little secret hush-hush for now. Is that ok? You see, here in the world you'll be coming to, they lock people up in funny places when they do and say crazy things. They'll *categorically* think this is one of those crazy things. So, for now... Shhhh! Talk soon through our *"Heart to Bump Conversations" porthole.*

CHAPTER 7

Oh No, Wait... Can I Really Do This?

I'm Now Questioning... Little one, can I actually do this? Sure, I'm talented. But, am I talented enough to be a fantastic mom, "kind of talent?" No doubt, I am creative. But creative enough to compete with the gifted moms with all their fancy arts and Pinterest Crafts activities, artistic ideas, and glue guns. Moms, who never miss a PTA meeting or a bake sale? I'm patient. But am I patient enough to raise a child?

Of course, I'm a loving woman. Without a doubt, this is true. But, loving enough to be there 24/7, selflessly, nonstop for every single baby experience, throughout your life? Forever? It's been said, I'm hilarious, a party to be around, and lots of fun to share almost anything with. But am I fun and entertaining enough for a baby, a toddler, a child, and eventually, (dare I say) a teenager? Oh, lord, a teen? Talk about scaring me to death!

Yes, I'm intelligent and I have my paid-off master's degree to prove it. Yet, am I smart enough to teach and guide you throughout school? I mean, I will humbly admit, I totally cheated the entire year in my geometry class. Points, lines, segments, rays, space, a right triangle, all meant nothing to me, other than a Sci-Fi film or positions when trying to get a tan. Give me a break, a pentagon, vertex, square, plane, or an acute angle? If daddy doesn't help you kid, I'm telling ya now, you're failing math! Geometry is way too out there for me. Jeez, in my world, *a cute angle* is a perfect selfie pose. And, a plane is how I got to spring break and back. Still, don't foolishly take me for a dumb blonde, either!

Mommy is clearly super dope and cool. But am I cool enough not to embarrass you with your friends? I'm sure I'll come in your room singing last decades' dated songs, hearing you scream, "Come on, mom! Get outta my room! Now! I mean it! Get out!"

Oh little Juliet, I know I will absolutely select the most amazing trendy clothes for you. You'll look girly-style-chic. Unless, of course, you are a Collin, and then daddy will definitely want to enter on this. So you know, we have a knack for fashion. "Just sayin."

I'm fairly good at all sports. I can teach you stuff. I know stuff! I think? Maybe? Daddy legitimately knows lots about sports. He once believed he could've been a famous baseball pitcher, had he not broken his arm senior year. However, mommy believes that daddy's story is similar to the tale about the guy claiming he caught the biggest fish in the world but threw it back. But please kid, don't ever tell daddy I compared him to this tale.

Sure, I can set boundaries, be strict, and follow through. Yet, will I be able to look into your innocent, sweet eyes and not cave? Doing so would only lead you to become a spoiled brat? I want to discipline you. Although, I also wish to be a fun, accepting mom.

(I'd like to buy some adjectives.) Will I be playful, caring, giving, whimsical, patient, warm and fuzzy enough to be an incredible mommy? I mean, I was, after all, a Girl Scout, baby Jane. I shamefully admit it was actually my mom who earned all the Girl Scout badges on my sash. Including the sewing badge, she also had to sew on for me because I couldn't sew. Whatever, I looked adorable in the uniform, if that counts for anything?

Baby Jeffrey, will I be strong, rugged, tough, brave, courageous, resourceful, fearless, and considerate enough to be an inspirational mommy for you. Will I be down for the annual Boy Scouts camping trip into the bug-infested, gross wilderness without complaining? OMG, I think I'm in over my head. I could so break a nail or a high heel!

I've been told, after you are born, your life will be my purpose. Contradictory, I have also been warned, that you shouldn't be my "one and only purpose." Confused, for 'they say,' if I do, and you become my entire world, then I won't be guiding nor helping you to become your own independent person. 'They say,' I must let you fail, let you figure things out yourself, and let you make your own mistakes. Whoever "*they*" are, I would like to tell those "*they people,*" it will be an impossibly arduous task for mommy to just stand by and watch you get hurt, go through hard times or disappointing and sad situations. I'll want to shield you from all of that and more. As a worried, overprotective mom, this will be like a stick in my eye. I only promise you, kid, I will play this by ear.

Through the heightened importance of raising you, I understand the routine aspects and tasks of daily life, as a new mom, will bring significant victories to the reality of the most mundane parts of every day. (Little Amanda or Camden, this is an example of a perfect run-on sentence. Teachers hate these!) Regardless, after such a fast-paced, successful career, will those victories be enough for me? Will being a stay-at-home mom be fulfilling or gratifying enough? You deserve the world's best mom. Can I be that for you? Yea, I seriously think I need to stop being so obsessively hard on myself, and chill. Indeed, Elizabeth or Boz, I'm overthinking this and consequently behaving absurdly.

What the heck! *I can do this.* It's a piece of cake. Yes, I can. I know I can, and I will. I might even take a math class or two. How about that? Yes, I must go Zen and hone in my confidence and mommy skills. I have 7 ½ months to brush up on all that entails. I vow to you little Maya or Liam, I will get this right, I promise. And if not, my immense love for you, my world-renowned humor, and unstoppable determination will get us through it all. Should you be afraid? Yeah, probably! I'd be if I were you. Oh, I'm just kidding, Baby Boo. Meanwhile, we'll laugh, giggle, and make fun of everything along our journey together. We'll probably be picking up a lot of broken mommy pieces, now and again. Potentially and conceivably picking up more of the, *"again, parts."* Come on. Give mommy a break. I'm new to this. No worries though, we shall do it till we get it right. It's funny, I'm not sure currently "Who will most likely be teaching who, more?"

One of the most charming, wonderful joys of having a baby is being a part of the miracle, bringing new life into the world. For now, though, we are a part of each other and you live within me, through me, and by me. Please know, I cherish every moment of the gift that is you. Later, when you're born, we shall separate, and you will have your own life. Regardless of the separation of our bodies, my life will always be an intricate part of, and forever amalgamated with, yours. I'll be right by your side, guiding and protecting you.

Oh No, But Wait. Can I Really Do This? To reassure you, sweetheart, you bet I can!

My beloved child, mommy will love you until the day I take my very last breath.

And, Evermore…

CHAPTER 8

"Sweetheart, are we Allowed to Have Sex?"

"*Yo, Asher?* Honestly honey, why are you '*Eye Sexing*' me with your perfect 20/20 '*SexRay*' vision? You are kind of freaking me out. '*SexPlain*,' please."

"I'm not sweetheart, not at all. I do have a question for you, though, but it's really unimportant. I'm only curious. Are we allowed to have sex? No worries at all if we can't! It's only a 'SexPloring' question. I can effortlessly remain celibate for 7-1/2 months, or even more? It won't be a problem at all, luv. If we're not allowed to, I can easily handle it? Darling Leona, you are the only woman I have ever truly loved. You mean the world to me. You took my breath away from the very first moment we met and nothing has changed since. I'm the luckiest man on the planet, for you're going to be the mother of my soon-to-be-born child. The significance of a baby, the magic of our relationship, love, trust, and respect for each other, compared to any 'SexPerience,' is so meaningless and trivial. My gorgeous, amazing wife, I don't think you truly comprehend how much I unconditionally worship, cherish, and adore you. You're the love of my life, 'L'!

That you are carrying our baby, blessing me with a child, and making me a dad is everything I've always dreamed of. Sex at this point is inconsequential. Besides, if we could, it would only be the icing on the cake. And, as you know, I'm not big on the icing. Have you noticed, I always wipe the icing off and only eat the cake? Truly, no problem if we can't have sex. It's A-Okay. Our love story and endless devotion will get me through. Leona, you are the dream. You are the fantasy. Sex, in comparison, is not even a concern. Just being with you is paradise enough for me! Enough, now! I'm going to stop rambling on. I humbly wanted you to know, I am blinded by the angel that is you... And not sex."

"Asher, seriously... This would be a good time to *drop the mic, and walk away!*"

I wanted to end the conversation right there, as my exit line was too damn perfect not to. Yet, I couldn't stop laughing from

"SWEETHEART, ARE WE ALLOWED TO HAVE SEX?"

all daddies' complete, excessive, overkill, and bullshit! Little Caleb or Jayden, this is how grown-ups say, 'full of crap.' Still, LMFAO!

"Ash, you are genuinely the only Rock-Star who ever lived that can't sing or play an instrument. Still, you are my Rock-Star, and yes, '*Sex,*' is totally fine and ironically recommended during the whole pregnancy. Hence, Mr. '*SexPert,*' all systems, are a go."

"Oh, Leona, thank you! Thank you, God! Sweetheart, I don't know how I ever could have survived being without you and our passion for an endless, 7-1/2 months!"

Then, mommy fell into daddy's loving arms. We made love, laughed, and sexed again...

CHAPTER 9

Why is everyone now accusing me of being bitchy? I'm bitchy? I must say, I'm rather tired of hearing that. I'm not frickin,' bitchy! Well, I'm not, dammit! Not even one little drop. Bitchy is arguably the most evil, hateful, nasty word. A word, confused so often with self-confidence. I question, why if a man is tough, demanding, or strong, he's brilliant? But a woman, she's bitchy? I'm only reporting the news. It's what I do. Ok, did.

ROBIN ROTH

Here are some actual, "Not Bitchy" examples:

Any normal woman would get angry or irritated if her husband called from his fulfilling, rewarding work, placating her daily with, "Are you having a nice day, honey?"

For God's sake, that is so absurd. Let's review: They fired me from my amazing job for not being a team player because I was having a baby. I'm home alone, pregnant, bored, fat, nauseous, and dealing with a million arduous things to become baby prepared. Bitchy?

And why shouldn't I be annoyed when I sent daddy to the store, he brought home 2 broken eggs out of 6, and nonfat milk due to expire in 2 days? And, it *wasn't nonfat!*

Furthermore, and get this, he brought Charmin toilet paper home instead of Ultra Plush Quilted Northern. I'm supposed to be okay with that? Charmin, baby! Charmin?

Oh, and this just in... When last week, for no reason at all, mind you, your daddy brought home an enormous bouquet of roses. For no reason! No reason at all! Like really, I'm not supposed to be suspicious about 24 random roses? A bit busted. Bitchy, indeed!

So, what? Snapping and yelling at my mom was entirely not bitchy. All I asked her to do was to please put some gas in my car. She then filled up my supreme gas tank with diesel-unleaded. Come on, wouldn't anyone yell? I was upset. Yelling was befitting.

It was also, *not bitchy*, little Amy or Joseph, when daddy shouted at mommy, (Well, he didn't exactly shout, but he sure looked at me funny) for abusing my credit card privileges and I reacted by vindictively cutting them up into tiny little pieces. Big deal, I bought the latest Louis Vuitton Purse. I simply had to have it. Amy, you get it! Besides, a purse never makes you look fat or pregnant. Anyway,

WHAT, ME? BITCHY?

whoopee-do, I needed clothes and Dior had a huge sale of 5% off. And when does that ever happen? Come on baby Joseph, I wasn't being entirely greedy. I bought daddy underwear, socks, a tie, and other stuff as well. I'm not bitchy! OMG, wait a second? Come to think of it... Perhaps my credit card massacre was a big, miscalculated mistake. Now I don't have any cards. Huge bummer!

Let me also state I did not behave bitchy when I had to stop months of vigorous training for the Boston Marathon, which I had been dreaming of entering for years. Any runner would feel the same way. I was a serious contender, able to run one-and-a-half miles straight, without stopping in only 48 minutes. Back off, I just started. Whateves! So I cried and yelled, and acted like a five-year-old brat for the day. Bitchy? Not at all! That childish conduct proved me to be competitive and sassy, which is a virtue. Also, I had a damn good reason to be disappointed. If I kept training, I know I would've surely placed.

And, what if I got angry when my mother-in-law questioned me at dinner about why I used lean turkey meat and olive oil, instead of the entire bottle of greasy vegetable oil and 100% fatty meat in my stuffed cabbage? The woman went on relentlessly, so I pursed my lips and sent her my incredulous gawk. As she looked me up and down, I swished my hair from side to side, "toss-toss," like in Wicked. I was not bitchy. Mother-in-law played hardball and had it comin'! Whatever, it blew over a month later. Maybe 3.

Meanwhile, giving a total stranger my stone-cold eye roll (my best facial, artistic mime trick), after she tailgated me, wasn't bitchy. Then, after that went down, I changed lanes, and she cut me off driving 30-mph, in the 60-mph *fast lane*. I quickly pulled up to the side of her car and screamed, "The left lane is for passing!" The nasty lady shot me a bird. I diplomatically let it go, acting like a gracious adult. Proving again, I am not bitchy.

I shudder to imagine how one could conceivably think I'm bitchy. While grocery shopping, some weird lady came running up to me and rudely put her hands on our baby bump. Without even asking me! I felt enraged and violated. Anyway, if that wasn't bad enough, the woman looked me straight in the eye, saying, "Oh, sorry, I thought you were pregnant!" Yes, that happened. Mommy raised an eyebrow, (which I haven't plucked in months) and added my perfected amazement of stupidity, slack-jawed, nostril-flair look. It's a noteworthy pose. Alas, I wasn't acting bitchy. I was horrified, furious, and stunned.

We all know what it's like to be ignored. But I mean, ignored and overlooked at Home Depot? All the guy kept saying to me over and over was, "Sorry, I will be with you in a moment." I waited 47 moments on my swollen legs for wallpaper and paint samples. Way too long to be snubbed. Therefore, it wasn't bitchy when I accidentally, *on purpose,* spilled the opened can of purple glitter paint on the floor in the Home Depot Store. It happens? Not bitchy for sure. As for my attitude, yes, possibly malicious, or maybe a tad *Glenn Close-ish* in "Fatal Attraction." A girl has to take control of matters now and then.

I'm pregnant. I needed frozen yogurt. *I needed it!* Daddy drove us to Yogurt-land, which closed 30 seconds before we arrived, at 8:45. They're supposed to stay open until 9:00. Kicking and banging the glass window, screaming, and having a hormonal meltdown are clearly standard behaviors for one in my condition. I was not bitchy. I was pissed off!

WHAT, ME? BITCHY?

And why baby Collin or Alexandria, is daddy always saying these days...

"Let's go out for dinner honey, so you don't have to cook."

"Wow, Asher? So my cooking is no good anymore just because I am preggers? What's the matter, honey-hon-hon? My culinary skills suck, so we have to go out to eat?"

Men... I'll give you bitchy! If you want bitchy, I can totally bring on the bitchy.

Lastly, just to clarify... Literally knocking over the woman at the bakery to grab the last red-velvet cupcake was not bitchy. Not one iota. That, my friend, was *selfish!*

Oh, dear Lord. A spontaneous, horrific, terrifying flashback just came over me.

I have No Credit Cards! This is profoundly a major travesty. It's a nightmare, I say.

I am most definitely going to be *bitchy* about this, and nonstop until daddy replaces them all. In fact, I'm gonna push for a higher limit. Yep, I'm gonna, dammit! Of course, in my scenario, this wouldn't be bitchy in the least, either! I would consider my behavior to be more like a magnificent, colorful cavalcade of passionate gumption and moxie. Not Bitchy!

CHAPTER 10

The Purest Sounds of Love...

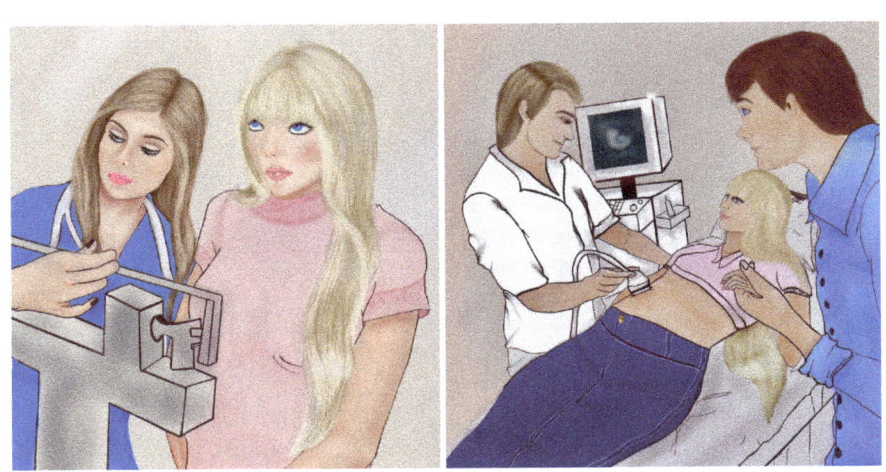

Today, sweet Cleopatra or Mark Antony, daddy, and I went to the doctor's office for our routine prenatal visit. I rang the bell, signed in, and was told to, "Sit Down, Please!" No doubt, the same woman who told me to, "Hold, Please!"

So, there we were, sitting in the waiting room together, staring at all the other pregnant women. You know all of those ridiculous, exaggerated, stereotyped clichés they say about pregnant women?

Well, for the record little precious, they are all accurate. Instead of reading a trashy, mindless, National Enquirer (damn, they were all taken), I spent the time waiting with my uncharacteristic, catty, devil-may-care, sarcastic thoughts.

"Where is that lady's glow? Gee, I thought I was bloated and gained weight! What second-hand shop did that tacky maternity dress from? Wow, talk about pimples and rashes?"

Need I bring up all of those poor husbands in the waiting room, feeling as out of place as a slab of meat in a vegan restaurant? I happily occupied the long wait with great amusement, watching the 6-9 month preggos trying to get up when their names were announced. Some of them literally needed a forklift or possibly a crane to help them up. Oops, hmm, I do believe that was way past catty and actually far into the bitchy category.

This behavior I was enjoying was so unlike me. Regardless, just as it was getting interesting, the nurse called our names… "Leona and Asher Robins, please come on in."

As daddy helped mommy up I thought, wait a second. Why are all the *bumpies* watching me trying to get up? That's not fair, although completely hypocritical! Then, the frisky, beautiful, skinny nurse said, "Jump on the scale." At that moment, I believed her to be the Anti-Christ. I gasped abruptly, "Sorry, nope. No can do. Just jot down I gained a pound."

"Mrs. Robins. It's very important to get weighed in. Please, step on the scale."

I snapped with a cynical lilt, "Yeah, not happening. Perhaps next time, or not?"

After countering me with her resting, dirty-look-face, she placed us in a room. We waited another 30 minutes for the doctor to come

THE PUREST SOUNDS OF LOVE...

in. Finally, Doctor Myers knocked and immediately slid through the door. Embarrassed, I threw down the National Enquirer that just happened to be in the room. He proceeded to do all the usual routine visit procedures.

Having not read all the baby books yet, as daddy and I listened to the comments by the doctor, we appeared rather naïve and unprepared. Shamefully, we virtually had no idea what he was doing, but we were eager and excited as can be if that helped us any.

While daddy (A Dr. himself) appeared nervous, Dr. Myers turned on this rather strange-looking machine and placed something gooey on our, cute as can be, little baby-bump. The Dr. explained, "So now, this gadget here is called a fetal Doppler. It's a hand-held ultrasound device that uses sound waves to hear a fetal heartbeat. You guys ready?"

And, all of a sudden, we heard the breathtaking, unforgettable, miraculous sounds. "Thump... Thump... Thump... Thump... Thump... Thump........... Thump!"

Doc Myers was so darling, rejoicing as if this were a rare and unusual novelty for him.

"There you are, mom and dad. That is your baby's strong, robust, and perfectly healthy heartbeat! I'm happy to report everything looks absolutely fine, dandy, and on target."

Completely humiliating myself, and not caring at all if I did, I cried tears of elation. All I could say over and over again was, "It's a miracle. An astonishing miracle!" Oh, dear little Bonnie or Clyde, Sonny or Cher, listening to your miraculous heart beating was the purest sounds of love and the sweetest sounds of happiness and love I have ever known. The glorious thumping of your heart made our dream a genuine reality. Little Giovanni or Gabby, if we had our doubts before, hearing your heartbeat today proved to us there is a real baby inside of mommy. Until now, it never quite seemed entirely tangible. There was always some apprehensive disbelief until this momentous moment.

To his own surprise, daddy completely lost it. He grabbed me by my now AWOL, long-departed waist, and kissed me madly, yet ever so gently. "Thank you, my beautiful wife. I love you, Leona!" How tremendous, little one, to hear your tiny life within mine. It is the closest sound to heaven. Amidst your beating heart, I sensed your voice, your cry, your laughter, your smile, and your soul. It was stunning to realize you've been able to hear mommy's heartbeat all along. Listening to your heart amazingly awakened mine.

"Oh my gosh Asher, we're really having a baby, this isn't just a silly fantasy." Daddy and I could have listened to your sweet magical heart all afternoon if they would have let us. Sadly, the doctor had to rush off as he had an important appointment to keep. His foursome was already waiting to tee-off on the golf course. It figures...

We left Dr. Myer's office all misty-eyed, sporting an exhilarating smile upon our faces. Although there were around eight other pregnant women in the waiting room as we exited, I couldn't help feeling as if we were the luckiest couple in the world. Then daddy leaned into us, uttering adorably, "You're the most gorgeous, stunning pregnant woman who ever lived. In fact, you should be on the cover of Pregnancy Monthly." Baby Cosmo or Jersey, thrilling experiences tend to make men say ridiculous comments, such as that.

Afterward, at our favorite restaurant, we celebrated the sheer bliss of you. Caught up in our exuberant, euphoric glee, we couldn't stop giggling. Daddy's immense smile of exhilaration (dimples and all) was so huge, it was hard for his face to display it all. You'll

THE PUREST SOUNDS OF LOVE…

be a dazzling chip off the old daddy block. To point out my point, *"Apple, meet tree!"*

Listening to the sounds of your beating heart was the most memorable, touching event daddy and I have ever shared. Being a sentimental, mush-gush, I recorded it on my cell and we played it over and over during lunch. For sure, it's going in the baby book.

Later that evening, passionately cuddling with daddy in our cozy love nest, he spoke with a shaky voice as tears cascaded from his gorgeous, vivid, ocean blue eyes…

"Leona, I am so proud and ecstatic about this gift you are carrying for us. The emotional awe of today made this the most wonderful day of my life. Thank you, luv." And just like that, your daddy always makes me feel like the prettiest girl at the ball.

In my comical mind, mommy thought of so many sarcastic, pretty funny things to reply with. However, I didn't have the heart to break his eternal, touching memory. You absolutely have to love him, and you will. So, baby Brad or Angelina, after the ecstasy of hearing the beat of your heavenly heart, daddy and I will feel its imprinted sounds forever in our hearts. For us, it is the purest sound of love, forevermore…

CHAPTER 11

I Very Often Wonder...

How are you feeling today, sweetness? I don't mean to burden you but... mommy is tired, nauseous, and constantly rushing to the bathroom. Quite embarrassing and challenging for when I sneeze or laugh, I never seem to get there fast enough. My boobs are sore, tender, and I'm constantly suffering from severe headaches. I'm hungry all the time. Ironically, I end up vomiting anyway. Barf, ick, and the status quo, normal. I seem to be forgetting just about everything. Mixed into the bargain, my legs are aching, and I have shortness of breath. Most humbling of all, baby Aladdin or Jasmine, I am continuously farting, and we don't have a dog for which I can blame it on. Anyway, don't worry about me sweetie, mommy will be just fine. Naturally, we'll dive deeper into guilt and passive-aggressive behavior when you get a bit older. That said, enough of mommy's complaining for now. Backing up and speaking of dogs, I suppose you should grow up with one. It's so important. I must put a pin in that. "To do, # 1,995... Look for a puppy."

You know, I have been wondering lately, what does it feel like to be floating around inside of mommy? Obviously, I don't remember. It's been too long since I was floating inside my mommy to have any memory of it. I bet it is awesome in a strange, bizarre way. I presume it's a cuddly, protective, safe, warm, and cozy feeling. I'm optimistic about it. I really hope you're having the happiest fun-in-the-womb-time, ever.

Come to think of it, is all of mommy's moving around making you dizzy or nauseous like I'm feeling? Tweak it. Think of it as jumping around on a trampoline or a bounce house.

How's the food working out for you in there? I am trying my best to eat and drink healthy cuisine for you. I eat spicy now and again, but you seem to like it. I can already tell, you have a sweet tooth. After all, you are my kid. I confess I do miss my junk food, Starbucks, and my vino! Don't be concerned, honey. I'll manage, I hope-I hope-I-hope-a?

I VERY OFTEN WONDER...

Are you comfortable in there? I warn you, it's going to get pretty crowded in a few months. I pray you won't feel too squished. Irrespectively, mommy is quite petite herself, so it will likely get fairly cramped soon. I'm optimistic your baby face isn't being bumped around too much, and you're not feeling overly jostled about while I workout. The Doctor said I could continue exercising since I normally partake in a daily regimen. Please know, I'm being as careful as possible, so you aren't being wildly tossed about in the course of a day. Bang on my belly button door if you're getting squeezed or crushed. Despite that I now eat *a lot,* (cause I'm starving!) I'm still trying to stay fit and trim as long as possible. You see, I don't want to give up on all of my amazing clothes just yet. Don't judge me. Mommy is a 'fashionista,' or I was before I got pregnant. Alas, FYI, maternity clothes are horrific. Feel my Chanel, couture-stylish pain! Much more about fashion later.

It has also crossed my mind whether you enjoy going out everywhere with mommy? Hah... it's not like you have any choice in the matter. Come on, you know you are having fun. Which reminds me, I'm sorry if you are hearing mommy's outrage and unladylike vocabulary. That is called cursing, vulgarity, or swearing. Mommy sorta does a lot of it. Forgive me if it's offending you. I am referring to the type of language you would be so totally grounded for using. I typically use these shocking words towards absurd people who do the dumbest things. Don't get me wrong. I'm a pretty nice person. And, because I am kind, (and a bit of a scaredy-cat), I don't say bad words or get angry with people, to their faces. Most of my ranting is by myself in my car, or at home alone. That's the main purpose of a mute button on the phone. Since I know you can hear me, I don't want you to stress or worry. There's nothing to be concerned about. There are never any brawls, police, yellow tape, ambulances, or danger involved. It ends well in the end.

I am talking about situations such as, and not limited to:

- A person standing in the middle of an escalator, blocking others who might want to pass. Also, hindering people from getting in or out of an elevator. *"F@#$%%*andK!"*
- A person letting the heavy door close right in mommy's face, even when they clearly see I'm pregnant. This is selfish, rude, and uncivilized. Therefore, *"F@#$%%*andK!"*
- A person taking forever ordering in line, then changing their mind 20 times. *"F#@$!"*
- A boorish person leaving their shopping cart in the middle of a great parking spot. This is offensive and self-centered. Put your cart back in the rack, people. *"F@#$%%*andK!"*
- When I'm sitting in a completely empty movie theater and 2 people show up late, then they sit down right in front of me and talk the whole time. *"Totally, F@#$%%*andK!"*
- The driver in front of me texting, not paying attention to the road. *"F@#$%%*andK!"*
- Meeting someone who is always an hour late without calling. *"F@#$%%*andK!"*
- A greedy person sitting next to me on a plane, taking up both armrests and their butt is on my seat, forcing me to contort my body into half of my full-fare seat. *"F@#$%*andK!"*
- Standing in a line and the person behind me is right on top of me, breathing down my neck. *"F@#$%%*andK!"* With a nasty cough, to boot! Scoring a double *"F@#$%*andK!"*

I VERY OFTEN WONDER...

- Someone who inconsiderately goes through the express checkout lane in the grocery store with an overflowing cart filled with 100 items. That deserves a major *"F@#*andK!"*

Baby Carson or Liv, I can come up with examples, all day long. Nevertheless, you get my point? I shall raise you to never do or say any of these selfish type acts. Sadly, though, mommy has a potty mouth about such ill-mannered situations, especially towards strangers. Again, get used to it. It isn't likely to go away anytime soon. But, I'm trying!

So, little Hunter or Bella, since we've already established you can hear me and listen to me talking, sharing our sweet conversations has become extra exciting. I often wonder, though, can you hear other people talking as well? Do you hear daddy? Can you hear the voices of all our friends or even strangers? Do you hear daddy's mommy and daddy? Without a doubt, you'll be able to tell your grandmothers apart. Nuff said for now about that. No concerns, Skylar or Hadley. They are both fabulous? Yes, indeedy, they are? Really, you will love them! We'll talk much more about *lying* later on...

I'm curious, do you feel daddy, hugging mommy? Do you hear us giggling, kissing, and having fun? Oh, no? Do you hear us having S-E-X? Even though the Dr.'s say it's fine to have *sex,* it seems icky and wrong on so many levels. If you do hear us, is it upsetting, troubling, or hurting you? Are you grossed out? If you are, I don't blame you. Being blunt and to keep it honest, if I heard my parents having sex (ewie-ew), it would for sure totally make me gag. You don't know what sex is yet, but I will explain to you, all about it when you are old enough... Like when you're around 30 years old or so.

Since you hear us, you already know that daddy and mommy are very much in love and blissfully happy together. I'm also hopeful you can sense the tender warmth from daddy's hand touching mommy's tummy, trying to feel you? Even though you aren't moving just yet, he still gets such pleasure from it. He already loves you more than words can express. Can you hear him talking and singing to you? Please bear with him. He's not the world's best singer. Truthfully, he's so terrible, but he gets an, 'A' for effort. Though you probably feel more of mommy's love, as we are together 24/7, daddy loves you equally. Because of you, he's excited and giddy all the time, taking endless pictures of mommy, and our bump (us) every week. I find his attention rather cutesy and adorable.

I've often tried to imagine what you know, think, sense, understand, or feel. I wish I knew all that you are going through. Are you frightened, panicked, confused, bewildered, or scared to come into the big new world? A world you know nothing about? You undoubtedly have no idea what is happening, do you? Everything probably seems so random and unfamiliar. Are you aware of anything at all yet? I can't believe you're just a blank slate with no thoughts. I imagine you certainly know more than I think you do. Yet, you cleverly find ways to tell me in our conversations, which all help me to understand.

Are you worried, apprehensive, concerned, or anxious you might not be safe when you are no longer inside mommy? I must admit, I feel all those emotions myself. Do you have any idea what being born is? Does God teach a class and prepare you guys for this before he sends you down to us? Did you get to pick us? Did you choose

I VERY OFTEN WONDER...

your sign? Did you get to select your sex, or what you'll look like? Can you feel our love? Honey, it's so obvious and you must be aware you've got nothing to worry about there.

Do you hear mommy singing to you? I'm not sure what music you like, so I'm mixing it up, just in case. Do you feel me nudging and poking you all the time, hoping to make you move? When you finally start kicking, I am going to make a fun tag game of it.

Little darling, you're going to be a lucky baby, enjoying such a wonderful life. Daddy and I promise we'll do everything in our power to ensure that happens. We are not perfect, (heaven knows) but when it comes to you, we will fiercely strive for perfection.

I smile, imagining what you will be when you grow up. I constantly question, are you a boy or a girl? We don't care, in case you're wondering. We want whatever God has given to us. Although we are only a few months of being *baby-bumped*, you are wanted and cherished more than humanly possible. Daddy and I can barely wait for your arrival. For now though, little one, we have so much to do to get ready. This includes working on curbing my *"F@#$%%*andK,"* rants. I imagine it's going to be a major feat to conquer.

I marvel, thinking about who you are. I wonder about the person you will become. I speculate on how you'll change the world for the better and what you'll do to give back.

My goodness, darling Raevyn or Kohl, I simply cannot stop imagining every single thing there is to know about you. There is no end to my persistent mind, endlessly pondering thoughts of you. I wonder about all that will be in the bright universe of you. And, I will wonder until the heavenly day you are born. Until then, I shall daydream, fantasizing with love and hope. Baby Lilly or Leif, it's so exciting. Let's "Heart to Bump" again soon.

CHAPTER 12

I'm Not Emotional... Well, I'm Not!

Why the heck is everyone, particularly daddy, accusing me of being overly emotional? I'm really not! I'm behaving as normal as always. I'm emotional, just because I was distraught when they preempted, "Big Little Lies, This is Us, Bridgerton and Ozark," all in the same week the British Royals are feuding? Hey, you can't do that to an avid fan.

Any good cook cries hysterically on the produce manager's shoulder if there's no fresh tarragon and garlic for the Russian stroganoff I was making that night for company.

Take me to court, so I also broke down and cried when they took the baby fresh softener out of my favorite detergent. I bet many women like feeling fresh, and cried too.

Emotional? I'm emotional just because I furiously held up the express line at the store, when the checkout girl refused to accept my 35-cent off coupon, and for having 11 items in a 10-item lane. Picky, picky, who can read those tiny expiration dates, anyway?

In addition, I don't consider canceling my Cosmopolitan Magazine subscription because I got the lowest possible score on the "Do you have a happy marriage quiz" as an emotional decision. It was insulting, and my answers were perfect, just like my marriage.

And how, I ask you, Baby-Boo, can anyone blame me for entering into an angry frenzy when my chocolate soufflé fell, just as I was serving it to a dinner party of my 8 closest friends. It was a supreme failure, an epic disaster. Not at all *emotional, may I add!* My tantrum was very normal and considered typical gourmet-chef behavior. Ask anyone.

So, I became unglued when my forever manicurist retired. 'Twas very rational...

Sure, I'm bursting with hormones and trying times as everything in my body is changing. I don't know why I'm crying all the time? But, I'm not *emotional*? Where's the Kleenex?

I'M NOT EMOTIONAL...WELL, I'M NOT!

Not to deflect, but to be clear, it's natural to become emotional with some wild mood swings when it appears that everyone is telling me what I can and cannot do these days. No drinking, no caffeine, not a lot of sugars, no soft cheeses, no sushi, and no tattoos. I can't go skydiving, helicopter skiing, scuba diving, boxing, climbing to the top of Mount Kilimanjaro, wrestling, motorcycling, bungee jumping, Jallikattu, or even bull riding. Let's not forget, no bull fighting either! I mean honestly, what the heck is left?

Emotional? Really? Simply because I went into a full-blown wrath when my hair stylist reversed my highlights and lowlights, making me look like a zebra. So justifiable...

And lastly... When my BFF, Shara called to tell me she'd be 10 minutes late for our baby-shopping spree, and I replied, "Forget it! Don't bother!" and hung up on her... That was not being emotional by any sense of the word. Now that, my little maverick or rebel, was just plain *bitchy!* Oh, and PSS... All normal people cry out loud watching the divine, beautiful, picturesque, Budweiser Clydesdales commercials! Case closed.

CHAPTER 13

On Being a Mommy...

Mommy's Complaints, WisDumb, and Other Stuff!

Arguably, being a mommy is clearly the worst paying job in the world. And yet, ironically, it brings the most riches. Yes, I want the job to the depths of my soul.

ROBIN ROTH

The Mommy Job Requirements and Career Descriptions:

This position is 24-hours-a-day, 7 days a week, no days off (Ever), no vacations, no sick days, and zero pay. Must have medical experience, teaching expertise, psychology skills, be kindhearted, friendly, compassionate, understanding, patient, fun-loving, a huge sense of humor, optimistic, inspiring, warm, loving, and spiritual. It is essential to be an excellent driver, personal shopper, housekeeper, and cook. Job requires being trained and skilled as a seamstress, mind reader, cheerleader, protector, and dietitian. Concerning this job, it's vital to be super-imaginative, artistic, creative, talented with arts and crafts, gifted psychic abilities, disciplinarian expertise, and best-friend-forever skills. Mommy applicants must be committed, selfless, and willing to sacrifice everything for the child. Candidates must clearly understand that their wants, needs, and desires come way after the child's, if at all.

I jubilantly accept this full-time, forever, job with all its requirements and zero pay. However, my little Ashton or Mila, it appears at this point in my pregnancy, mommy is somewhat (ok, a lot) overloaded with questions, fears, and worries. I feel like my head is spinning with endless issues, qualms, and apprehensions of what is, what isn't, what to decide, and infinite queries on 'to-dos and not to-dos.' I am vexed by a cacophony of deafening worrisome sounds and alarm bells. There is a vast menu of troubling concerns.

For Example...

- Will a baby change or even hurt my marriage? Will I love you more than I love daddy?

ON BEING A MOMMY...

- Will the sonogram or ultrasound hurt you, my sweet angel? Or perhaps even scare you?
- When going to the doctor's office, must I continually face the enemy? AKA... The scale?
- What if during pregnancy your heartbeat stops or isn't normal? Or I lose you, God forbid!
- Will I be one of those women, viciously attacked by the dreaded Postpartum Blues?
- Why was I told, I'll most likely have to take a diabetes test? I don't have diabetes?
- Will I have to get an amniocentesis test? It could be exceedingly dangerous for the baby.
- Should I get my baby the vaccination shots or protest? You know, they're controversial?
- When should I sign up for a mommy and me class? I can't have my baby socially deprived.
- Should I enroll my baby in prep-kindergarten and get in line for a Harvard-type prep school? I don't want my child left out. I probably should jump on all of this immediately.
- What if you're colicky, Baby-Boo, and won't sleep all night like my girlfriend's baby?
- What if (*Not to sound shallow!*) you're ugly? Like the Elephant Man ugly? Clearly, an elephant has never trampled over me. Though judging by your ultrasound pictures, you looked weird and distorted, sweetie. Surely it's fine and just bad, ultrasound-type photos?
- I categorically and positively don't want to know if you are a boy or a girl! Or gosh, do I?

- I worry about an emergency C-section because I want the *skin-to-skin* contact right away.
- Being pregnant, I can't color process my naturally blonde hair like I want to. Bummer.
- Should we save the umbilical cord? It's expensive, but it can help with over 80 diseases.
- Should I get an epidural? It can be quite dangerous... In fact, it could paralyze me! Scary.
- Breastfeed, or not BF? Of course, the breast is best. But, sometimes mommy needs wine!
- Should I take advantage and have my baby, "Room-In" with me in the hospital? Or stay in the nursery, so the nurses can give me a break? Might be my last chance to sleep. Ever!
- Diaper rash worries? Not all creams work, leaving my baby crying with painful sores.
- When should I enroll you in a safety swim class? Should I get a pool gate? Learn CPR?
- I worry with great fear and trepidation about SIDS! They now advise putting the baby to sleep on their back. But, yet they keep changing it? I'll never feel at ease from this scare.
- Will I know for sure when it's time, or if it's Braxton Hicks, false labor, or the real deal? Will I wind up going to the hospital 3 times, thinking I am in labor only to be mocked?
- Not to mention, what if I can't handle the ordeal of birth? I might need to be knocked out.
- What if I'm not a good mother? Wow, that'll keep me up for the rest of my pregnancy...
- And lastly, my biggest question! When should I tell people we are with child? They say it's bad luck to tell people too early,

and we should wait for at least three months to make the announcement. Some people say, even after that. I profess I am pretty *stupidstitious.*

"The Whys and The Pregnancy Guilt!"

In a nutshell, this is how being pregnant makes mommy feel, all the time....

- Why are my legs swelling? And why are they swelling in tandem with my puffy face?
- Why are there ugly, bulging, unsightly red patches on my face? Really... Why?
- Why do I have so much damn water weight gain? (Massive internal eye-roll there...)
- Why can't I fall asleep? I'm tired, fatigued, and absolutely exhausted? So then, why?
- Why am I suffering from constant heartburn all the time? OMG, I never had this before?
- Why am I hot? Why am I so cold? Why am I never just right? I've become Goldilocks.
- Why am I farting all the time? I feel like a cross-country truck driver, eating baked beans.
- Why am I dizzy? And, little one, don't even reference the dumb, old cliché blonde jokes.
- Why am I so Thirsty? Even an ocean couldn't quench my thirst. Now wine, that's doable!
- Why do I have all kinds of skin changes invading my face and body? Thoroughly, yuck.

- Why does everything I read or hear about pregnancy always involve stretch marks? Not happening to me! Won't allow it. No *f-in* way! Wish they'd stop stretching the truth!
- What is that gross, visible blue on my legs? Is it varicose veins? It looks like a road map.
- Why am I snoring? I never used to snore. Lord, it sounds like a freight train. Poor daddy.
- Why are my feet getting bigger? I'm a serious "shoe girl," so they better go back to size 7 right after you're born. No way I'm losing my shoe collection, I'll tell you that right now.
- Why am I feeling heart palpitations? I haven't felt those since the first time I met daddy.
- What is this nasty facial hair thing that's happening? This must cease at once. I mean it!
- Damien, why am I having weird, scary, vivid dreams? Exorcist-style like a horror film?
- Google: What is this disgusting thing in my butt? "A vulgar, hemorrhoid?" Oh, hell, no!
- Why can't I have more coffee? Seriously? You're going to be up all night anyway, baby?
- Why can't I have a Margarita? Really, why? I believe this *no-no* needs further tweaking.

Mommy's WisDumb and Loving Words...

Little Lancelot or Guinevere, when I pick you up in my arms, I know I'll instantly sense all the history of the collective generations, which have come before you. This is quite phenomenal. There will be a feeling of immense pride within the entire family bloodline.

ON BEING A MOMMY...

Mommy believes that every child born makes the world a better place. (Well, mostly?)

It frightens me little one... For I've discovered, the more I grow into an amazing mother, the less you will need me. There's no greater proof of success, wisdom, and love!

Not to put too fine a point on it, but being pregnant with you, Tyler, Justice, or Thomas, has opened my eyes and placed everything into a new crystal-clear perspective.

I'm beginning to understand, being your mommy will cause me to worry, question, and wonder about everything you say and do. I am certain of this scenario.

I've come to realize all the love and feelings I hold for you inside... I was actually born with. This distinctly proves you're an essential part of my whole makeup and spirituality.

Just so you know, daddy's lap is the sweetest, safest, and most tender place on the planet.

They say (Again, whoever *they* are), cuddling your baby changes their DNA. However, I say, cuddling your baby changes everything. For this embrace is a piece of heaven.

By design, the creation of a baby is so perfect and miraculous it is utterly impossible to improve upon, by any stretch of the human imagination.

Random, but I can only guess how many tries it'll take to swaddle you, till I get it right.

It's been said, "We enter the world alone and we leave the world alone." I don't believe this idea is true. As we enter or leave this world, hopefully, our family greets us, or says goodbye with open arms of love. Baby, our loving arms are wide open, waiting for you.

The umbilical cord falling off really freaks mommy out! Regardless, if we don't wind up saving it for medical reasons, then for sure, that sucker is goin' right into the baby book.

Mommy will finally understand the infinite joy and experience, the ultimate ecstasy and fulfillment when I witness your happiness, laughter, and all of your dreams come true.

Fact... Don't mess with Mother Nature or any other mother, for that matter! Don't even think about it. The consequences never do end well. BTW, there is a vulgar name for that.

Baby Grant or Ari, a mother's love is the purest love you'll ever know in your entire life.

Giving birth to you is like opening the door to everything extraordinary and dazzling.

I now understand being pregnant (AKA a mother-to-be), and going to childbirth classes with daddy... exactly why women were selected to carry and give birth to a child. Period!

As a new mommy, baby Spencer or Emma, I imagine when you drop your pacifier on the floor, I'll sprint out to sterilize it in a pot of boiling hot water before giving it back to you. In contrast, when my next baby drops the pacifier, I imagine I'll be chill and scream out to the dog, "Go get it, girl." Then, happy-go-lucky, plop it right back in the baby's mouth.

Being a newbie mom, when you need a clean diaper, I guess I'll dash off to change you. As for the next baby, after pulling back the tabs and checking it, I fancy I'll be chill and think, no biggie. Only half-full, it's still fine. What? Diapers are ridiculously expensive!

It is oh so spiritual that before you are born, I carry you with love in the very center of my beating heart. On the day of your birth, I will cradle my love for you, both on the inside and the outside, forever. You see, baby Hercules or Amalfi, you are my heart.

No matter how bad my day has been, how much stress I endured, how awful I might have felt, it will only take one little baby kick from you to transform everything into enchantment. One little kick will make mommy feel all is perfect in the world. One little baby kick from you and life will be joyful. *Please start kicking!* I can hardly wait.

Becoming a mother, I feel as though the day of your birth will be the start of every possibility, wonder, dream, and hope that is conceivable. Meeting you and seeing your face will be a revolving loop of unparalleled exhilaration. I visualize it will feel as though mommy will be looking into her own soul, totally naked, with everything revealed. Sweet darling, Liberty or Bell, you are my dream and all the magic that will exist in my life.

On the day you are born and no longer within me, and a part of me, it will be bittersweet. I will desperately miss the sensation of you moving inside me. It will feel as if my heart exists outside of my body. For now, I hold and protect you, carrying you in my tummy. Soon, I will protect you in my awaiting arms. As time goes by and I can no longer hold you, I'll still protect you till the day I die and the end of time.

Well, thank you to the moon-and-back for listening, sweet Harvard or Piper. Mommy loves you with all her heartburn, rashes, swelling legs, weight gain, dizziness, thirst, and exhaustion. No worries and don't feel guilty. I'll be fine. Let's chat real soon.

ROBIN ROTH

Oh, no! Wait just a minute! Is that? What is that? Is that a gray hair? No way. Oh, hell to the no! Where are my *F@#$%*andK* tweezers! *For this one kid, you owe me a kick!*

CHAPTER 14

The Second Trimester... We're Showing!

Good morning, my handsome Lucas or beautiful Sophia. With my head way up in the clouds, I jubilantly announce, *"We Are Showing!"* Mommy is elated and proud. *We Are Showing!* Staring in the mirror, I took in a deep breath of happiness and screamed out loud, "Hooray!" Being pregnant has undeniably had its challenges, but now that we are showing, I am bursting at the seams. (Literally!) My situation, having to endure these past several months being pregnant and not showing, has been rather a precarious state of limbo. Now that we are out, and sporting our bump for all to see,

I have never felt more empowered and confident in my own skin. Thrillingly, in accordance with my desires, the long embarrassment of looking chubby has concluded with a favorable outcome. People finally know for sure, and can obviously see that I am not just overweight or plump. Mommy is ecstatic and proudly flaunting the cute baby-bump look. It's so odd, gazing into the mirror and realizing the pregnant lady there in the "mirror-mirror, on the wall," is actually me. As I see my reflection and in the spirit of positivity, my growing bump is a source of immense bliss and pleasure. I'm lost in the euphoric abyss of my baby rapture.

With humility, I feel supremely fortunate to be among the lucky pregnant women who look cutesy, pretty even. How adorable are we? I dare say gushing, "I've never felt sexier or more lovely than I do right now, whilst joyfully showing off our precious bump."

Until our grand reveal, I tried to conceal being pregnant. I also didn't want to let the cat out-of-the-bag to the world too soon. And just like that, my belly rounded out, and we are officially showing. It's surprising how people are now coming up to us and saying the sweetest things. It's endearing hearing a perfect stranger calling us beautiful, especially when mommy hasn't been quite sure about it these days. Still, it's nice to hear, anyway. I'm feeling excited and awkward at the same time. But, at least now people can see exactly why mommy is smiling around the clock. I guess the jig is up. No more hiding my wonderful secret. We are no longer just a rumor or even a...*'womb-er.'* Feeling butterflies in my belly make me giggle knowing it's you, my angel. I'm obsessed, relentlessly wanting to feel or hold my tummy. I often wondered about that, seeing pregnant women constantly holding or rubbing their bumps.

THE SECOND TRIMESTER...WE'RE SHOWING!

Currently, everything's changed and many new experiences are happening in our lives. The days seem to be rushing by at warp speed. I've unmistakably noticed since our condition went public, we seem to inspire the best in people. I mean, just look at all of the help and attention we are presently getting. People are opening doors for us, instead of slamming them in my face. The bank manager, even for my nine-dollar deposit, put on an extra teller so we didn't have to stand and wait. Normally, they close my line right when I'm next. The grocery bagger helped us out to the car, without me even asking him to.

Mind-boggling as it is to fathom, people everywhere relinquish their seats so we don't have to stand. Can you imagine that? You don't know yet, sweetie, but that's not typical human behavior. My number one favorite, special-pregnant-treatment (drum roll), was at a concert. When daddy took mommy (for no reason at all) to see Lady Gaga, the ticket guy took one look at mommy climbing up to the nosebleed seats and gave us the best seats in the house, front row center. So lucky! I suppose management didn't want me struggling to climb up 45 flights of stairs to our original awful seats. Now, don't you go thinking daddy is cheap! He would have gladly bought mommy the good seats. Sadly, the concert sold out within minutes. It is *Gaga,* after all! Come to think of it, that will most likely be your first word, "*gaga.*" I do hope it will be daddy, instead. Actually, mommy, would be even better? I mean, honestly, I was fired from my job for you! Note... That is called guilt. It's something you'll become quite familiar with. Get used to it. I'm kidding? Though because of mommy's bad language habit, I am praying, that "F@#!$%%*andNG," won't happen to be your first word. Anything would be better than that. Daddy's mommy would go ballistic with me if you did. Although, the mere thought of it makes me snicker!

Another matter I find quite altered and humorous since we recently started showing, is how most people refer to me as Mrs. instead of Miss, as they did only a few weeks ago. Not so pleased giving up the Miss, as it typically denotes a younger woman. Oh well, you're worth it. Further astonishing, all the salespeople, yea all of them I swear, speak to me kindly and politely in a pampering, "How may I help you, way." I like that!

Also remarkable is how people run up to my car, falling over themselves to assist me in filling my gas tank with the correct gas and a smile. I imagine they think the gas pump is too heavy for me to handle? Willy-nilly, I can emphatically adapt to the splendid thoughtfulness of perfect strangers. This outpouring of kindness and assistance could no doubt turn me into an *attention whore*. And a big one too! I best attempt to be careful with this notion. Further puzzling is how other moms smile at me all the time with a warm, compassionate grin. I suppose it's a solidarity thing or initiation membership into the "Special mommy sorority." Naturally, I eagerly smile back. What else could I do? Oftentimes these moms and I stop to chitchat. We compare mom notes and sage old advice. It's sorta sweet if you think about it. I've actually gotten quite a few helpful tips.

When I drop anything, anywhere at all, at least 2 people quickly lunge to pick it up for me. Even the spiteful paperboy now angles the paper near the front door, instead of slinging it perfectly onto the wet and dewy, morning grass bordering the street, like he used to. Yes, little Tribune or Post, I still read newspapers. After all, I am, ok was, a journalist.

THE SECOND TRIMESTER...WE'RE SHOWING!

Just like royalty, all this kindness and help really makes me feel like a princess. Which reminds me, I should start wearing my tiara again. Thinking about it, if a princess is treated like a princess normally, I can only imagine how a princess is treated when she is pregnant? I'll admit it, baby Prince William or Princess Kate, legitimately being able to wear a tiara or a crown in real life (and to justify it alone), makes me envious. Let us not ignore the millions of other perks like jewelry and butlers. There is always the next life!

Mommy often thinks silly things like that while alone with my random thoughts. I also wonder, as my tummy grows, if my innie will become an outie? Similar to the old jack-in-the-box... You never know what or when something will pop out. Thinking out-of-the-box, how awesome would our bump be, as a fabulous canvas for some creative abstract body art?

Ya know, I hear women all the time complaining about being pregnant and how they can't wait for it to be over. I don't feel that way. Perhaps I'm weird, Baby-Boo, but I love being pregnant. It all seems wonderful to me, and our sweet bump is a constantly growing reminder we're doing something astonishing. We, you and I, are an absolute miracle and my body is an unbelievable, miraculous vessel to be able to do this work. Super-Woman, work.

As time passes and we grow even bigger, I am not sure how I'm going to feel when people come over to us and touch our tummy without asking, especially strangers. I hope they have the good sense to at least ask my permission first. (Even though I will say no!) Mommy is a splash *stupidstitious*, so I clearly don't want just anybody running up to touch us. I suppose it would help walking around backward, as I don't look pregnant at all from the back. Well, as of yet. Gosh, does my possessive, protective boldness make me a helicopter-mom already? Eeks! Legend or Arabella, I know for certain you'd hate that kind of behavior when you're a teenager. I'll try to tone it down if I can. I said try!

Gosh, my tiny prince or princess, I'm noticing this pregnancy thing ultimately appears to have lots of royal benefits and silver linings. For instance, soon our bump can be used as a laptop table, or a book rest. It can be a comfy armrest, a human tray, a coffee table, or a pillow for daddy to lie down on. It can double as a cup holder, a coffee caddy, a cellphone nook, snack shelf, crumb catcher, or a manicure table. Our bump can be a fab get out-of-jail-free-card, for talking my way out of a speeding ticket. Ultimately, our freshly noticeable bump is a happy reminder that you are always with me.

Baby Austin or Australia, here are a few important things you should know now:

1. You are the product of your daddy and mommy's immeasurable love for one other.
2. There has never been, nor will there ever be, someone like you. *You* are unique and there will never be another *you*. There is no one like *you* anywhere, in the entire universe.
3. I shake my head in awe, thinking how impossible it is to comprehend just how much I categorically love you more and more each day. It is astonishing.
4. It's comforting to realize I am never alone, for I always feel your presence within.
5. The sheer creation of you is beyond mind-blowing. It's like when an artist paints the colors yellow, pink, blue, green, and red images on a canvas, creating a masterpiece. Designing an amazing original, with glints and shimmers of purple and orange,

THE SECOND TRIMESTER...WE'RE SHOWING!

along the edges, dripping and spilling until the conception is perfected and finished. It's what God, mommy, daddy, and you are creating right now, a one-of-a-kind, colorful, baby creation.
6. As you grow, Fraser or Xiomara, you will naturally have many doubts and uncertainties. Nonetheless, never doubt that you're loved and wanted unconditionally.
7. Oh, how mommy adores our pregnancy. I'll miss our bump profoundly when you are born. I'll feel empty without you within me. The thought of it makes me sad, even now.

Although you are the best thing that life has ever brought your daddy and me, don't kid yourself, beloved one. You are not scot-free, nor out of the woods. Brody or Maddie, need I remind you about the many things mommy had to give up for you? And let's not forget how I lost (cut up) all of my credit cards. I'm still totally sick about it.

Don't even bring up my swollen ankles, headaches, and my aching back from carrying you. Now, that right there is a tiny portion of guilt training just to get you going. Thought it best to jump-start you early, though the guilt technique isn't my thing. Yet, it's never too early to get started. Talk soon. Sending you a huge muah and a million hugs.

CHAPTER 15

Ya Just Can't Win!

Early this morning, I woke up to a beautiful, gloriously sunny day. The Robin birds in the apple trees were singing away. The splendid geraniums, radiant roses and orchids in my window box, now in full bloom, never looked lovelier or healthier.

A cool breeze blew gently through the opened Louis XV walnut French doors, while I savored my one allowed, delicious hot cup of coffee. Life was perfect, and I felt wonderfully blissful.

Astonishingly, I also developed that lovely glow described in all the baby books. Then, suddenly, as scary as a Stephen King novel, I witnessed a menacing, chilling, terrifying situation, as bloodcurdling sounds spawned from my lips. A vision so dreadful, it was hard to believe what my own eyes had seen. This couldn't be happening to me? All I managed to utter was, "No, this only happens to other women." Yet, there it was, plain as day. Were my own eyes betraying me? Woefully, I couldn't deny it. It was real. "Lord, why? Why me?" I cried out as if I'd seen an exorcist, a terrorist, or a ghost?

Stretch Marks!!!!!!

Dammit not this, anything but this. Not the dreaded stretch marks, also the best friend of the devil himself! Dant-Dant-Dan-Dah. There it was, facing me with its ghastly haughty, arrogance. *Stretch Marks!* Aha, *Stretch Marks!* "AKA, tiger stripes, gut wrinkles, lightning strikes, noodle belly, stretchies, lion claw, skid-marks, and ominous bands."

As cute as all of that might sound, there's nothing darling about this dilemma. By what *stretch* of the imagination befell upon me, to be cursed with this ugly mark on my belly?

Obviously, and as one might expect, you and mommy dashed off to every store within 50-miles. We frantically searched for the finest oils, vitamin E gels, cocoa butter, tummy butter, coconut oils, Shea butter, StretcHeal, Mama Mio, StriVectin, TriLASTIN-SR, Clarins, Burt's Bees Mama Bee, Basq Butter, Botanic Tree, Mederma, and Mustela creams. With my new (higher limit) credit cards, I even bought Chrissy Teigen's $375 stretch-mark cream, (plus tax, shipping and handling). This little outing of ours cost your daddy around 3 million dollars or so, and that's only for *one* stretch mark. Yet sadly, as we all know, like with ants or bugs, where there is one, there are plenty more to follow. I could throw up. Forget about it, stretch marks! That is utter nonsense. This mark will be the only *one* I'm going to suffer through. Well, if I have my druthers about this quandary.

Regardless, that most doctors claim these creams and ointments are a waste of money, I didn't stop there. I spent hours on Google conjuring up potions, mothers' time-proven recipes, grandma's and witches spells, and remedies used by every culture. Not taking any chances, I rubbed every one of them on my bump. I was an icky-sticky mess, head to toe. As they say, "Faith wouldn't be faith if you only believed when things are good." Thus, I have ample faith in the creams. Maybe it couldn't hurt to call an exorcist?

I'm now living with nightmarish fears of growing more tiger claws and stretch marks that want to invade my entire body forever. It appears in all the books I've read, every woman who's had a baby offered unsolicited horror stories of how stretch marks plagued their lives. They say it is the bane of their existence. As if I needed to know that? But nothing could be scarier than today, when I awoke to the dreaded, feared, seemingly crawling tendrils of my one blossoming stretch mark. Singular, and it better stay that way. Hoping to make this my reality, I purchased vitamins A, C, and E. Also, I will now eat a lot of Zinc-enriched foods, and foods rich in gelatin. Moreover, I will constantly keep my hydration levels up. So much so, I should probably move into the bathroom.

Being totally anal, I started a new bi-weekly ritual of body scrub exfoliation with natural abrasives such as coffee grounds and sugar granules. Leaving nothing to chance, I bought fancy ones, too. Furthermore, I purchased the most expensive Extra-Virgin olive oil, imported from Italy. I smell like very sexy chicken Parmesan, Caesar salad, or spaghetti with clams. I've read stretch marks fade into thin stripes, blending into the surrounding skin in time. So, what the hell does that even mean? Do they fade or not, yes or no? Someone once said, "Stretch marks are a badge of a real woman." I'd like to leave my own mark on that guy! Gimme a break, that's something a male therapist, would say. As I've stated many times, I'm *not emotional*. Nevertheless, the thought of any more of these things sprouting, zigzagging from my tummy, or spring-boarding their way up my thighs, boobs or hips, will make me freak out and scream at the same unemotional time.

Without that much-needed glass of wine or second cup of java, I went to lie down with my feet up. Looking down at my growing baby bump, I pondered, how much could my stomach stretch before it explodes? I wonder if that ever actually happened? I was only starting my 4th month and already beside myself with the notion of turning into a big huge disastrous *stretch mark*. "F@#%!*k!" OMG, will daddy fall out of love with me if that ensues? That's preposterous. He probably won't even notice the mark. Or will he?

The baby books say to love, embrace, and be proud of your *stretch marks*. Oh, *please*, get real. I don't know which one is more ridiculous… to love, embrace, be proud of, or the stupid badge of courage comment. They say to tell everyone about them. Show them off with delight. I promise, little Zorro or Catherine Zeta-Jones, not only will I not do any of the above, I shall never, ever admit to experiencing the marks, 1st hand. I'll simply tell everyone who might see them in the future on my tummy (or if they spawn others) that you, baby Tara or Garth, wrote on mommy with silver and red markers. Done.

YA JUST CAN'T WIN!

Such as life and so classically, typically typical... Just when I had made all of that luxurious extra room in my bathroom, after having thrown away all of those industrial-strength Maxi pads, heavy-duty Tampons, Pamprin, and Midol pills... now my, *Magical Stretch Creams,* are overtaking the entire space.

It's true "Nature abhors a vacuum." *I swear on Dior and Prada, Ya Just Can't Win!*

Don't worry, sweetie. And no, of course, it's not your fault. Well? Hmm? No, no, it's not? Hey, dammit, is that another frickin' tiger-stripe I see? Are you kidding me?

CHAPTER 16

OMGosh! Baby, was that you? I'm *overwhelmed* and ecstatic if it was! For real, was that a kick? Oh my, did you move? Did you just kick mommy? I could feel tears of affection cascading down my cheeks. What a stirring and wonderful surprise.

Little Adam or Eve, do it again! Kick me just one more time, please. Oh, honey, for sure, that last one was definitely a legitimate, honest-to-goodness, real-life baby kick. What a tremendous sensation. Gee, I can hardly wait for you to show daddy that you're kicking now, when he gets home. I am absolutely so blown away. I cannot adequately explain what your very first little kick did to my heart. To feel you finally moving inside of me was extraordinary. No, astonishing, unexpected, and startling. Your kick helped me appreciate that we are really, truly a part of each other. We are two people who are now joined as one. For the first time, I fully understand that I am giving you life. Goodness, how I desperately want to hold you in my arms and tell to you how gigantically you are loved and what you mean to us. How long I have passionately wanted you. How grateful I am that God chose to give, *you to us.* Funny how this simple kick of yours makes all the woes of pregnancy quietly disappear. Well, mostly, and except for the *Stretch Marks...* That stands firm. Besides them, your kicks magically and instantly make it all worth it.

Wow, gee, I felt you kick with my hand this time. I felt your little body with my fingers. I think it was a leg? That was sensational. Really epic and without a doubt, the best feeling I have ever experienced. And let me tell you, kid, I've known a whole lot of supreme feelings in my day. It's crazy, you are not even born, and yet you are fully alive. You're not entirely developed, and yet you have already shown me the best moments, out of all the moments I've ever known. My darling unborn child, you have given me new

YOU KICKED!

life and all the colorful, glorious joys it brings with it. Not to mention a few extra pounds!

Kick again. Pretty please. Bahahaaa, it makes me giggle! You're adorable. I have so often tried to imagine what genuine ecstasy (out of bed) is and what it would feel like. There are surely many descriptions. But your little kickoff, Emma or Owen, is the perfect example of happiness for mommy. Without question, it is the best part of being pregnant. Each time you move, it gives mommy such peace of mind knowing you are healthy and having fun. So, don't worry about bothering me, kick away, little munchkin. Oops, there you go again. LOL. I know you're now punting, since you hear mommy talking to you. I can already sense your perky, fun personality by your impish kicking trick. Uh-oh, I gotta go. Daddy is walking in the door. I want you to Super Bowl kick him later. He's going to freak out over this.

Talk to you later, baby Rockette or Justin Tucker. And thank you for your fabulous gift. I'm elated and completely jazzed about this latest part of our journey.

CHAPTER 17

What Do You Look Like?

Often I find myself wondering what you're going to look like, little Chopin or Adele? Definitely, one of the hardest parts of expecting is the huge mystery about you.

Will you look and act like your daddy? If so Kurt, you won't have a thing to worry about. He's awesome in every way possible. It's almost obnoxious. *"That's Called, Sarcasm!"*

Now mommy, on the other hand, is a whole different story. Don't get me wrong, "As I've been told," I am pretty and terrific, too. Honestly, though, it took considerable effort for me to look this way. Just ask my Jr. high school best friends. They'll tell you. For example, Aimee, if you have my teeth, after 5 long awkward years of wearing braces, you too, will have beautiful, pearly whites. I guess if you get my big blue eyes, very long lashes and all, you'll be happy. Like mommy, they'll look even better once you are old enough for awesome contact lenses. You can even pick pretty, violet-colored ones. I hope you get my nice hair. I was lucky with this one. Plus, I don't get many bad hair days.

Now suppose little Nino you have daddy's Italian nose. Personally, I love his nose and find it extremely sexy. But if you happen to be a Nina, it's amazing how simple and successful plastic surgery can be these days. You can easily get a new nose in no time at all. *"That's Called, Offensive!"* I am so joking, Tess or Mac. Your nose will be perfect.

Daddy is 6'1", which is great. Mommy is 5'5". The blend should leave you, just right. If not Logan, just look at all the wonderfully successful and happy short men like: Mahatma Gandhi, Charlie Chaplin, Tom Cruise, Picasso, Houdini, Pacino, Alexander the Great, Isaac Newton, Spielberg, and Aristotle. Even Daniel Radcliffe is only 5'5". Not a problem. As for you, baby princess Sky, there's Kristen Bell, Reese Witherspoon, Ariana Grande, Lady Gaga, Mila Kunis, and Scarlett Johansson. You're in good, short company.

WHAT DO YOU LOOK LIKE?

With any luck, you might be one of those annoying people like daddy, who can eat anything he wants to and never gain weight. I mean, what is so great about pizza, fries, and chocolate fudge cake, anyway? Keeping it real, all of those goodies are a joy to behold. Don't stress. Daddy's overactive thyroid will smooth that out for you, too. Unlike mommy, who simply walks by a pastry cart and gains weight! *"That's Called so Unfair."*

I wonder if you'll have my dimples? And the ones on my cheeks, too, *"Ba-Dum-Chhh!"* Will you have daddy's sexy, Hollywood-star, cleft chin? He's really entirely gorgeous. According to daddy, "mommy is gorgeous," too. But as they say, "Love is blind." I believe you won't have a thing to worry about in the looks department. FYI, you embody roughly 100,000 genes, which is a great deal of substantial physical traits to mix and match. God's helpers are busier than Santa's elves. *"That's Called, Trust and Faith."*

You will undoubtedly be a very intelligent person. Mommy and daddy are very smart and highly educated people. Don't let that tiny detail about grandpa having to hire daily tutors so mommy could get through elementary school, throw you one drop. Things picked up in Jr. high, and by the time I reached high school, all was good. I was finally making straight C's and even an occasional B. I'm teasing, kid! Mommy and Daddy were straight 'A' students, for real. No pressure or worries, though! Baby-Boo, you're going to have to learn we're witty, we joke around frequently, love to laugh, and enjoy having fun.

Although I am *("Ok, Ok, I WAS,")* a successful journalist, if you're like mommy, you'll be blessed with extraordinary acting and singing talent. I'd be a famous mega-star if it weren't for my 1st-grade teacher, Mrs. Holland. To this day, I'll never forgive her for making me the only kid in the school chorus, excluded from performing in the 1st-grade play. What's the big deal if I sang a little off-key and hit a few bad notes? I was nervous. Nasty woman. She ate her words when I got the lead in the 2nd-grade play. And, *"That's Called, Karma!"* Today, I'd have #1 hits on the charts if not for her. I'll sing, you judge.

If you are like daddy a respectable doctor, you'll have the patience of a saint. He always stays calm and relaxed during any intense situation. He is solid, like a rock. Just don't let his football team lose, because that, little Tom Brady changes everything.

If you turn out like mommy, you will possess a super great sense of humor. Gosh, I even laugh at your daddy's jokes. Speaking of which, I hope you have his smile. He sparkles, totally lighting up a room, making everyone around him beam with delight.

So chill... Whether you are like daddy or mommy, with a little hard work and parental tweaking, you'll turn out to be an astounding, incredible person. And humble too. LOL.

Indeed, you'll come to appreciate we are a smidge different, unusual, novel, and imaginative, with a quirky way of thinking. Let's say we're rather unique. But that's a good thing. Being different is special, and you'll grow to love that about us. You'll see?

Sadly and unfortunately, being good-looking in this world is important. I'd be a lying hypocrite if I said it wasn't. Still and all, being beautiful and sexy is not everything. Not in the least. I must tell you, precious Pollyanna or Everett, I have met so many people in my lifetime who were unimaginably gorgeous, stunning, exquisite even. Yet, I found them to be the most horrid-looking people I had ever known. They were such awful, atrocious people that their beauty vanished right before me and all I could see was their

WHAT DO YOU LOOK LIKE?

ugliness from within. Meanwhile, I have known many individuals who were not at all attractive, but they became the most lovely, divine-looking people I had ever known. You see, sweet Beauty or Beast, their loveliness within, sparkled through. True beauty comes from the love and kindness a person embraces in their heart and soul. You'll see one day.

Speaking of ugly, there are all kinds of mean people who tease, pick on, mock, or poke fun of others, regardless of their appearance. It's hurtful and insensitive. For bullies will always be bullies. Don't ever put up with it. We'll tell you more about this when the time is right. Remember my darling child, whether you are a girl or boy, no matter who or what you look like, whose eyes, nose, hair, smile, or mouth you have, how tall, short, or smart you are, through our eyes, we'll only see your beauty, wonder, awe, and bliss. To us, you'll be the most glorious baby ever to be born. Most importantly, your heart and soul will be magnificent. I know this is true, as I already feel and see you from within me.

Oh, how my heart skips a beat merely thinking about you. We are desperately excited beyond any emotion we have ever experienced. And... *"That's Called Love!"*

When you are born, daddy and I will know at once who you are, just by looking into your eyes. Your eyes are the doorway and the path into your heart, soul, and your entire being.

CHAPTER 18

Growing Up Baby...

Little Han or Leia, they'll be so many fabulous times ahead in your new world. There are astonishing things for you to see, do, face, learn, discover, achieve, master, and accomplish. You'll know unlimited triumphs, stages of success, and wondrous journeys to experience. Life will test you with unending challenges to meet, conquer, and realize. Darling Baby, there is immeasurable happiness and fun in your future. You'll enjoy being a part of awesomazing events, and exciting, fantastical jaunts.

To begin with, there will be tons of swaddling, diapers filled with whatever you create, blankets, mommy's breasts, and bottles from daddy. They'll be a crib (if you don't wind up in our bed, which they say is a big NO), playpens, high chairs, strollers, rattles, cars seats, bassinets, swings, bibs, and oodles of *vital* pacifiers hiding all over the house. Olivia, mommy will dress you in lots of pinks, over-the-top ruffles, and huge fancy bows. Mason, daddy will have you wearing his sports teams' caps, helmets and numbered jerseys.

I assume there will be endless crying and late nights in our future. I suspect, Ed or Viv, some of the tears will even come from you! Indeed, we'll sing, "Peekaboo, A Bushel and a Peck, When you wish upon a star, Row, Row, Row your Boat, Wheels on the Bus, Twinkle, Twinkle little star, and Old MacDonald" types of songs and other such lullabies.

On the subject of nursery rhymes, I'd like to jump in and examine them further. Frankly, I find most of them to be tragic and horrible, with disastrous, dreadful endings. I am pretty much against most of them. I dare to beg the question... With all the brilliant writers in the world, why can't they come up with happy, sweet rhymes? Here are a few examples, to demonstrate my point. And Baby Boo, you do the math! So, there's, *"Incy Wincy Spider," "Rock a bye baby," "London Bridge is falling down," "Jack and Jill," "Humpty Dumpty," "Ring around the Rosie," "Goosey-Goosey Gander"* and *"There was an old woman."* Each one ends in catastrophic horror. Can't we do better than this? They scare the crap out of me, and I'm not a baby. Hell, they'd scare a serial killer away! I question how they ever became famous in the first place? "Not at all child-friendly." No worries, baby. I'll never recite them to you. Well, maybe when you are around 12 and go through puberty. You might deserve a little scare by then and probably have it coming!

Next, some eventful firsts shall arrive. Such as... your first shots, first outing, first words, and your first smile. The first time you turn over, the first time you crawl, your very first steps, and your first giggles. How I will love hearing you jabbering away on the monitor, alone in your room. Your first food tastings will be such fun. You can expect I'll be giving you a lemon or 2 and maybe a taste of wasabi. I forewarned you, I'm a jokester. Your shocking faces in the pics will be hilarious, and worth it alone. Then, potty training, which sounds fun? Alas, your first haircut. I'll cry more than you. Playing with your first friend, favorite toy, first time watching TV, and talking on mommy's phone. Sadly, there will be your first boo-boo, first fall, and the first time you get really hurt. Oh, my heart!

When you're a bit older, you'll discover, "Disney, Mickey and Minnie Mouse, Sesame Street, Dora, Blue's Clues, Muppet Babies, True and Rainbow Kingdom, Barney, Octonauts, and Helpsters." Mommy will be crying in every photo. How embarrassing for you! As a child, you can surely expect that some of your fairy-tale-dreams will come true. You'll enjoy (take in a big breath here for a *run-on sentence*) swimming, bicycles with or without training wheels, dancing, singing, jump ropes, jacks, puzzles, Lego, balls, parks, crayons, chalk, marbles, finger painting, hop-scotch, swing sets, a cozy teddy bear, holidays, birthdays, parties, and brand new toys. Can't forget, Simon Says, Candy-Land, hide-and-seek, rock-paper-scissors, and tic-tac-toe. Such grandiose fun you have to look forward to. I'll kvell with every giggle, smile, and joyful moment watching you play, as I sit on the floor taking endless videos and photos. I'm not sure who'll be having more fun.

Of course, mommy will feed you healthy foods to help you grow big and strong. But, let's be real for a tick-tock. I pinky-promise you'll get to devour all the delicious, unhealthy, fun stuff, too. Junk like: (take in another big breath) cupcakes, Oreos, pizza, brownies, shakes, Mallomars, chocolate, candy, McDonald's, cotton candy, ice cream, fries, spaghetti, grilled cheese, tacos, gum, and pancakes with gobs of syrup. I mean, being a kid, daddy will insist on it. He'll give you candy even if I don't. But never tell *his* mom!

You'll enjoy great days going out to movies, theme parks, the zoo, play dates with friends, the beach, water parks, picnics, lakes and boats, and also fun trips on airplanes.

School days will creep upon us, and boy will you ever have a lot of learning to do, little Shrek or Fiona. Wow, would you just look how tall you've grown, overnight! Soon, you'll be bringing home progress reports and report cards for us to brag about. But, no pressure. Oh my, where did you go? Where'd my little baby go? You've grown so fast. Time flies by, like a rocket soaring into space. And then poof, you've become a child.

Liz or Adonis, there will be many tears of sadness, tears of joy, and some tears for no reason at all. Growing up is not always easy or pleasurable. However, daddy and I will be right there by your side. We guarantee to encourage you with our love, patience, understanding, and compassion. Our constant support will guide

GROWING UP BABY...

you towards becoming the best person you can be. We'll never stop giving, helping, loving, or caring about you.

I have a silly belief that all babies come to earth with a message from God within them. Kind of like a fortune cookie, (But without all the MSG!) way more important, not as general, with divine insightful guidance. As you grow, you'll come to realize your own personal mission, intuitive lessons from God, and what it all means to your life. It's a gift of knowledge, a rare treasure map containing all the, who, what, when, where, and why.

As for daddy and I, the best part of your growing up is how we get to grow up with you. We'll get to do things we missed out on as kids and redo some we didn't quite get right. I'm completely jazzed on the notion of a second chance to be a kid. There are loads of things I never got to experience that we will be able to share together with you. How cool is that? Maybe, daddy will buy us a pony? Yeah, probably not, we'll stick to a dog. Oh, so cute, you kicked when I said, dog! I love that. Cutie-Pie, let's chat later about many more firsts in your life.

What the what? Is that another *stretch mark?* Oh, Hell No!

CHAPTER 19

Gaining Weight... WTF?

Hi BABY-BOO, My Boop-De-Doop! Gosh-dammit! No, mommy's not upset. I'm just trying to hold back my girly-girl angst emotions. You see, "Argh, ugh, eek, phooey, and hiss," are code words

I use to mumble feelings under my breath. Essential, as I've been told to stop my *"F@#%!cK-ish" words.*

Let me expound little Oprah or Stedman. That big sigh is justified, for it appears mommy is gaining too much weight! Actually, to put it nicely, I'm getting pretty chunky. "Mumble-mumble, argh, ugh." Ok, I'm fat. There, I said it. I'm fat. Are you happy now?

It's all totally confusing. So on one hand, you have the medical theory expressing, "Keep your weight down. Moreover, watch your food intake and calories carefully." The other philosophy suggests, "Don't starve your child. You're eating for 2 now. Eat!" To be outspoken and upfront, I rather fancy the latter, more delicate, softer approach, far better. It sounds logical and besides, I'm hungry. I am hungry all the time. Ludicrously hungry!

Anyway, what's so wrong with eating 3 breakfasts? After all, I get up fairly early.

To be blunt, when I go out to eat, is there a problem with ordering the whole left side of the menu? Including all the daily specials... for the week? So, what of it? I'm famished.

What is most concerning, I now find myself eating yucky foods I don't even like. At all!

Some women have cravings for pickles and sardines. I have cravings for utterly everything. Even more mind-blowing... mommy, who has never cleaned a plate of food in her whole life, is now virtually licking it clean. Yes, licking with my tongue, fingers, or a piece of bread, if need be. Even in family restaurants that serve so much food, people always say, "Who can eat it all?" Well, my little Esther or Abraham, your mommy can!

Before you, honey, I would always notice big numbers to the right on the doctor's scale and wondered what they were even there for? Well, sadly, I know now. Which, of course, guarantees I'll never wear a skimpy bathing suit ever again. The upside though, is I'll be able to shop at, *Additionally You,* the oversized tent dress store, after you are born. They're all made with cheerful sailboats and slimming material cut on the bias. Big sigh!

Furthermore, being pregnant, I've discovered dropping anything on the floor could very well ruin my day. I stop to ponder, "Just how badly do I need this diabolical thing that just fell?" The fallen object typically wins, at least until daddy gets home to pick it up. Wait, a sec. There really is a positive side to gaining a little too much weight. The pimples on my face are now enveloped in chub, and my nose appears much smaller. Barry or Zia, you see that? There's always a silver lining. You just have to look for it.

Particularly problematic from all this extra belly weight, I'm finding it supremely challenging to arrange my legs comfortably, as I can no longer cross them. Moreover, I woefully can't tie my sneakers either. I lost that battle weeks ago. It's ok, *"I will survive."* For the *record,* not being able to bend over to shave my legs these days has been a real predicament. I'm insecure about my "hairy situation." I wonder if daddy believed me when I told him, "All the women in Europe have hairy legs. It's considered sexy-chic."

Another biggie is trying to get up off of the couch without a helping hand. Worse yet, is when I have a helping hand and they aren't physically strong enough to get me up. Really, who is? The hulk would probably reject me. This is not attractive or fun to watch.

Little Tori or Travis, mommy is currently sitting at our OB-GYN appointment pretending to look at magazines, which my photos of stars and celebs used to grace the covers of. Needless to say, it's all a charade. I'm using magazines to peek-and-hide from all the other preggers in the waiting room. "Heavens to Betsy, do I look that huge? Am I as big as the lady to my left, or the humongous girl to my right? Shocking, but do I?" Whatever. I feel secure because daddy hasn't said a word about my newly stretched-out silhouette. Blimey, do I turn him off? Mommy is really freaking out. There is no way I look like that colossal lady sitting in the corner. Talk about falling from denial and facing reality? If that wasn't scary enough (and believe me, it was more than enough), why am I talking to Betsy? Who the heck is this Betsy chick, and why do we always associate her with heaven? Then, I suddenly appreciated how greatly I missed and needed my soothing wine. Discouraged and despondent, I thought, "Well, for damn sure I'm not getting on the scale today." Not happening, unless the National Guard chains me to it. Ironically, the chains would add 10 more pounds to the problem. I'm not getting on that monster. Darn, the enormous pregger across the room caught me staring at her. I smiled, nodding back as if it were a camaraderie gesture. Eek baby, clearly my eyes, fearfully bulging out of their sockets, had nothing to do with solidarity, in any fashion. I continued smiling anyway.

I was relieved and rescued when I heard my name called by the nurse... "Mrs. Robins, come right in. How are you doing today? Come on back, Leona. Follow me."

FYI, It's not all bad, little Sonia or Eduardo. There are plenty of good days, soaking happily in denial, in which I completely forget about my increasing weight gain situation. But alas, it all comes rushing back to me when the *"Please, step on the scale"* happens.

Regrettably, although I still fight it, I am now forced to get on the *evil numbered demon*. Your angelic mommy demanded, "Hell No! Nope, not today... Still, thanks for asking."

GAINING WEIGHT... WTF ?

"Leona, come on. Step on the scale! You know you have to. We've already debated this."

The nightmare broadens when the perky, strawberry-blonde, cruel and insensitive, 98-pound, skinny nurse says to me in that obnoxious voice the entire office clearly heard, "Wowza, big jump there. That's a huge weight gain! My gosh, huh?" I retorted harshly...

"Perhaps, Nurse Annie Wilkes, the scale is reflecting a whole lot of water retention?"

"Well then, Mrs. Robin's, I would venture to say a *whole lot*! Don't cha think?"

Since I like my doctor *a whole lot*, I didn't think it proper to call her a bitch. So, I refrained. But I did say it quite loud in my inside voice. Instead, I responded like a dainty lady from the 60s, giggling, "Well then nurse, it's either that or a 46 and ½ pound baby!"

The weight gain chart during pregnancy suggests that if your weight is normal before you conceive, you should gain: 25–35 lbs. If you're underweight: 28–40 lbs. If you're overweight: 15–25 lbs. If you're obese: 11–20 lbs.! How impossible and rude is that?

Baby Boo, I don't think mommy falls anywhere in those ridiculous charts. I say the heck with it, I'm gonna eat for 2. Then, I'll soldier-march my *baby weight anxiety,* down to the beach (no bathing suit), and throw it right into the ocean. No problem, my weight is fine!

CHAPTER 20

I'm Not Jealous! Well, I'm Not!

Okay, so why is it your father and all of my friends are now accusing me of acting jealous all the time? What are they talking about?

In my defense, my big breakup with Geri, my oldest and dearest lifelong friend, had nothing whatsoever to do with jealousy. Who cares if she lost 25 pounds and now looks like a model, all slinky and sexy, while I'm turning into a beached whale? And, I couldn't care less if Christa and 3 other journalists (I worked with) won the 500,000-dollar lottery a day after I was fired. Good for them. I don't care if Tululla's boss, (new lover) gave her a gigantic raise and a huge promotion? So, her hunky beau is taking her around the world on his Learjet. "La-dee-da, La-dee da!" Big deal. Ok, maybe a smidge envious? I said envious, but I'm *not* jealous!

Jealous? Not me! Not one iota. Meanwhile, it's summer and I get that, but why is every woman dressing in a style that pretty much screams, *Naked*? A cotton ball would cover their boobs better. There ought to be a law. And precious, Beyoncé or Jay-Z', don't even think of suggesting to me that your father is not looking. Not like he has to look very far. I suspected it, when his tall, blonde, fake, busty secretary, *Bubbles La Rue,* with junk in the trunk of her motorized rear, said, "Good morning Leona, how are you?" Aha, yeah, tell me that wasn't packed with a butt load of sly innuendos? And when did *we* get on a first-name basis? I might also interject your dad's been coming home from playing tennis 10-minutes late for the last 4 consecutive Saturdays. Hmm, why is that, I question?

Jealous? Me jealous? Not that I admit to it, mind you, but why is it every time daddy answers his cell, he listens intently and then claims it was only a solicitor? Indeed?

My little baby, in retrospect, reflecting back, I don't understand why daddy was so unreasonably upset with me, simply because I refused to go to his little sister's 21st birthday event. It was a pool party, for heaven's sake. "Sexy Bathing Suit Required!" Really? I'm pregnant! How nervy to even expect me to attend a bikini celebration with a gaggle of 21-year-old, perfectly toned, gorgeous, single, horny, snickering girls? Besides, why would that make me jealous, anyhow? I was just not in a *"partay"* mood, that's all. When we discussed it, daddy added insult to injury (with obvious lies), that his sister's friends were all ugly, anyway. Not jealous, still that would piss off any pregnant woman.

What about the way your father flirted with the counter girl at the ice cream shop? This rendezvous was not a happy situation to witness, especially in my condition. Making matters worse, he accused me of having a vivid imagination. Aha, if that were merely my imagination, why then did he get 4 Maraschino cherries, a free scoop, gobs of dripping fudge, and oodles of whipped cream on his 3, (4) scoop sundae? While I only got one teeny tiny cherry, a trickle of fudge, a whisper of whipped cream, and 2 skimpy scoops? Hardly my imagination! While we are on the subject, how dare he accuse me of hiding his naked, perverted, girly magazines from him? Not that I have to defend myself, but in a charitable fashion, I donated them to the Veterans' humanity drive. I admit it! I'm a serious patriot!

Maybe it's me? Truth is, I'm exhausted after schlepping you around all day. So why does daddy get to go out and hang with the guys all the time, calling it, "Guys night out?" He's off drinking beer, enjoying football games, bowling, and playing cards, while I'm alone, growing you by myself. Wrong emotion Asher! I'm aggravated, not jealous!

Furthermore, why and I do mean why, am I accused of being jealous, just because I snuck daddy's phone to, *'Sherlock Holmes spy,'* on all his photos and the websites he's been frequenting. Yep, busted. I almost left him too, when I found totally naked photos of a gorgeous blonde. After I calmed down, I was relieved to realize the photos were of me. Phew, great shots though. Hence, not jealous, that was normal, standard, female behavior.

Moreover, just because I now hate all the nurses he works with, what does that possibly have to do with jealousy? Honestly, my little Nurse Betty or Greg Focker, they are constantly flirting with daddy while *"busting out,"* (literally busting out *with a capital B)* of their too short, trampy uniforms, like he is some Svengali. Thus, it's logical not to trust any of the seductresses and hussy nurses who get near him. "Jealousy, schmelousy!"

As you know, baby Avery or Kimmie, your daddy and I are happily in love. I'm not jealous, but as I grow bigger, I feel unattractive and not at all sexy. He might wander. How can I compete with these 20ish-year-old perfect girls, with fake boobs, phony butts, and flat bellies, desperately vying for my man's attention? Ironic, pre-pregnancy, none of that concerned me. Sure, I trust him, but I don't trust them. I'm with child, not stupid!

Just because I am going a tad, *CSI Detective*, and keeping my eyes *wide open,* has nothing to do with jealousy. I'm self-confident. Why would anyone detect jealousy here?

Ya know what, this is all preposterous and ridiculously stupid at best. I am Zen. I am peaceful and serene. I'm not jealous, envious, or even bitter. Still, however, "Back the hell away from my man, you trollops, femme fatales, vampy nurses, and sleazy bitches."

That said, and in my defense, all the above are not defined nor classified as one who is behaving in a jealous manner by any fumes of fancy, or facon de parler.

I'M NOT JEALOUS!

Sure, acting a little crazy, paranoid, and hormonal might suggest that I am possessive. Of course, but they're not symptoms of jealousy. Besides, it's simply all part of the many joys and normal reactions of pregnancy. Being suspicious, protective, cynical, skeptical, green-eyed, and distrustful with sneering squinting eyes is not jealousy, emotional, or even bitchy. It's not like I'm shackling him up in dramatic emotional bondage. It does sound pretty sexy, though. *Note to self: Try some hot, erotic, pregnancy sexual bondage.*

Murphy's law and wouldn't you know it? This month, People Magazine did a whole story including photos of famous men cheating on their pregnant wives... Front cover and all. Whatever! When all is said, done, and spied on, Asher is positively faithful. Therefore, I am not, nor do I have any reason, to be jealous. Still, come to think of it, why wasn't he wearing his wedding ring last week at the family barbecue, after he came from surgery? He alleged he took it off to scrub in, put it in his pocket, and forgot about it. I suppose I can believe his BS, tall-tale, while exhibiting piercing eyes of skepticism. Right? My distrust is understandable and reasonable coming from a pregnant woman who is essentially pissed off! Ugh, it is what it is. But for sure, it is not jealousy! Just saying...

CHAPTER 21

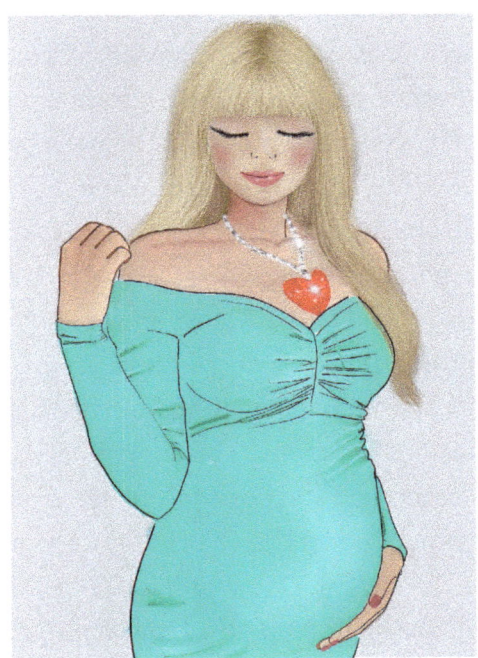

Rainbows... are made with pink, red, yellow, green, blue, and you! Tatiana or Trevor, mommy is now experiencing what they call, *"Maternal Feelings!"* Feelings, that all the books I've read and rummaged through, predict. It is a condition, which makes one feel very motherly-*ish*. It has something to do with countless hormonal changes. Not only am I supposedly *"glowing"* on the outside (And trust me, I don't see it either!) the books imply, I'm *glowing* on the inside too... Allegedly! I assume this divine inner glow is responsible for my being scorching hot. More accurately, sweating my guts out. Poor daddy, the air 24/7, is set at 50°. He's a real prince and truly deserves a crown!

These days, baby, my whole world revolves around you. You are the giggle in my laughter, the joy in my smile, the excitement in my heart*burn*, the unibrow above my nose, and the hair on my legs. I go about my life contently dreaming of you, little Collin or Reign, with my eyes wide open. Did I mention I am not sleeping much these days? Hence, I pass the hours baby-dreaming of cradling you with tenderness and adoring you for hours on end. You're my miracle. I visualize myself playing with you, caring for you, and protecting you from the world. Frustratingly, I wait impatiently for your arrival and I find the days are moving by in slow motion. Every tick-tock on the clock seems endless.

Nowadays, as the maternal feelings ensue, my heart expands wildly with a medley of emotions. You come into the world bringing new meaning and renewed purpose to our lives. You create insurmountable significance, beyond any priceless treasure. You are the ultimate gift to be cherished. Drew or Tiana, you will arrive bursting with goodness. We shall help you grow strong, noble, mold, and teach you all that we know. We'll share our world with you. I've never known such overwhelming fulfillment or this beguiling sense of blissful inner peace. It's as if I had been sleepwalking through life until you were conceived. You're the total celebration of mommy and daddy's affection. Whatever the magic is which manifested, "our *2 hearts to beat with love, as one,*" also manifested you.

Mommy dreams of turning all your frowns into smiles, transitioning your tears into laughter, and erase all your doubts with certainty. I hope to expunge all your failures (if any) into accomplishments and success, and magically reverse all fears into calming faith.

I will venture to edit your anger or frustrations into peace of mind and hope. I want to help you imagine your dreams, whatever they may be, towards possibilities and realities. Mommy envisions making a beautiful home for you, abundant with happiness, laughter, compassion, and, above all, love. It's the type of home you wake up to, feeling as if every morning is a holiday. Although snow may be falling, we're all cozy and snug, cuddled in family warmth and bliss. You will enchantingly turn a devoted couple into a real family.

"Maternal Feelings arise through a Mother's Love for her baby!"

Her love is pure and powerful, with its unique, mysterious, embracing harmony, infused with a calming peace and serenity. The best part, it need not be acquired, earned, or even deserved. A mommy's generous, continuous soul of affection is an unending blessing. Even when a mother's heart is overflowing with emotion for her child, while thinking it's impossible to hold or contain yet another inch of love, she'll always find a way to expand her heart, enabling her love to grow eternally. Baby Meg or Pip, important to understand, this devotion arrives together, alongside, through, and infused with the splendor of God.

Every mother, if asked, will delight in describing how being a mom is the greatest achievement and joy in her life. She sees the very best parts of herself reflected within her child, only better, far more perfect, remarkable, and extraordinary. A mom's love for her child leaves an indelible, permanent, inerasable mark, which remains evermore. For her adoration is an intangible, abstract concept, indeed. Understand, precious, my love for you is already grander than the universe and wider than any galaxy. It shines more vibrant than the moon and warmer than the sun. My love for you is the brightest guiding star and the sun to my planet. You and daddy are my entire world. All I am, or will ever be, revolves around my devotion for you both. *Aristotle* said, (Hey, that's a possible good name for you!) "Love is composed of a single soul inhabiting 2 bodies." So right, he was.

Woefully, the day will come when every mother knows instinctively (dragging her feet and clenching her heart) when it's time to let go and cut the strings. When her baby must go off into the world, make their own path, and follow their own personal destiny. Regardless, a caring mom waits and watches over her child amidst the shadows. It is her warm voice and radiant guidance, which always sheds light and direction for her child.

Through these legendary "Maternal Feelings," (AKA, hormonal hell) I've allowed myself to be persuaded by my beliefs and convictions that, the light, which sparks from my inner star of love and emotions for you, cannot be diminished, and its sparkle is limitless. However, I have heard all that glittery sparkle might be left behind in the dust during your teen years. Whatever? We'll wait to see what happens there. But, ugh, don't!

MATERNAL FEELINGS

Baby sweet pea, throughout my childhood, I would always say to my daddy...

"I love you."

He would continually respond with an exuberant, "I love you more!" I never quite understood what he meant by that. Maximus or Tabitha, now, at last, I get it.

Hence, I love you more, my sweet Boop-De-Doop. You have mystifyingly stolen my heart and anchored it directly into your soul. Thank you, sweetheart, and thank you, God!

If everything good and wonderful had been erased from life as we know it, and only a mother's glorious, massive love remained, the earth would prevail and flourish.

And, little Dorothea or Donovan, if my love for you had a color, it would simply be the whole, entire rainbow. It would display colors that shimmer and glisten for all to see, every single possible color amid a perfectly arched, stunning, full-circled rainbow.

Rainbows are made with the promise of:

Luck, rebirth, joy, magic, bliss, wonder, peace, awe, pink, red, yellow, green, blue and you!

CHAPTER 22

Lunch With Colette...

The Obnoxious, Catty, College Sorority Sister

"*Hey, Leona!* GIRRRL, O-M-GOSH, are you seriously still pregnant? Are you kidding me? Jeez! Holy Moly and Yikes! What month are you in?"

"No. Not kidding! Just starting my 5th month. Yet, so nice of you to ask, Colette?"

"For real, you're only starting your 5th month? I mean, it seems like you've been pregnant for a year. Two, even! I don't know, girl, I just remember you being shockingly huge the last time we met. No offense, but could you be having twins? Perhaps, triplets?"

"Could be? Doctors are wrong all the time. No offense back, Colette, but actually I haven't really gained all that much weight. I'm within the projected statistics of what to gain. And good Lord, Colette! Your comment is awfully insensitive, don't you think?"

"Testy aren't we honey? Whatever babe, I've heard the raging hormones do make moms-to-be very emotional and bitchy. Understandable, but do calm down! I didn't mean anything by it. Although, I gotta ask, *do you have a full-length mirror?* If so, have you looked at it lately? Gosh, I think you should. How much weight have you gained so far?"

"Somethin, somethin, and not really any of your business, pounds."

"Fine, just don't let yourself get out of control, or you will so regret it later on."

"Well, my doctor told me I'm retaining a lot of water and not to worry."

"Ah-ha, ok, retaining an ocean, I'll bet? Never mind, just forget that I asked. So, will you be doing the whole scary, nonsense, antiquated, natural-birth, drama thing?"

"Not certain just yet. We're still mulling it over. So Colette, how have you been?"

"If I were you, I would sincerely start mulling, and quickly. Definitely, there will be no natural anything for me, thank you very much. I want to be put directly to sleep if they can. I hear the pain is excruciating and crazy unbearable. Do you even think you can handle it? They don't scream in the movies like that for nothing! You know what I'm saying? Nothing for nothing, they better meet me in the parking lot with an epidural."

I thought to myself, that's actually not a terrible idea. Yet, I still replied crossly, "Thanks, by the way, for terrifying me, Colette. Can always count on you to add drama."

"What? I'm only asking? Oh, I see! Are you still blaming me and holding that Frat Party, fiasco against me? How could I have known they were spiking your tequila? Besides, we all did ultimately rescue you after you drank the date rape drug. No credit, no thank you? Huh, nothing? Ok, whatever. Sorry, I didn't know you were terrified of labor. Wow, look at you. Gosh, I just realized, how does it finally feel for you to have breasts? Why you must be in 7th heaven. Good for you! Asher must be unequivocally diggin' it."

"I've always had breasts? Just not huge jugs like they are now. Honestly, I'm not thrilled at all. They're way too big and uncomfortable. You'll see when you're pregnant."

"Too big? What? That's impossible. Man, Leona, did your mother ever fail you! 'Diamonds, houses and boobs can never, *like ever*, be too big!' Those are words to live by. And why are you getting so upset? I gather it really is true what they say about preggers being overly sensitive and emotional. Beware girly, from what I hear jealousy is next?"

"What? I'm not being sensitive! Why are you even saying such things to me?"

"Never mind. I'm only saying that Asher is quite dreamy, so be careful there."

"Colette, I am not bitchy, emotional, or jealous. Asher and I are totally great."

"Fine, perfect, enough said! E-gads, chill out... I didn't mean to rile you all up. Moving on, you are aware that all the sisters heard about you losing your awesome job. It must've been an enormous bummer. You're probably completely devastated over it?"

"Nah. It's cool. I have more time now to prepare for Azazel or Oaklynn."

"You've got to be joking about those names. You're messing with me, right?"

"No, we haven't decided on names yet. Simply throwing around a few ideas."

"Ok, well, you can throw those 2 into the garbage, if you ask me. Hold on, wait a minute. You don't want to know the sex of your twins or the triplets ahead of time?"

"Very funny. It's only one baby and no, we really want to be surprised."

"Wasn't the two red lines on the stick surprise enough? Well, I'd want to know. I hate surprises, especially about that! I'm having another. You want a glass of red, too?"

"Colette??? Umm? Hello? I am pregnant. Come on girl, you know I can't drink!"

"And that's another reason not to have kids. You're eating for 2, I'll drink for 2."

"Aren't you such a good friend? I'll admit I really do miss my wine and coffee."

Colette went on, as I enjoyed the perfect bite of my double-double cheeseburger and fries.

LUNCH WITH COLETTE...

"Girl, I couldn't live without my wine or café. BTW, not to state the obvious, but Leona, your roots have like 5 inches of growth! What's the deal? Have you decided to let yourself go, or only letting your so-called, natural blonde hair go back to, *whatever that color is*? You're pregnant, but you can't allow yourself to get lost in it all. Keep in mind, there is life after the baby. No worries, I'll hook you up with my colorist, with one call."

"Girl, you are so damn catty. Give it a rest. Besides, they say color processing is not good for baby. I'll get there. Not letting myself go, but what's your excuse, Colette?"

"LOL, touché! You still have your spunk. I'll give you that! Though, looking at you now, it makes me petrified to ever get pregnant. Asher must *really, really,* love you!"

"Wow. Ouch. That comment was a textbook, '*Nonpliment.*' You... You're good!"

"My pleasure! Anyway, would you like some of the other sisters and me to throw you a baby shower? Or would that ruin the surprise, too? It would be such a blast to do."

"Thanks for asking. Can I get back to you on that? My mother-in-law has inquired about it. I think she has things in the works, but I'm not sure yet. She's very mysterious."

"And how is that nasty bitch doing? Mysterious, what an adorable word for her! How you can deal with her, I don't know. You are a better woman than me, for sure."

"LOL, for sure I am that. Regardless, she is actually... well actually, very lovely."

"You are such a bad liar. You always were. Whatever, if you say so? Although, clearly and mysteriously, some of that weight has definitely gone straight to your brain."

"Ha-Ha-Ha. You are the funny one. Yet again, I really haven't gained that much."

"Ah-Ha, OK? So, Leona, speaking of Asher... How is your gorgeous, successful, hot-and-sexy, hubby? Take care of him, doll. You don't want to lose a winner like Ash. Men feel left out when their wives are expecting. Don't be naïve. Who knows where that could lead? Wake up, Leona. Single girls are on the prowl for a hunk like Asher. He looks like sexual-manna from heaven. I'd surely keep my eyes glued-open if I were you!"

Unfortunately, I wasn't able to hide my cold gaze of lethal daggers. And, I found it difficult to stop my mean-girl words from spewing off the tip of my tongue... "What are you implying, Colette? I hate to throw shade, but jeez, speaking of nasty bitches! You are more unkind and harsh than I remember. What's happened to you? Are you not happy?"

"Of course I'm happy. I have a perfect life. I'm blissfully married. I have a lovely house, car, and an amazing job. I am thin, toned, pretty, and my hair and skin are flawless,"

"Wait... You forgot humble and modest... OK! Great, then I am happy for you."

"Leona, forget I asked. Anyway, how are you guys managing financially? I bet it must really hurt not having that *little extra bit* of money from your job that fired you?"

"Colette cut the crap. You know Asher is a successful doctor. We are super-de-duper fabulous, ecstatic, excited, in love, and having a baby. Nothing could be better. As a matter of fact, every night Asher makes it a point to crouch down, to kiss my belly, and marvel at the life we created together. I am the luckiest, happiest girl in the world."

LUNCH WITH COLETTE...

"I'm going to throw up! Thou dost protest too much? I'm teasing, glad to hear it. I think? I couldn't be happier for you. You know I luv you. But a word to the wise... I do hope Ash is doing more than kissing your belly while he's already crouched down there!"

"Good to know, nothing's changed. You're still a dirty girl. Let's order dessert."

"Hell's bells, you're still hungry? How is that possible? Fine. Sure, let's do it. After all, this is a special occasion. And, unlike you, I can afford to gain a few pounds."

With a whiplash of emotions and a massive internal eye-roll flying freely, aimed directly at her, "Yum, I want the extra rich, double-double fudge, chocolate-chip cake."

"I won't say a single word. Dammit... I have to. That's really fattening, Leona!"

"Yep, so it is! Perfect, 'cause I'm eating for 2. I'm not sharing, so get your own!"

"Leo, you were right... yummy, luscious, and worth a few pounds. *Well, for ME!*"

"You're such a bitch! And yea, their desserts are fab. I'll get a few to take home!"

"I won't say a single word... Anyhow, Leona, I'm thrilled we got together for lunch today. Really happy we did this. You need to stay in better touch with me, and the rest of the sorority gals. Naturally, we all have such busy, successful, fulfilling lives. But... we still miss you. If we don't do a shower, we should all get together real soon.

"Ahhh, nice to hear, ditto, and that would be wonderful. Tell everyone I said hi!" (I couldn't help wondering if God smites pregnant women for lying through their teeth?)

"I will do that, for sure. Let's get the check and by the way, lunch is on me."

"No Colette. Thank you so much, anyway. So, let's just split the bill, OK?"

"I wouldn't think of it!" Then she continued with her razor-sharp tone, "You have enough to worry about and besides, you're out of work. It's my way of helping."

With a laborious effort to remain civil, "Thanks, Colette. Umm, it 'twas fun?"

"It 'twas. Hey before we go, tell me, and do be honest. How bad are the *Stretch Marks?* Leona? Leona? Leona! Where are you going? Leona? Was it something I said? Leona! Leoonnnaaaa, come back! Where are you going? We are not finished lunching yet. I was only curious? Stop running! You're going to hurt yourself. Leona stop running away. What-eves bella. Ciao, Leona! Bye, bitchy, emotional, jealous, hormonal, beeyotch! Wow! LOL! Bhah-ha-ha-ha! Yikes, her *Stretch Marks* must be epic!"

CHAPTER 23

The Rollercoaster of Worries...

Pregnancy, without a question of a doubt, brings along with it a loop-di-loop rollercoaster, of ups and downs, to be troubled or worried about. Feasibly, even more than stretch marks and gaining weight. (If you can imagine that?) Obviously, there's a bevy of uncertainties, uneasiness, fears, concerns, anxiety, angst, apprehensive emotions, and buckets of unwanted stress. Now, add to this upsetting equation all the baby planning, finding the right doctors, the perfect delivery birth plan, all the insecure body changes (there is much to reckon with here), and let's not forget the list of endless "Dos and Don'ts." Then sprinkle in the astonishing fact that there's a tiny human growing inside of you. Being with child is obviously a high-stakes endeavor and quite worthy of freaking out. I remember the quote, "Bravery hides in every heart, and one day you will be summoned." I believe that day has come. Granted, and being earnest, it's natural to over-obsess about every little thing while a baby is blossoming within. *For instance:*

- What if I have a Miscarriage and lose the baby? I can't even bear the thought.
- There is too much stress to cope with. Will I succeed in dealing with all of it?
- What if I have a premature birth? I have a million questions on that prospect.
- What about the unbearable labor pain? I'm worried, uneasy, and afraid. Can I handle it?
- Is it true no sushi, wine, caffeine, soft cheese, junk food, etc.? Ugh. Gosh, what's left?
- Breastfeeding? Can I do it? Will my baby want it? Does it hurt? Will I like it?
- What if something's wrong with my baby? God forbid! But will I be able to cope?

THE ROLLERCOASTER OF WORRIES...

- Pregnant weight gain! Hell, was bitchy Colette right? Is it possible to lose it later on?
- I'm having dreadful morning sickness! Is baby getting enough to eat in there?
- I'm constantly worried that it's harming my baby if I eat or drink the wrong foods?
- Is my daily stress hurting the baby? Ironically, it's the vast baby worries that stress me.
- I'm crying all the time. I'm not even sad? Is it upsetting my baby? It's upsetting me!
- I'm now laughing and crying together. Is it confusing to the baby? It's confusing to me.
- I can't stop fearing my baby might have a birth defect. It's a scary and legit concern.
- Though it's rare, I am a little concerned I could die in childbirth? It does happen.
- What if I have terrible complications, like preeclampsia or gestational diabetes?
- Not to be negative, but I'm obsessed and troubled about *everything*. It's awful.
- Will I hurt the baby if I exercise? Dr. said I could, but won't that tangle the cord?
- Worried, sex will never be the same. Tell me it's absolutely not true. Or just lie!
- I was told my vagina after birth would be huge, like the Holland Tunnel. Will it?
- I'm not getting much sleep. Is that hurting the baby? I must say, it's hurting me.

- What If I am crushing the baby running around, or constantly moving too much?
- What if I need an emergency C-section? F#$%andg. Hell no! Yet, it could happen.
- What if my mother-in-law never leaves? Kidding, she's wonderful and mysterious?
- What if I think I'm in labor? How will I know if it's Braxton Hicks or false labor?
- What if I'm not cut out to be a good mom? What if I'm not up to the task? Sigh!
- Will I have a life after baby? They say not to make baby your whole world, but...
- Will seeing the birth turn Asher off, never wanting to have sex with me again?
- What if I don't love my baby? Even worse, what if my baby doesn't love me?

Evidently, little Amal or George, I need to meditate and get my Zen going. I need to go spiritual, cosmic even. Still, all pregnant women panic and worry, right? Moreover, what about all of the, *"Should I's, and what if's?"* For example:

- Should I even consider Llamas Natural Childbirth? Or, definitely stick to an epidural all the way. I'm terrified, plus I've heard they can be dangerous?
- Should I make my own baby food from scratch or go buy it? Does it matter?
- What stroller, crib, mattress, swing, car seat, playpen, bath, bottles, changing table, diapers, and toys should I buy? A bad choice could piss-off the baby at hello.

THE ROLLERCOASTER OF WORRIES...

- Should I use pacifiers? If so, which ones? Still, I've heard they're bad for teeth?
- Should I let the baby cry through the night? If not, when should I step in? I can't imagine letting my baby cry all night? That would likely keep us all up, crying.
- Should I wear a baby carrier? It looks ideal and offers lots of baby bonding.
- What will I do if the baby has a very high temperature in the middle of the night?
- How will I find the best pediatrician? And will I ultimately pick the right one?
- Is it true doing Kegels help delivery muscles get in shape and ease pregnancy symptoms? Or, is that just BS mansplaining, to keep women in good vagina shape?
- Should I quickly sign up for a mommy and me class? Don't want us to be left out.
- Will I likely suffer from postpartum blues? Can it be prevented? Me, no likey!
- Should I enroll my baby in an Ivy-League, preppy, private, pre-school right away to ensure my child gets into an Ivy college? I don't want to ruin my kid's life at *square-1*. It's very competitive out there for dreamers? #Harvardorbust! Just hoping!
- What if my baby is totally colicky and won't sleep all night like my girlfriend's baby? She never stops complaining. For real, I really think she hates her baby. Egads.
- What if baby is really ugly? Will I still love my baby? #Superficialandshallowmuch?

- While costly, should we save and store the umbilical cord for future medical reasons?
- How do I baby-proof? Presently, the house is a battleground of baby perils. It is virtually, a baby war-zone. It's one big baby trap, teeming with unsafe cords, outlets, electrical wires, chemicals, choking hazards, sharp edges, stairs, toilets, and cabinets.

Baby Nora or Luke, have no fear. I can do this. Anyway, that's what I keep telling myself. I'll figure it all out by the time you get here. I will be ready for you, I promise. I'll even request a dossier of baby proofing philosophies. Trust me, my love for you will get us through all obstacles. In other breaking news, I'll love you no matter what, even if you are ugly. Especially then! Ya know, "As only a mother could love." I'm sorry, that was radically cruel and hurtful. But I'm totally joking. Mostly...

CHAPTER 24

A Call From Mommy's Mommy...

"**Hello Leona, Sweetheart.** It's Mooom...

I know I called you earlier, but that was over 2 hours ago and I'm still worried about you. How are you feeling now? Is your nausea any better? Remember, eat crackers and toast."

"All good, mom. Please stop worrying. You're going to drive yourself crazy and take me along with you. It's all normal pregnancy symptoms, but thank you for caring."

"Sorry, I just love you so much. OK then, I'm delighted to hear you're doing fine. How is your husband? Is he treating you well, catering to you, and being supportive for a change? I pray that he is! You're the best wife in the world and I hope *Aster* realizes it."

"Mom, his name is Asher. He treats me like a queen, an angel, and you know it!"

"Great, then! Listen, darling, I hope you are being careful and not overdoing too much. After all, in your condition, it wouldn't be wise. And, I really want you to stop bending and lifting from now on. Go ahead and let your husband do all of that for you. While I think about it, show him how to run the washing machine and dishwasher. Does he even know where they are? Let him do the laundry! You need your rest. Your body is creating life, and mundane household chores shouldn't be on your to-do list. Also, honey, I meant to tell you yesterday, you're too thin. You realize you're eating for 2 now, right? And, while I have your ear, stop cooking all those big, fancy meals every night. It's not necessary. Who the hell are you trying to impress? Get off your swollen legs and put your little feet up. You don't want to risk getting a blood clot to your heart, do you? There's nothing wrong with serving the big-fancy Dr. a few TV dinners. They are actually made very well nowadays. BTW, there are companies who deliver fresh meals for the week. Better yet, tell what's his name, to pick up healthy food to cook for you both when he gets home. Frankly, *Ashshum* can stand to lose a few extra pounds! Listen to your mom."

A CALL FROM MOMMY'S MOMMY...

"*ASHER* is clearly *not* overweight and you know it! He's a total sexy hunk, with a perfect 6-pack. Leave him alone! You are such a tough crowd, mom. Besides, Asher is a very busy Dr. and is working his ass off. He is doing everything he can and I don't expect him to come home and have to start cooking and cleaning, too. Why can't you see that? He's the most wonderful, caring man, and I love him. Newsflash mom... *So should you!*"

"Well, I don't know about that dear, but I certainly love you, my precious Leona."

"Please understand mommy, I'm truly the lucky one here. The man is a diamond."

"Blah, blah, yada, yada! About that, tell *Ashani* to put a bigger and better diamond than the pebble that's currently sitting in your ring. OK! I'll try harder, because you love him. Here's a thought! Tell *Archie* to hire a housekeeper, at least until you deliver. Make it easier for yourself, hon. BTW, did I tell you already you're going to have a baby girl?"

"Yes! Yes, you did, only about 100 times... This week alone! Good Lord, Mom."

"Leona, be nice to your mother. My memory is going. I'm almost 50 years old, you realize. Understand, you won't have me forever and you'll miss me when I'm gone! God knows, we don't know how much longer I'll be here to protect you. Remember, a mother's love is the greatest, most giving, selfless love in the world. You'll soon, see."

My little Sienna or Wyatt, that's the perfect example of guilt and passive-aggressive behaviors combined. Grandma has made an art form out of them. She's utterly brilliant.

"Anyway, Leona, *it's a* girl and I'm never wrong. It's 100% a baby girl, princess. So exciting. Now that I'm certain it's a girl, we must start buying the entire layette, plan a shower, and decorate the baby's room. Or better yet, you stay in bed and I'll do it all. For sure, I can't count on *Aiden*, as he is so very busy saving lives. Besides, I have the time to start at once. Ya know I have exquisite taste and I'll happily do the whole room in pink."

"It's Asher, and mommy, no thanks! I'm not far enough along yet, so I don't want to jinx anything. Just lie low and chill for now, OK? Really, thank you so much, though."

"OK darling, and as always, I will respect your wishes. Give *Alonzo*, Mr. Perfect, my, my-a, my love. Let's talk later. Now get off your sore feet, call DoorDash for dinner, go lie down, and get some rest. By the way Leona, are you keeping all of your Doctor's appointments and taking your prenatal vitamins? It's very important, so don't forget."

"Seriously, his name is Asher! Yes, to the appointments and yes, to the vitamins."

"Very good. One last thing, honey. I wanted to know if I should look through baby announcements and pre-order them? Or, I can cherry-pick some online for you to look at, if you'd prefer. Whatever makes your life easier, I'm glad to do it with pleasure."

"No thanks, mom. Too early and I'd prefer to choose them myself. No offense."

"None taken. All righty then, I love you? Oh, wait. Leona, hold on one more sec. I just had another thought. Would you like me to come over and clean the house for you later? Maybe do laundry, toilets, and leave a fresh brisket with potatoes and vegetables cooking in the oven. It'll last a few days. Plus, I can bring over my legendary fresh apple pie with the chunky crumbs and cinnamon on top. Apples are so good this time of year."

A CALL FROM MOMMY'S MOMMY...

"That's so sweet, but no thanks. I'm good, but I love you to pieces for asking."

"Oh, I also wanted to tell you, I am so proud that you are going to breastfeed. It creates a wonderful bond with the baby. It's such a healthy, loving way to start off your little baby girl's life. You'll both love it! Ok, ciao for now. Say hello to *Ashton*, for me."

"It's Asher! Wow, clearly no man will ever be good enough for me in your eyes."

"Yes, that is a very true statement. I'll admit, no man will or could ever be good enough for you! Talk to you later, honey. Muahhh. I Love You, a Bushel and a Peck!"

"Bye Mom... I Love You a Bushel and a Peck, and a hug around the neck!"

"I'll call you later tonight my darling!"

"Wait. Mom, No! Mom, Please, Don't Call. No, mom, stop. Ugh..."

That's when mommy heard a click and a loud dial tone. Gosh, darn it!

Little Darwin or Kylie, it's funny, fascinating actually. Somehow, being pregnant has made me love and appreciate my mom so much more than I ever have. Yes, without a doubt, she is by far the biggest, most relentless, overbearing pain in the ass, ever!

When she gets a thought into her head, she never stops. But, come on, she loves me dearly and her soul is so caring and compassionate. I do feel guilty sometimes for all the unkind words or mean things I've done to her in the past. Well, almost? Ok, all of it. Sweetheart, I give you my promise I'll try not to be an overbearing mom. I'll try, at least!

CHAPTER 25

A Call From Daddy's Mommy...

"*Hello Leona, Dearest!* How is my son doing? Your better-half? I worry so about my Asher. These days, no one seems to be looking out for him. That's what a mom is for, I reckon. It never really ends, huh? Although I did assume your "Till death do us part" vows meant that was supposed to be your job? Right, dear?"

"He's happy and well, mom. No worries, we take excellent care of each other."

"Delightful, good to hear. I was only wondering because the last time I saw the 2 of you, or should I say the 3 of you, he appeared extremely unhealthy to me. He looked pale and way too thin. I do hope you're at least feeding him well. After all, and to be perfectly blunt, you don't have a job anymore. So essentially, you have loads of free time on your hands to cater to him. Aren't you the lucky one, being a woman of leisure and all?"

"I was fired, mom. Fired for getting pregnant. And Asher's eating super healthy."

"Wonderful. Gosh, silly me and, of course, how are you doing? I couldn't help but notice you are packing on the pounds and visibly eating super well. Meanwhile, dear, you mustn't let yourself go. You have a gorgeous, desirable husband. You don't want his eyes to wander. Do you? It's crucial to watch those unsightly pounds. If not for you, dear, do it for Asher. A baby only averages 7 pounds. How are you going to lose the other 50?"

"Ouch! And mom, I haven't gained a lot of weight! *BTW, Did you raise Colette?*"

"What? Pardon? Colette, who? Well, suit yourself. I'm merely extending a gentle and helpful heads up. So, Leona, I have recently done a lot of reading since you became pregnant. Boy, I must say, times have certainly changed from my day. They say bending or lifting is healthy now, and a good form of pregnancy exercise. You must get off the couch and start moving. It's unhealthy keeping your legs up and doing nothing all day. You need to stop all of this pampering and indulging yourself. All that *'doing nothing'* laziness would push me into a dark depression. They say in the books and

A CALL FROM DADDY'S MOMMY...

literature I've read, self-coddling is now considered passé and detrimental. Thus, pull off the covers and go deep clean the house. Lord knows it could use a spring cleaning. (Summer, winter, and fall, too.) Read the latest opinions. Once upon a time, you ran with modern-day views?"

"Mom, honestly, where are you getting all of this fake news? I assure you, I'm not pampering myself and I exercise daily. Though, I do appreciate you caring about me?"

"Excellent. Now, listen up. I don't know if you've thought about it yet, but I want you to appreciate this is a very difficult time for my darling Asher. I felt I needed to bring it to your attention because it's actually not just all about you now. He is killing himself to make a good living to support you, the baby, and to give you the life that you evidently expect. On that note, I pray you aren't neglecting him and his important, essential needs. If you would dear, please at least, try a little extra hard to be patient and understanding with him. I hope you can realize how another mouth to feed in this day and age is a huge responsibility, bringing additional stress for any man. I'm sure *even you,* grasp this fact?"

"Mom, I grasp it entirely. His needs are met, we are totally fine, and very happy."

"Perfect. Incidentally Leona, I know you said you were fired, but don't you think you could contribute a little and look for a new job? I think it would be a positive boost to your self-esteem. If you ask me, I don't think giving up your career as quickly as you did was very wise. I mean, the girls around here, as I did when I was pregnant, worked right up until our water broke. And, weren't our husbands ever so proud! But surely, you know best, dear. You know me, I stay out of things. I don't intrude or butt in. It's not my style!"

"Thank you mom for your subtle advice and input. I shall keep it all in mind."

"Oh, heavens, I almost forgot. I wanted to tell you in advance to prepare you. You and Asher are having a BOY! Heed my psychic advice, for I am never wrong about these matters. Congrats, my little pretty, it's a boy. Start buying all blue. Boys are the best!"

"Thanks, good to know, mom. Though for us, a healthy baby is our main focus."

"One more thing Leona, before I let you go back to your, *relaxing*? Please, tell me you are not thinking of doing natural childbirth! You aren't? Right? Forget the fact that Asher is a surgeon, but you know how squeamish your devoted husband is about seeing people he loves in pain. I don't feel you should put him through something as traumatic and disturbing as all that hideous screaming and yelling throughout the whole birthing drama. It's so unnecessary. Certainly, you agree? Still, as you know, I never meddle."

"OK mom, we'll think about it. We haven't decided anything definite, as yet."

"Brilliant, I got it! Leona, there's one last thing I wanted to ask. Of course, you're not considering breastfeeding my grandson, are you dear? In earnest, do you really want to lose your perky breasts? Moreover, breast surgery, later on, to put them back up where they belong is so costly. Besides, breastfeeding is totally bourgeois and old school. Don't you agree? You're a modern girl, aren't you? You'd hate it, anyway. Meanwhile, there's nothing wrong with formula nowadays. They're all healthy and nutritious. The closeness, affection, and bonding with the baby are the same when using a bottle. You want to stay beautiful and sexy for Asher, don't you, dear? I do recall him being a staunch boob-man."

A CALL FROM DADDY'S MOMMY...

"Umm, yeah mom, way too much information. Really, far beyond way too much."

"Nuff said. I wouldn't dream of interfering, intruding, or telling *you* what to do!"

"Mom, my breasts will stay perky and sexy. Clearly, we'll do what's best for baby."

"Indeed. Well then, I don't want to keep you from your... chores? Or, whatever it is you do with yourself, all day long? I've got an idea! Why don't go prepare a fancy dinner for 2? Google a Martha Stewart recipe. Also, remember to do your Kegel exercises. They keep your honeypot tight, you know. Ok, goodbye now, Leona. Don't forget, think blue!"

"Bye, mom. Thanks for calling. You're always so... *helpful*. Have a lovely day."

And then I heard her blow a perfunctory kiss to me through the phone.

All of a sudden, I had the urgent need to call my mommy, your magnificent other grandmother. My baby Joan Crawford or Captain Von Trapp, I feel as if I just got run over by a Mack Truck, charged by an angry rhino, or dare I say, knocked down by the wicked witch of Oz flying on her broom. I'm a joking, silly-dilly. Grandma Robins is divine. You'll love her?

Phew! Yikes, little Riesling or Merlot, daddy's mom is definitely a massive force to be reckoned with. Oh, how I desperately need a glass of wine! The whole bottle, even!

CHAPTER 26

About Babies

A baby, a newborn, encompasses the heart of the human spirit... Holden or Anika, most babies begin their journey into the new world after nine months of being carried and cradled inside their mommy's bump. Babies are typically made with mystical sprinkles of love that blossom from a mommy and daddy's love for each other. A baby brings pure innocence, delight, inspiration, hope, and sunshine to every life they touch. One baby smile can warm and melt an entire universe, even if it's covered by ice. A baby is a spark of God, and moreover, God's greatest gift to the world. A woman endowed with the privilege and honor of carrying a child is blessed with unbelievable enchanting magic. She's blessed with a new soul to cherish, to embrace with love and awe.

Silly as it seems, when I was a little girl, I used to wonder how much love one's heart could hold. Amid the heavenly news of discovering we were pregnant with you, I learned a heart could actually grow enormous and immeasurable with a love beyond anyone's imagination. My angel, you have the extraordinary advantage of experiencing and recognizing my love for you. As you are growing within me, you are able to feel and hear my heartbeat. It's phenomenal how easily a wee fetus awakens, reinvents, recharges, inspires, and beguiles every thought, emotion, and concept into one's life. It's *Amazable*.

I don't know what you'll become in this world, but I do hope you'll come to appreciate you mean the world to us. Despite everything miraculous my hands have touched or my arms have held throughout my life, holding or touching you will be the greatest sensation they have ever known. When I pray, searching for a miracle, soon all I'll have to do is look into your eyes to know, "I possess all the miracle I will ever need."

With you at the center of our universe, we'll indeed sense our life's true purpose. To daddy and I, you'll be indescribable fulfillment, twinkles of excitement, bliss, elation, pureness, and oodles

ABOUT BABIES

more adjectives, all swaddled in one teeny blanket. It's sad to think, we'll only have your hand to hold, your heart to protect, time to teach, moments to enjoy, laughter and memories to share, for only one tiny moment in time, as you'll grow so fast.

God brings to the world renewed hope and optimism through the birth of each newborn. A new soul is the beginning of all things... the seed level of wonder, hope, dreams come true, endless possibilities, boundless opportunities of euphoria, and perfect harmony. A new life can bring fresh potential as far as the imagination can reach towards amazement, optimism, creativity, and impossible, unrealistic, crazy possibilities. Somewhere on this earth, 250 babies are born every minute. Each one of those babies will journey alone all the way to earth, with their own important mission to accomplish and crucial astonishing lessons to teach the world. We must listen intently! Each human life is uniquely essential, significant, critical, and vital to the human race as a whole. Thus, why we must teach them with gentle love and care, kindness and understanding.

When you're born, Legend or Arabella, I know I will stare at you adoringly for hours on end, marveling at the life that your daddy and I created. It will be startling to fathom, we together with God, made this mind-blowing, stunning perfection, that is you.

It's imperative if you grow up knowing one thing, know that you are our total world and reason to live a divine life. Above all, throughout your life, never doubt "You are loved."

Our child, sent to us from above, you'll unwittingly be making us better people. Consequently, as your parents, we must become the extraordinary people that we hope and want you to become one day. For us, it's necessary to achieve greatness, which will then enable us to guide you to grow into your best self. We'll strive in every way imaginable to support you toward becoming an exceptional, well-rounded person.

News Flash... Daddy and I are counting milliseconds till we meet and finally get to embrace you for the first time. Regardless, and despite both of your grandma's insistent psychic predictions, how exciting it will be to find out if you are a boy or a girl. Either way, it will be gloriously thrilling. My beloved Jonathan or Sandy, I giggle with delight, pondering the newness of your sweet baby smell, while gently tucking you in, singing songs, and kissing you goodnight. I imagine rocking you to sleep will feel like paradise.

In the quiet hours of the night, I find myself constantly thinking about you. I keep reminding myself as to the importance of appreciating every moment, not allowing a single experience to be taken for granted. To cherish every day we spend with you. Daddy and I will value every smile, delightful activity, every hug, kiss, snuggle, your sweet sounds, adorable baby talk, and all of the memories we make together as a family.

Your happiness will bring us power and your laughter will build our strength. Your joy will bring us immeasurable inner peace. We will endeavor not to waste, lose, or miss out on a single second with you. For these are the wonderful times we can never get back. Mommy will probably spend most days basically watching and marveling at every little thing you do, which will, of course, appear brilliant. I could be a tad prejudice? But I know your smile will wash away any problems that life may bring your daddy and me.

ABOUT BABIES

Sitting here alone in your room at 4:00 A.M. dreaming of you, as I so often do, it's hard to envision any form of real happiness that isn't about you or doesn't involve you. Being pregnant with you has proven to me that fairytales and wishes realistically do come true. For I made a gigantic wish and soon, I am going to be a mommy. I am going to be your one and only, forever mommy. I do hope the mere suggestion of that works for you!

You have grounded us with stunning promise, higher morals, potential, and lasting commitment. Little darling, your daddy and I are profusely excited and we can hardly wait to welcome you with a powerful tsunami of love. So you know, we have more enthusiastic, flickering fireworks flying around awaiting your arrival than a fourth of July parade. The promise of knowing you're coming colors our world with everything perfect.

In a garden teeming with flowers, you're our radiant, flawless, divine lovely rose.

I find it rather astounding, "How could your tiny little baby feet (before you are even born) leave such gigantic footprints in our hearts?" It is inconceivable. But yet, you did.

And all at once in a nanosecond, I stopped in my tracks understanding and accepting... "*You*, sweet Ledger or Cassidy are mommy's everything!" No other words needed.

CHAPTER 27

Women Always Know...

Friday...

Since I am now "The mommy-to-be," it grants me the power and authority to announce, "You are a girl," my baby Celine. And yes, "My heart will go on." Ergo, I declare I am 100% scientifically, physically, emotionally, psychically, undoubtedly sure, and theoretically positive that you are a beautiful little baby, girl...

Ta-Da! My God, it is so ridiculously apparent and incredibly obvious. It's almost silly.

First of all, I am carrying extremely round and high. You are kicking and moving ever so gently, as only a little delicate baby girl would do. In addition, my biorhythms are very elevated, which in-and-of-itself, alone is concrete evidence. Wait, there's more. My face is covered with gross pimples, your heartbeat is super fast, and I can't survive this heartburn for another minute. I've also researched the many sage old wives' tales, which clearly prove it's a girl. And like years gone by, when I dropped my scarf at the mall, the lady *bent over* to pick it up instead of *stooping*. A fact verifying you're a Rebekah. A girl.

Last but not least, confirming beyond a shadow of a doubt that you're a girl, I am depressed on Mondays, Wednesdays, and Fridays... Ok yes, Sundays too, on occasion. Now, I ask you, how could a woman be more certain than that? My goodness, it's all so very exciting. Soon, I'll be having a feminine baby girl, dressed in pink bows and ruffles. After all, God wouldn't give me a boy. I know nothing about boys. Mommy's the biggest girly-girl in all the land. Seriously, I'm a woman and we know these things. We always know. If you don't believe me yet, I have further out-and-out, absolute scientific proof.

1. I've noticed a change in my body temp. I am always feeling hot and sweaty. It's a girl.

WOMEN ALWAYS KNOW...

2. I am craving sugary sweets and carbs way more than usual. (That's a lot) Yep, it's a girl.
3. Wait, it gets better. I tied my wedding ring on a string and hung it above my pregnant belly. It swung back and forth, *not in a circle.* Come on, plain and simple, it's totally a girl.
4. I've been as graceful as a ballerina and not the least bit clumsy at all. It's a baby girl.
5. I have been having crazy pregnancy dreams about boys. This alone verifies it's a girl!
6. My urine is light and dull instead of a bright yellow color. Confirmed, it's a girl.
7. I'm temperamental with enormous mood swings. *So, I've been told?* It's a frickin' girl.
8. My left breast is much larger, which sadly makes the right one look stupid. Aha. A girl.
9. My hair is dull, not shiny and I'm having far too many bad hair days. So clearly, it's a girl. And what an ungrateful brat? Sorry, but really Erin, stop messing with my hair!
10. My face is fuller. No, rounder. Heck, to be candid, it's fat. Little Shaina, why are you doing all of this cruel stuff to mommy? Are you a mean girl? Yo, kid, *I'm your true BFF!*
11. My bump line extends, running its unsightly line from my belly button down. Girl?!?
12. I threaded a needle (like the old wives' tales say), held it over the palm of my hand, and it swings in circles. Yep, flat-out proof and scientific opinion is... I'm having a girl.
13. I'm constantly drinking orange juice lately. I can't get enough of it. For Pete's sake, I literally hate OJ! I'm definitely having a girl. And who the hell is this Pete guy, anyway?

14. I picked up a key by the short end. Voilà! Yep, without a doubt, it's absolutely a girl!
15. I lie in bed on my right side, which distinctly signifies I'm carrying a girl. No-brainer.
16. I even took the baking soda/urine test, and it barely sizzled. Aha, a girl is arriving!
17. I embarrassingly did the nude bump test. Because of the way my hands cupped the side of my bump, curving around the side of my belly is explicit proof it's a girl! Done.

It couldn't be more apparent. All the evidence points and indicates... Girl, Girl, and Girl!

Tuesday, 11 Days later... Goodness, hold everything ~ Oh no? No! No?

I don't understand what's going on here? What? It's Tuesday, and I'm depressed! Really depressed. And would you just look at that? My face is clearing up beautifully. Ouch, ouch, little one. You are kicking mommy extremely hard, like an offensive tackler. Ouch, owe, and cool it. You're vigorously moving all the time now. *What sup* with that?

Gee, that's funny? Isn't that something? Staring at the mirror, I didn't realize it before. It seems I'm carrying low now? When did that happen? However, my heartburn is still there. I'm so confused. Wait, a darn second here... *You Are A Boy?* A little Emerson, Gerard, or Keaton? How can that be? How is that possible? This is a curious twist of fate.

But, of course, you are a boy! What was I thinking? It's a no-brainer. Looking at the signs, God would unequivocally give us a baby boy. Daddy's *'male-azing,'* and very boyish himself. Naturally, you'd take after him. Sure, I can do boys. Clearly, mommy is crazy in love with all sports, camping, boating and fishing. I've even read a few copies of "Mechanics Illustrated" cover-to-cover. Or was that "Hustler?" Hey, most of the kids I grew up with were boys. I was a tomboy that summer when I was 7 years old. Moreover, I have 2 brothers and I dated lots and lots of you guys. Lots, but shhhh! Don't tell daddy.

That's it then, you're a boy! Fine, I'm good with that. How fantastic, a son, a baby son. What a relief. I am 100% scientifically, physically, emotionally, psychically, undoubtedly sure, and theoretically positive, you are a handsome little baby boy! Ta-Da! My God, it's so apparent and obvious. Seriously, I am a woman and we know these things. We always know. If you don't believe me yet, here is further out-and-out, absolute, precise, academically, systematically, methodically, and totally scientific proof.

1. My skin is glowing and flawless... It's a boy. BTW, baby, that's so sweet, and thanks.
2. I have noticed a change in my body temperature? I'm feeling cold and icy. It's a boy!
3. I'm craving salty, spicy, sour foods, and no sweets. I'm carrying low now, too. A boy!
4. Unmistakably, this darn wives' tale is always accurate... I tied my wedding ring on a string and hung it above my pregnant bump. It swung in a circle. Gimme a break. A boy!
5. My legs and ankles are completely swollen, like 2 stuffed sausages. It's a boy!

6. My urine's yellow. Been real clumsy lately. The ballerina has left the building. A boy!
7. I'm having crazy pregnancy dreams of girls. So, it's a boy. I do love the tiaras, though!
8. I'm experiencing frequent, terrible headaches? Totally a boy! Ouch, and cut it out, kid.
9. My mood is so happy, cheerful and mellow. Wow, I really am expecting a boy! Cheerio.
10. Right breast is larger and areolas are darker. Sad, the left one now looks stupid. A boy.
11. Not that I can see my legs anymore, but the icky fast-growing long hair to the touch reflects that I can now brush them. It's a boy! Ewe and *no thanks* a lot for that, Lil buddy.
12. Big yawn. Not sleeping at all these days. Go to sleep so I can, will ya? Such a boy!
13. The plus side and quite the perk, I'm happily looking somewhat radiant. It's a boy!
14. Darn, my thin nose has changed and appears much wider now. You are a baby boy!
15. My feet are always cold, even with my fuzzy socks. Slam duck and boom, it's a boy!
16. I put the soles of my feet together and saw a lump on the right and left foot. Not quite sure I understand this one myself. Regardless, there's a lump. Yep, therefore, it's a boy!
17. Nowadays, I'm sleeping on my left side. Thus, Wesley, you're genuinely a baby boy.

Apparently, it couldn't be clearer. All this substantiates and points to Boy, Boy, and Boy!

WOMEN ALWAYS KNOW...

Friday, 10 Days later... What the heck?

What is happening? I don't get it? I have a round high belly, it's Friday and I'm so depressed. I've got pimples all over my face like a 13-year-old. I look like crap. I am in the moodiest mood, and I can't help falling asleep all the time. I am dreaming of boys and my legs are not swollen... I am certifiably baffled.

So, you aren't a Rex or a Mason? You are a little Shaquille or Charlotte? Of course, God is sending us a girl. This is not an Agatha Christie mystery. When you get right down to it Mila, mommy is a high-heel, tiara, fancy-outfit, bow wearing, makeup, and long pink nails, girly-girl. If you are a boy, I'd still put it on you. You'd so hate it.

All righty, that settles it! Since I am now "The mommy-to-be," it grants me the power and authority to announce that I'm 100% scientifically, physically, emotionally, psychically, entirely sure, and theoretically positive you are a beautiful little *baby girl*. Ta-Da! My God, it's ridiculously apparent and incredibly obvious. It's almost silly...

I'm a woman and we categorically know these things. We indeed, always, always, know!

But still... Hmmmmmm?

CHAPTER 28

Now I'm the Mommy and You are the Baby...

Hey, Baby-Boo... What are you doing up so late? Honey, are you aware that it is 2:00 in the morning? Precious, you should be sleeping right now and not wide-awake kicking mommy like Tristan

Vizcaino. I guess it's fine, considering I probably woke you up in the first place. Now then, since you're already up, what would you like to do? We can enjoy one of our lovely conversations, or go raid the Twinkies, Oreos, Doritos, and cold pizza. That's my pick. OK, yes, you're right. We really should be good. I hear Colette's voice on a loop, infesting me with her bitchy guilt about weight.

Ya know being pregnant brings a greater focus to my life. It creates crystal clarity, vision, and insight. Reflecting over my lifespan, I can only think, how did the years fly by so quickly? What happened? Where did the time go? My point being... I was just a baby, a toddler, and a little girl growing up myself. And poof, abracadabra, hocus-pocus, and now I'll be the mommy and you're going to be the baby. Very Houdini and serendipitous.

Soon I suspect, before I know it, your friends will be calling me, "The old, nerdy, uncool mom." It's funny how fast time ages us and changes our roles. Honestly, I find it a tad bittersweet, and besides, "I'll never be old or nerdy, and I will forever be cool!" Yet, I can still remember laughing at my mom for being so uncool and embarrassing me as she tried so desperately to be nice to my friends. I now understand she struggled really hard to please everyone because of her deep love for me. I teased her terribly for speaking lame words like gag me with a spoon, gnarly, grody-to-the-max, bogus, as if, da bomb, stoked, peace out, oh snap, sup, that's hot, and barf me out. I was totally humiliated by her robust determination to be part of my sleepovers, to hang out with my friends, and wanting to have fun with us. Looking back, we were so mean and cruel, rudely kicking her out of my room. I should have a heart-to-heart with her one of these days to apologize for all of it. I don't need a soothsayer to predict my karma is going to be quite the bitch. I also mocked her for using endless jars of ridiculous anti-aging creams that, ironically, I now have plastered all over my face. So where's that magical *Poof* when you need it?

I absolutely remember everything about growing up...

I vividly recall the awful day my mommy collected all of my pacifiers, telling me, "It's time to give them up, honey." I still remember my hurt and pain, wondering, "Why is this woman who I love being so cruel and evil?" I don't think I ever forgave her for it.

I remember being three. How I cried my eyes out when I burned my whole hand on the stovetop. I heard my mommy screaming, "NO, no, Leona, stop. Don't touch the stove!" Naturally, I didn't listen. I pray you'll listen to me better than I did with my mom.

At four and a half, the single most frightening experience that could happen to a child happened to me. I dropped my mommy's hand, left her side, and got lost in a busy, gigantic department store. I still feel that panic, even today. My eyes were flooded and blinded by my tears. Scared to death, I called out, "Mommy, mommy, where are you? Help me, Mommy!" Next, some kind lady who worked at the store found me and located my mommy. Seeing my mother's relieved, beautiful face, thirty long minutes later in the security office, was *almost* better than getting a brand new pair of roller skates. Needless to say, it didn't happen again. I never loved my mommy more than at that very moment.

When I was five, I hurt my foot, falling off my training wheel bicycle. Daddy and mommy to the rescue swiftly rushed me off to the hospital. Lots of blood and 16 stitches later made this a painful, terrifying childhood memory. But I was pretty lit about the huge cartoon bandage the Dr. put on my foot, and the ice cream

I devoured after all the drama. I take pride in this scare as proof of my staunch, brave and courageous resolve. It took me a long while to get over this tragic ordeal. Still, even now, I can't watch Grey's Anatomy.

At the big *girl* age of six, I enjoyed my fondest birthday celebration. I was able to invite 20 friends over to my house for a party. Mommy hired a clown and also four very beautiful Disney Princess's. I quickly ascertained on the spot, "*I hated clowns!*" I found them to be the creepiest, freaks ever. May I just ask... does anyone really love clowns?

I do believe my friends felt the same way I did. Thank goodness my daddy quickly sent away the ugly, gross, red-haired clown who kept destroying, popping, and breaking his animal balloons. Regardless of the scary clown, it turned out great since we all loved the angelic, beautiful Princess's. How very special I felt because my party had authentic true-life princess characters. They sang telling us to "Wish upon a star and all of our dreams would come true." Gosh, I loved mommy to the moon and back that day for hiring them.

When I was seven, my teacher took turns letting us take the... "*Science Class Chicken Project,*" home to monitor and watch for 3 days. It was all fun and games until the 2nd day, when my brother ran into the house, stepped on the chicken, and killed it. And I thought clowns were the creepiest freaks ever! I didn't like my brother Jeff, either. Needless to say, I got an F on the project and I never forgave my brother. Yes, he claimed it was an accident, but I certainly didn't believe him. I ate the last chocolate cupcake the day before the murder, and I believe he was just punishing me. Not to mention the poor chicken! After that, I didn't eat poultry for years. I ate cupcakes though. I'm not crazy!

NOW I'M THE MOMMY AND YOU ARE THE BABY...

When I turned eight years old, I ran away from home forever and ever! Forever turned out to be when it got dark late that afternoon. You see, I found out the ugly truth. There is no such thing as the tooth fairy. The severe anguish and grief I endured were as horrible as the parental betrayal I felt that day. My tooth fairy was awesome and special. She wrote me such sweet notes. Because she'd fly away so rapidly, it caused her wings to get fiery hot, burning the edges of my notes. But my fairy gave me far more than money. Her words of praise and encouragement were life-changing. Also, I shall never forget that she gave me my first Barbie Doll. I was devastated. My own mommy and daddy deceived me so intensely and crushed my faith. I know now, (*kinda*) it's among the things (LIES!) parents tell their children. Little one, since I was so shattered over this, I'll need to decide what to tell you regarding these types of matters. And don't even get me started on Santa.

Anyway, sweetheart, the emotions and memories of childhood remain with you throughout your entire life. It's like your own personal roadmap. I remember at age nine, how ashamed and mortified I was when I froze and forgot all of my lines in the school play. I literally ruined the whole show. Sadly, I had the lead too. Everyone in the entire audience viciously laughed at me. My mom told me they were laughing because I made the play funnier and better. She explained, "Honey, you single-handedly made the show a big hit." Chelsea or Donavan, I don't know if I'll be able to tell you such overt lies like that, right to your face! Regardless, the class was already furious with me. I mean, the kids were still blatantly upset over the chicken, and ruining the play didn't help matters.

The following year, *the most awesomazing event in the world happened.* I enjoyed pure elation on my 10th birthday, without any clowns or princesses. That was the day I got my own puppy. I thought I'd freak out from the sheer happiness and surprise of this happening in my life. I had asked for a dog for as long as I could remember, and here she was. Obviously, I named my cute lovable King Charles Cavalier pup "Princess," with her crown and all. For 14 years, she was forever by my side and the glue of my childhood. Later, after college, Princess moved in with me till she passed away. Huge, painful sigh.

At 12-13, if getting one's disgusting period wasn't bad enough, I've got nothing to add. Well, yes, I actually do. My brothers teased and laughed at me for days. Jeffrey the chicken killer added, *"Bwaaak-Bwaaakk!"* They really were satin's spawns. Still are.

At 14, I snuck my mother's family heirloom necklace, made of fine pearls, from her jewelry box and wore it to a party. I accidentally broke it. I'll never forget the panic and utter fear I sensed as the pearls flew everywhere, all over the party floor. At 14, all girls are brats, and I was no exception. But the caring way my mom handled the accident made me love her even more. So much so, I stopped being bratty for three whole weeks. At age 14, that's a lifetime! Things went along great until, that is, the boyfriend situation occurred. After all, I was growing up and getting bigger. Consequently, my problems, of course, got bigger. I justifiably and deservedly didn't talk to my mother or father for a month because they wouldn't let me date, 17-year-old, Larry Samuels. "Give me a break, he's my 2nd, *true love!*" (Greg Brown was my 1st, at the tender age of 12.) They had absolutely no right whatsoever to meddle in my personal love life the way they did. After all, I was 14 and *quite* old enough to go out with whomever I wanted to. So I thought! For support, I listened to that prehistoric 60s song "They tried to tell us we're too young" over and over. If we were allowed to date,

NOW I'M THE MOMMY AND YOU ARE THE BABY...

Larry and I would've lasted far longer than the month my parents and I fought over him. Sadly, it would've been true love forevermore.

And let's not forget the overwhelming pride I felt at 15 when my mom came to school to talk to the class on career day. She's a lawyer. Shamefully, I was never proud of her until that day. As mom spoke to the class, she was impressive, humorous, and very adorable. It's funny how you never forget the little things. I guess I was too self-centered and stupid to care about her life and achievements. But it all changed on that day, for great respect ensued. I hope you'll be that proud of me one day, little Scout or Dawson.

Later that year, my life turned into one big sore throat of endless agony and pain. I finally had to have my tonsils removed. Let me tell you baby, the tons of ice cream I was promised would help? *Didn't!* Big Ouch. More, white parental lies as well, I suppose?

I always wanted to go to sleep-away camp and finally, I went as a camp counselor the summer I turned 17. That summer involved lots of boys, mischief and campfires. We'll discuss these experiences later on. Roughly in about 40 years. And, no, I don't feel guilty about anything! Well, I don't? Even though I never told my parents any details about that summer, I know you'll share everything with me. Surely you will? BTW, they were very cool and calm when I came back home with pink-purple-blue hair and a belly button ring.

I recollect only too well, as if it were yesterday, all the times my mother yelled at me for keeping a messy room, for throwing my things on the floor, for not helping around the house, for smearing on far too much makeup, sometimes neglecting my school work, for wearing outlandish clothes, and endlessly being on my phone and computer too often. Here's a heads up, baby. One big hug and an "I love you, mom," can make it all go away.

However, I believe the most trouble I ever got into was my senior year. I skipped school with my friends and went to the beach on "SAT" test day. The trouble evolved from my clumsy, ultra inept explanation. I foolishly and ignorantly told them that my sunburn was due to the roof on the school building being repaired. I was disgracefully busted and grounded forever. Thank God, they had a make-up "SAT" test the following Saturday. The good news and silver lining... I scored at the top 1% of my class. Whew! BTW, if I didn't have to sneak out to meet Larry all the time, none of this would have happened. They never did discover I snuck out. So Shhhh, Baby Boo! Don't tell them.

Another little ditty (you'll *never* pull) was during that same senior year, I was punished and not allowed out for something I did. Whatever! Naturally, I climbed out my bedroom window anyway and went to a party. I can still capture that furious, angry look on my parent's faces at my ridiculous attempts to climb back into the house through my bedroom window. The crashing sound of the priceless Tiffany lamp falling off my desk was horrifying. Poor Princess, it scared the daylights out of her. Foiled and punished again.

I do believe the worst thing I ever did though, was one Saturday night when your grandparents-to-be went out with their friends in dad's car. I, without permission, took my mom's car and got into an accident. I wrecked the car, and yes, the accident was my fault. I only had a permit and needed someone over 21 to be in the car with me. That was such a disaster. Lawyers needed and all. Thank God, mom was one of those. I genuinely don't know how I ever lived to tell these stories to you, little Angela or DeAndre. I am fully confident you will never put mommy through any of these crazy antics. Don't get me wrong. I was an amazing kid? Go ask grandma and grandpa about it one day. Or not!

So, my still innocent baby, I feel free to share these stories with you now, because you're not born yet and won't really remember these tales of glory and woe later on. But have no fear. I'll retell all the crazy stories to you again one day and many others. Perhaps when you are going to be a mommy or daddy and waiting for your child to be born. Poof!

How well I remember growing up. I had a wonderful happy, childhood. I was a very fortunate, lucky girl to have such amazing, understanding parents. I promise your daddy and I will do everything possible to bring you magnificent, fun, happy experiences growing up. I feel every child deserves immense love and fabulous childhood memories.

You should know, life isn't always a bed of roses. Inevitably, darkness will pop in from time to time. Yet, I look at darkness as a blessing. Without some darkness in our lives, how would we be able to appreciate the shining light, blissful times, and the sparkle of happiness? They'll always be good and evil. AKA, Uncle Jeffrey... the chicken killer!

So precious, it seems I'm no longer the baby, the toddler, or the little girl growing up. That was my lovely past and your wondrous future. Amazing, for it's now my turn to be the mommy, and your turn to be the baby. How breathtaking and thrilling for us both! It's late precious one. Go wish upon a star, and then dream yourself to sleep. Goodnight!

CHAPTER 29

Sex... And Pregnancy?

Maybe it's because I'm feeling altogether maternal and loopy, but having sex these days seems weird, worrisome, and pretty freaky. It's sort of like those photos that beg the question, "What's wrong with this picture?" On one hand, I'm tenderhearted, motherly and pure. Diversely, sex doesn't match the angelic pregnancy puzzle on the box.

Let me explain. Mommy is fiercely concerned that you can feel or see daddy's penis thrusting its rather scary head into your safe nesting domain? A penis invasion would terrify anyone, especially if you don't know, *what the what*, it is. Heck, maybe more if you do? Are daddy's strange, unholy, odd moaning sounds flipping you out? It would certainly be understandable. Not to mention the bam-bam-bam, of it all. Are we bouncing you around mommy's womb too much? Just so you know, those screaming, groaning noises you hear from mommy, it's not pain, sweetie. It's more like ecstasy. But if this is way too traumatic for you, I get it. I'll tell daddy we can't do it anymore. After all, he can't ground you yet. Don't be shy. Tell mommy how you feel. I'm worried how you're coping with all the surrounding chaos. Your thoughts and emotions concerning the *"Ins-and-outs"* could officially put you on a therapist's couch in the future for years and years.

Pregnancy makes mommy feel surprisingly sexual. Oh my stars and garters, I so love surprises! I suppose it's why they refer to the second trimester as the "Honeymoon Phase." Since my belly size is still manageable, it is not too difficult having sex. Plus, my breasts are larger than normal. Daddy likes this aspect a lot. I think he finds *busty mommy* incredibly sexy these days. My nipples and genitals are more sensitive, embarrassingly making me horny and wanting lots of sex. Then, a few days later, as quickly as the horny urges erupt, they burn out. Leaving me wanting nothing to do with sex. Thus, I sneer intensely and scornfully at poor daddy to stop in his tracks, back off and walk away. It's basically equivalent to being "Sexually bipolar." Is that even a thing? Wait, there's more!

SEX... AND PREGNANCY?

Darling Lancelot or Guinevere, because much of what your hearing or experiencing might be confusing, let's take a quick sidebar and an informative, cautionary update alert, concerning *"Sex, hormones, and growing up."* Once upon a time in the far distant future, when you are around 12–13 years old, as much as you love and adore us both, that will change and you'll feel very differently. This is called *puberty*. Thus, we won't recognize, who in tarnation you are anymore. Like you've had a spiritual walk-in. Although it'll be a great challenge, with any luck, we'll love you as much as always. You'll start to think we are total nerds, stupid, uncool, and not the best at anything, in any way, anymore! You'll be convinced we are crazy, clueless, and assume we know nothing about everything. You won't want to listen to a single word we say and most likely won't. You will desperately crave using words, which you are not allowed to say, at least without getting grounded. I will go into grounding more later on. During these hormonal years, you'll say lots of things like, "Hey, that's not fair," "Go to hell," "You never let me do anything," "I can do whatever I want to," "I don't have to listen to you," "You mean nothing to me," (ouch) "I'm running away," "I wish you'd die," and the always predictable, "I hate you both!"

Everything we do or say will embarrass, humiliate, mortify, and creep you out. To be sure, you will let us know that too. You won't want to hang out or do anything at all with us anymore. If imperative, you'll have to be forced, bribed, or paid to do so. During these charming years, you'll only want to be with your cool friends. You'll resist any (all) affection, hugs, or kisses from us. Daddy and I will no longer be permitted to open your bedroom door without knocking. Even so, you'll scream at us, "Get out of my room! Now!

Now!" We won't take it to heart, as we know you don't really mean it? Hopefully?

Amid this passage into puberty, I tend to believe that "aliens from another galaxy far, far away" come to earth and take our perfect, sweet children away. They fraudulently replace our teenagers with perfect genetic copies, abundant with acute flaming hormones, and major bad attitudes. However, when the time arrives that the alien child's hormonal changes are completed, our teens are willingly returned to their families back on earth. Have no fear. They will indeed return you back to us within 5 or so years... more or less?

When it's time, we'll talk more about hormones and growing up. Don't be nervous. We'll explain all about sex to you when you're older. Like really older, around 30ish? By the way, we don't want you to think sex is bad or dirty. Because when it is right, it's a wonderful, beautiful, extraordinary expression of sharing love. Indeed, daddy and I enjoy this awesome, flirtatious, intimate, sextacular, *whoopi-ride.* We jump on that fantasy trip every chance we get and treasure this validating communication of our love. Appreciate love and commitment are important and essentially key here. Now back to Preggo sex...

Note most doctors encourage sex during pregnancy. Moreover, they claim it's very healthy, relieves stress, and provides relaxation for both mommy and daddy. So they say! In fact, daddy reminds mommy of this all the time. They advise pregnancy need not end the intimacy and affection between expectant couples. Dr.'s also recognize, having sex is not only safe but also, romantically beneficial to enjoy until the last few weeks of term.

You mustn't be scared Baby-Boo because my OB-GYN told mommy, and I quote, "Not to worry Leona, your baby is well

SEX... AND PREGNANCY?

protected by the amniotic fluid in your uterus, and by the strong muscles of your uterus itself." He informed us that sexual activity wouldn't affect you whatsoever. I'm not exactly sure I believe the Doctor on this, even though daddy wholeheartedly does. Like Duh? He explained further, "Asher, try to find comfortable positions for Leona to make it easier and more enjoyable for her." A bit of a no-brainer there, I thought, standing before Doctor Myers with my, *"Ya think?"* face!

During the same appointment, Myers reiterated that daddy's manly-man penis unquestionably couldn't penetrate beyond mommy's vagina. He assured us, there's no way you could tell what's going on from your angle. While, unlike daddy, mommy is not wholeheartedly convinced and my editorial view is still out on it. Meanwhile, if the Dr.'s advice isn't correct, please give mommy a red flag or tip-off signal. We'll stop instantly.

I have spent hours, literally hours, trying to find and discover some comfortable and enjoyable sexual pregnancy positions. Which includes drawing precise charts and trying to visualize the whole activity. I've read books written by sexual therapists on, sex during pregnancy. I'm not proud. I'll admit that. In conclusion, I've determined doctors are glib and evasive on this sexual topic. Why? Because they know it's an exhausting challenge and well aware success at best, is shaky till the couple figures it out on their own. They're probably inwardly laughing, discussing this subject with parents-to-be. In the end, I said let's go for it. A *very happy daddy* and this indulgent, very tolerant mommy did just that.

Our goal with our pregnancy sex is to be unusually unique, extremely limber, and remarkably original in hopes that we might be written up in, "Ripley's Believe it or Not!" We're still waiting for their response on that... I think we actually might be contenders.

After all, is tried and done, I chose to lay back and let daddy do all the hard work! He doesn't seem to mind. Besides, your rational daddy wasn't about to let sexless weeks of no affection pass us by due to pregnancy. What a guy! We did totally triumph on the whole sex with a baby bump predicament. The biggest challenge that we found is kissing because our bump gets in the way, separating us. Honestly, without tooting our own horn, we could (and should) write our own book on "Sex during pregnancy!" Wow, an "Aha moment" baby Kurt or Goldie! Daddy and I have successfully achieved so many fantastic sexual skills and positions, all the while having to contort, twist, and bend our bodies... we can easily and confidently audition for any "Cirque Du Soleil Show" in Las Vegas!

On our last visit, mommy questioned the doctor as to why I want sex more than usual at this point in my pregnancy. He illuminated that a boost of hormones and increased blood flow to my girly parts might be increasing my sex drive, particularly in the second trimester. It was just a lot of *yada, yada, yada, yeah, aha, and whatever to my ears.*

More to the point, here is the good stuff he showed us about sex during pregnancy...

- **Better orgasms:** Increased blood flow brings an increased number of more powerful orgasms for mommy. "*Seriously, no one is going to argue with that.*"
- **Keeping fit:** Sex burns calories. "*Well, you know I workout hard and like staying trim, right? Plus, Colette, burning calories means an extra piece of cake for me!*"

SEX... AND PREGNANCY?

- **Bonding between partners:** This act of love brings parents closer together. *"And Baby Boo, you know what they say, a happy home means a happy baby."*
- **A boost to the immune system:** Sex increases *IgA*, an antibody, which helps keep colds and other infections at bay. In other words, sex keeps us healthy. *"Yeah, I agree Lila or Payton. It sounds like a bit of male malarkey to me, too."*
- **Increased happiness:** Orgasms release endorphins that can help mother and baby feel happy and relaxed. *"Tell mommy, it's working? Are you happy and relaxed?"*

So little one, since you won't remember this chat, I felt free to discuss sex with you. In closing, baby John or Yoko, if you're not comfortable with our sexual encounters, we'll stop at once. Trust me, we don't want to get you mad or pissed at us before you are even born. We're confident you'll come up with 1000s of things to hold against us, all on your own. So we don't want to start off on the wrong baby-foot now. If you don't mind, daddy and I are going to continue our sexual interactions. If it's not Ok, just kick me. I'll get the hint! Honey, I'm sorry to burden you with such an inappropriate "Heart to Bump conversation," for a fetus. Gotta go! Oops, daddy's coming with a lustful, amorous gaze.

CHAPTER 30

Goin' With The Flow...

Goin' With The Flow! Go with the flow? That's what the *"They say-ers"* and the books on pregnancy advocate. Really? They have the nerve, (without laughing) to recommend this to women who are pregnant? News Flash... "Where can we muster up this so-called

FLOW?" More terrifying and in other breaking news, "I haven't had a sip of wine for almost 5 months... In a row!" Gimme my wine back and I'll categorically go with any flow *they* propose! And FYI, that is not the notorious *"With child, pregnancy glow"* I'm sporting. It's simply your basic everyday detox occurring. I'm just clarifying.

"They say," while pregnant (and going with that infamous, unattainable flow), it's imperative to relax and de-stress. Easy for the *"They say people"* to suggest. Care to know what *"I say?"* Pregnancy is like living in a paradox. A mystery set inside an emotional bubble, secretly circling in a vortex of intense mishmash and frenzied feelings. Moody? Yep! I now exist in a potpourri state of temperamental dispositions and attitudes. All of that is a nicer way of saying unpredictable, erratic, volatile, or unimaginably crazy. BTW, were *these, know it all's,* ever pregnant? And you *"They say, people,"* stop saying we waddle. To be precise, I believe you're referring to our sexy pregnancy strut and our preggo swagger. It's adorable if you ask me. So, apologize and *"go with the flow!"*

I have read obsessively and heard by *"The sayers,"* that during the nine months of pregnancy, a woman's moods and emotions can alter drastically. They can go from the highs of feeling ecstatic and enthusiastic about having a baby, to the sinking depths of darkness, being impatient, irritated, edgy, and fearful. This can worsen as the eminent delivery and motherhood near. Pregnancy creates enormous transitions and such extreme changes to a woman's life. It's no wonder we suffer through a complex mixture of both good and bad emotions and sensations. *I say the sayers' rumors are unfairly negative.*

At a biological level, my hormones, estrogen, and progesterone are now firing up intensively. *"They say,"* some women are more sensitive to changes in progesterone, and could make them more irritable. Oh blah, blah, more blah, and easy for them to say, blah! Gee, will I be one of those unlucky emotional women? Hell no! Not happening to me.

Experiencing weepiness? OK, sure! Listen, Brooklyn or Kennedy... mommy is dealing with a full plate of weird eccentricities and many diverse varieties of stress here. Feel my pain. Big deal, so I found myself crying hysterically at a sappy reverse mortgage commercial? Or I got pissed off opening up late, a life insurance policy notice. Or going ballistic at the 4 Mormon missionary guys, dressed in full garb. Seriously, they rang my doorbell and woke me up, selling me... *I don't know what,* because I slammed the door in their faces. Not sure if I was being bitchy, emotional, hormonal, or if they had it coming? In addition, I'd say it was totally normal to burst into extravagant tears after throwing my guts up. It was gross, and even sadder, for no one was around to hold my hair back. Ewe!

As I said, mommy is living through a complex mixture of emotions. Incidentally, I felt terrible for that old couple having to reverse their mortgage. And in my defense, it's natural to sob hearing Sarah McLachlan singing on the ASPCA commercial. FYI, I'm an animal person. And who cares if I cried, believing the Geico Lizard got run over by a bus.

Dammit, *"Hormones, schmormones,"* I give up. I'm crying all the time, even when I'm happy. I do feel pretty bipolar. I also say with great anger, all of this crying better not give me wrinkles. I'll tell you that right now. Stretch marks, all by themselves, are more than enough to deal with. Plus, what about my boobs? Will they really end up down by my knees after breastfeeding? Will my vagina return to normal after parting the red sea? Likewise, will I ever look like my old self again? And, *"They"* wonder why I'm crying?

Ok, *"They say-ers,"* tell me... how is it possible to go with that fab flow of yours? News Update and Alert the Media... I am completely exhausted from barfing. Plus, I can currently vomit and pee simultaneously. I'm tired of being tired, feeling nauseous, coping with swollen legs, ankles, and feet. I am suffering from endless headaches, bloody bums, heartburn, rashes, bloating, insomnia, pelvic pain, acne, facial hair, and backaches. And that's all before noon! Worse yet, I am hungry all the time. I'm talking 24/7, all the time. I have a heightened sense of smell. This means I detect every one of daddy's uncouth farts, whether I hear them or not. Even scarier, I've discovered I have pregnancy-brain, too. This syndrome, which is also called mommy-brain, causes memory problems, poor concentration, and absent-mindedness. Though, it is sorta cool because it's my all-around excuse for everything I forget to do or mess up. Good thing I'm not going on Jeopardy. Seriously, baby Kinsley or Gianna... I totally saw that! Don't you dare roll your eyes at me! You're not allowed or expected to do that until you're at least 10 years old. Eleven, even. Anyway, science has proven mommy-brain is real. All of us 'bumpies' have reported it.

Mommy is having lots of trouble recalling words lately. Thankfully, though, none of my necessary, critical words. Hey, I need my curse words now more than ever. Also, I'm constantly forgetting names and completely confusing important things. For example, I was standing in an elevator the other day, like forever. Then I realized I didn't press any buttons. Likewise, I tried to pay for my Chinese food takeout with my driver's license. Even more embarrassing, I was infuriated and insisted that the card I gave him was good.

GOIN' WITH THE FLOW...

It doesn't end there... I've left the oven and the stove on for hours. I forgot the wet clothes in the washing machine for 5 days, stinking up the whole house. I forgot to lock the front door and left the garage door open all night. Wait, it gets better! I put the ice cream in the pantry and the aluminum foil in the freezer. No doubt, forgetting to turn my car off before running into Target was a total mommy-brain moment. And leaving my straightener on all day, almost burning down the house... *not good!* When the pharmacy guy asked, "What's your DOB," I gave my social security number, angrily quarreling that it was my DOB.

Still, I want to recap that even through it all, I am in no way emotional, jealous, or bitchy! I am merely a normal, pregnant mom-to-be, dealing with enormous insanity, and very unpredictable, odd things happening every day in every way. If you ask me baby Sheena or Lamar, I'm doing a brilliant job keeping it together in my delicate condition.

Guess what, "You smug *they say-ers?*" About that little FLOW devil, you want me to go with? NO! But it reminded me of a different flow. I won't be seeing her for at least a year. There's a Happy plus! Damn, gotta go Hue or Safari. I left the bathtub running...

CHAPTER 31

So Bored... I Mean, Really Bored! I hear so many pregnant women today complaining about being bored during pregnancy. I confess they do have a legitimate case. Especially if they had loved working, and were fired unfairly from their ideal job, banished for being pregnant! Sorry baby, I can't seem to let that go as yet. Meanwhile, I've come to discover, there are plenty of rewarding and exciting activities to enjoy making any expectant woman fulfilled, busy, and super happy.

For Instance...

At long last, I finally have the time to place all those random coupons I've been saving and forever collecting into an organized folder. I found this profusely rewarding, as I was never able to find the coupons I needed when going to the store. For real, people get their grocery bills down from $150 to $0 with coupons. I'm actually making bank here. Gosh, I might also be victorious in the grocery store game "Win a free trip to Italy."

And of course, there are the 4 million things I must accomplish to get ready for your arrival, precious baby. I have already tried over 40 sample colors of paint for your room. Nothing seems right to me, though. Have you any idea how hard it is to find that, "Perfect, not pink or blue, I wish I knew the sex of my baby, color?" It's a lot of pressure.

Let's not overlook the hours of enjoyment and relaxation reading unrealistic romance novels filled with torrid love, searing ecstasy, passion, and sex on windswept cliffs and barren moors. Naturally, they all have that gorgeous, long-haired, Fabio look-alike guy gracing their covers. All stories women relate to through experiences of their own. Or not! This could be risky, falling into passion quicksand and becoming a Harlequin Romance junkie. Forget it, Asher's more gorgeous than any of those photo-shopped guys.

BORED?

And, how long I have wished for the frivolous time to marathon shop every store, in every mall, within a 100-mile radius. Mommy would totally hate that. Hello, Amazon!

How fabulous. I now have all the time in the world to enroll in the many online intriguing college classes. I mean, one is never too old to keep up, to learn, and to grow.

Fascinating Intellectual Courses, Like:

(FYI, all actual, *authentic* courses!)

1. UFOs in American Society (*"Old News! Haven't you heard? They live among us."*)
2. Zombies in Popular Media. Surviving the Coming Zombie Apocalypse: Disasters, Catastrophes, and Human Behavior (*"Or simply drive on any Los Angeles freeway!"*)
3. The Science of Superheroes (*"UMM, isn't that a perfect example of an oxymoron?"*)
4. Underwater Basket Weaving (*"I need to interview the weirdo who signs up for this."*)
5. The Unbearable Whiteness of Barbie–Occidental College (*"Stop! Barbie's timeless."*)
6. Introduction to Beekeeping (*"Really? Was this the very last course left or available?"*)
7. Lemonade, Black Women, Beyoncé and Popular Culture (*"True, Je ne sais quoi."*)
8. How to Stage a Revolution (*"Seriously? Go turn on the daily news. Save the money."*)
9. Alien Sex (*Ok, for real, my brain just exploded! Probably lots of this, in Hollywood.*)

10. Nip-Tuck-Perm-Pierce-Tattoo-Embalm Adventures with Embodied Culture (*"Ouch"*)
11. Demystifying the Hipster (*"Like, honestly, does anyone really care? Well, do they?"*)
12. Those Sexy Victorians (*"Could be good. Every art museum proves this is spot-on."*)
13. Mail-order Brides? Understanding the Philippines in Southeast Asia (*"No. Just no!"*)
14. Joy of Garbage (*"That just made my eyes bleed! Ugh... I can't even be sarcastic?"*)
15. FemSex (*"Hmmm, I'm listening. I'm always willing to learn some new tricks."*)
16. Ways to Make People Angry (*"Come on now? Who needs a course for this one?"*)
17. Practical Jokes to Scare Strangers (*"Fun, but didn't we learn this in Junior High?"*)
18. Patternmaking For Dog Garments (*"Horrible. Back away from the poor dog, now!"*)
19. How to Get Away with Lying Every Time (*"Please we conquered this in our teens!"*)

There is so much to learn and endless topics to study. So how could one possibly be bored?

I ask you little Jeremiah or Eliza, how could expectant women complain? I stop to ponder. Am I the crazy one? Gosh, I've used this time to clean out all of those nasty, hard to get at places in every room in the house. I have eagerly tooth brushed all the bathroom grout... twice! My entire house shines. I finally get that feeling of a gratified, proud Suzy homemaker! I should call

BORED?

daddy's mom. She'd be so thrilled! I beseech preggos, why not use this perfect time to write every company you've complained about the past 10 years?

Bored, one might ask? Not bored at all!

Just look at the wonderful gift of time I now have to put into albums, all those 100s of loose elementary, Jr. high, high school, and college pictures taken before phones had cameras. Let's not forget the photos of friends, trips, weddings, and awards I've now had time to put into scrapbooks? My goodness, they're all placed between the pages now, and ready to exhibit. Plus, all the photos are decorated with confetti, stickers, buttons, and bows. You'll quickly learn your mommy is a scrapbook, sparkle and glitter, kind of girly-girl. This completed task gave *my* mommy indescribable pleasure, reliving happy, proud, heartwarming memories of my life all over again. The *extra time* options are infinite.

What is wrong with these bored, lazy, querulous, whining, pregnant women, anyway? Heck, I wish it took 10 months to have a baby! FYI, female elephants are pregnant longer than any other animal. Their pregnancy lasts anywhere from 18 to 23 months. And us women think we have it bad, and much to complain about? Those poor elephant moms! Maybe that's how the phrase, "The elephant in the room," got started?

OH God, I'm lying... I am lying! I am so Freaking Bored! Wait just a second. Perhaps there are other options I can do to keep busy?

I can learn Kabbalah.

I can discover Gandhi's philosophies.

I can study Deepak Chakra.

I can educate myself with Reiki for its power therapy.

I can watch Tony Robbins' videos.

I can binge-watch every single show on Netflix, Hulu, Prime, HBO Max, and Apple Plus.

I can also study Sufi-style whirling dances, performed by women like the Ghoomar Dance of Rajasthan that has been popularized in Bollywood films. Something to ponder.

I can make random calls scaring and freaking people out like we did when we were kids.

Or, I can spend time disassembling and assembling the refrigerator. Why? Just cause.

I can study ants or the wisdom of African monkeys. Possibly amusing? Or creepy as hell!

It could be fun to watch a foreign language movie without reading subtitles. Try to guess what they are saying and enjoy acting it out. I declare, to hell with the annoying subtitles.

So hilarious, if I went to my *brother Jeff's house, the very OCD, chicken killer.* I'd laugh changing his things, moving his stuff around differently in every room? He so deserves it.

How about attempting time travel? That would be awesome and quite historic to achieve.

I can go to a movie and stare nonstop at the person next to me eating popcorn and candy.

Or better yet, I can go to the grocery store and follow someone around and copy them, putting everything they place in their cart, in mine. That would be entertainingly comical.

BORED?

It appears my precious baby, mommy is pathetically bored and pitifully losing it! However, I have learned that you, on the other hand, are not bored at all judging by what mommy has been reading. You are doing all kinds of shocking things besides growing and kicking, mommy. Not only are you learning to move your fingers, toes, and limbs, you're sometimes dreaming, breathing, opening and closing your eyes, and yawning. You are also turning away from the light that enters through mommy's belly button. You're smiling, sleeping, sucking your thumb, holding your hands, crying, and shedding tears. Sweet baby, you are listening, tasting flavors, masturbating (Umm, mommy says to stop that now, please!), and doing countless other truly astounding things. Plus, you are forming vocal cords, hiccupping, smelling, and you can even get startled now. BOO!

Believe it or not, you're literally peeing inside mommy, to the tune of one liter a day. Keeping it honest, that's actually pretty disgustingly gross. I could've done quite well not knowing this. Did you know, that every 2000 babies are born with teeth? Little one, don't do that. That's just too ewe and weird for mommy. I believe I'd prefer having you pee instead. If you're Lexie, a girl, you're developing all the reproductive eggs you'll ever use. How crazy is that? You're very busy, Ely or Smith, and not bored at all in there.

Big perk... I was so bored (So Bored), that daddy took mommy on a "*Babymoon* vacation" for a whole week on a Ship Cruise. It was wonderful and the last time, we'll be alone like this for a long while. However, you were there too, having fun right along with us, happily peeing away inside me. The only negative thing about our *Babymoon* was mommy's hormones were raging and I couldn't have alcohol. This is textbook irony.

Ok little, Ashley or Simon, I must run along now. My online class, "The Perfect Excuses For Any Reason," is just about to start. When mommy's finished with that, it will be time for my scrapbooks and glitter activities. Next, I'm going to make a Kentucky Derby hat from scratch. Frightening, since it's not even Derby season! Hey, I got it. I can learn to read tarot cards and start a business. Another great idea! Later! Have fun in there.

CHAPTER 32

Spoiling a baby? Can That Even Happen?

Morning baby Shayla or Beckett... My precious little angel, are you up? Let's chat. Hey, you up? (Pound! Pound! Pound!) Oh gee, sorry, did I wake you? So lately, mommy's been watching and observing every baby I see passing by me. Since you'll be coming soon, I want to learn everything there is to know about babies.

With that thought in mind, yesterday afternoon, I overheard the most ridiculous statement I've ever heard. Observing a couple of new moms eating lunch, I accidentally heard, (yes, accidentally) one of the mothers saying, *"I won't ever, never, ever, spoil my baby!"* Her friend responded, *"Unequivocally, I can't agree more and I wouldn't either."*

Unable not to, I rudely laughed out loud, alone at my table. Sorry my Addilynn or Sloan, it's an indisputable statistic that babies (through no fault of their own) are the most spoiled human beings ever to crawl the face of the earth. They are chiefly born that way.

Honestly, how could this mom say that, and with a straight face, no less? Even worse, out loud for all to hear? Come on now, she won't spoil her kid? Her baby girl was royally attired in pink satin ruffles, hand-sewn couture threads of Irish lace, a glitzy tiara, gloves to match, and real diamond earrings. The infant was luxuriously cradled in a gold Rolls-Royce baby coach. The pretentious woman was holding a Tiffany and Company silver rattle, and a Waterford Crystal baby bottle. She was sitting, waiting intently for her perfectly unspoiled baby to indicate when the royal princess was ready to sip-sip-sip...

Right then and there was the defining moment I smugly decided to breastfeed! The mom, visibly a high-society, overindulged socialite, was cooing adoringly at her baby while struggling to think of anything more she could do for her child, all the while ignoring her friend. She was too busy indulging every cue from her baby. I don't even know why she ordered food, since I only saw her consume a nine-ounce pour of red wine.

SPOILING A BABY? CAN THAT EVEN HAPPEN?

Before I knew it, two classically British nannies loomed and scooted the spoiled infants away. Question solved. I now understood why she ordered food. Huh, nannies are an amazing luxury, I can only assume. At this point, I seriously needed mouth duct tape.

Babies are picked up constantly, held in someone's warm cozy arms, gently laid down, fed, washed and changed, diapered, powered, caressed, catered to, rocked, played with, fussed over, pampered, adored, loved, indulged with things and gifts (toys, stuffed animals, clothes, etc.), pacifiers, time, and permanently marked the center of attention.

Maybe it's just silly ole me, "fiddle de-de and all," but doesn't a newborn baby's total dependency and helplessness, in-and-of-itself, prove this philosophy? Which, in fact, shows *a baby cannot be anything but spoiled!* All babies, in the beginning, are spoiled, and rightfully so. Not in a spoiled, bratty way, but in a "Wahh" I'm a helpless baby" way!

All this coddling and attention would deem any adult hugely spoiled. Well, unless they happen to be a famous movie star, then it's normal! Yes, infants are spoiled, but in a necessary, essential fashion. A baby's every wish is our command, as it should be. By design, they need us to survive. Which ironically means they are, in fact, not spoiled at all. Confirming you really can't spoil a baby until they get a little older. A resounding "Ta-Da" on my "can't spoil a baby theory." Relish it sweetie while you can, for it won't last forever. The sad part, being a baby, you won't remember it. Meanwhile, and just my own personal belief, moms should be spoiled and pampered every now and again as well.

Don't be anxious little Paris, Kourtney, Kim, Armani, Sheikh, or Haji. Since it's impossible to spoil you, daddy and I will spoil you with every ounce of love in our hearts. That is our job and nothing could make us happier. Nonetheless, at least we won't be oblivious and we'll know we're indulging and pampering you, for Pete's sake and yours.

For it is simply a well-known statistic… Babies have an easy life, as indeed they should!

Only the rich, famous, privileged, dogs, cats, and royalty have it this good, or maybe better.

Needless to say...

Here are a few heads-up warnings for your future, my soon-to-be coddled, Amadeus or Ava, when your baby pampering days have left the building… All non-negotiable!

- Little sweetheart, never, ever call me… *mom, mother, or Leona*. I will always be *mommy* to you. Anything else? Yea, that'll get you in timeout for like… Forever!
- Don't pick your nose baby Jeremy or Chaya. And by the way, that's just disgusting.
- Don't bite your nails.
- Don't color or write on the walls.
- Don't eat your hair Devorah Basha. Besides, that's far too weird, anyway. Don't!
- Don't wipe your buggies on the furniture or anywhere else. We see you! It's gross.
- No, means No! Yes, means Yes!
- Now, means now!
- Stop, means Stop!

SPOILING A BABY? CAN THAT EVEN HAPPEN?

- No cheating, stealing, cursing, or lying. (*As tempting and fun as they might seem!*)
- Always say please, thank you, you're welcome, and absolutely, be grateful.
- Be thoughtful, kind, helpful, and never act bossy, be rude, or behave cruelly.
- You have to take a bath and brush your teeth every day. You heard me, every day.
- Listen to what daddy and I say, and don't roll your eyes about it. We hate that...
- You must share, be caring, compassionate, and be a good person. Never be a bully.
- Sex is fine and absolutely permissible. After you are around 35 years old, of course.
- No drugs or alcohol allowed! I don't care what your friends do or what the law is!
- You will have to go to College. Period...
- God is good. God is great. God is astronomically amazing.
- You are loved my darling Jennifer or Jordan, more than humanly possible.

Hmm, in hindsight, little Suri or Dylon, that Waterford Crystal Baby Bottle, and Tiffany and Company Silver Rattle were exquisite! I think I might have to check them out. Don't judge me, little one. Whatever? I'm just sayin? Ok baby, go back to sleep now... Hugs!

CHAPTER 33

God's Splendid Creation... Grandparents!

Regardless, and no matter how perfectly perfect, parents might strive to be, sometimes they might need some extra help and support from their family. There will always be occasions when mommy is occupied or unavailable, and poor daddy may be far too busy, unable to be with you or take care of you in the way he so desires.

And that's precisely why God's loving, concerned hands created Grandparents!

These people prove God's ultimate genius. They were flawlessly fashioned to bring a child everything in life parents don't think of, don't want to think of, and even more of the things their parents do think of. Grandparents shrewdly find things to bring, give, and do, even when the parents say no, by setting limits and boundaries! They offer willingly everything imaginable from toys, love, time, experience, knowledge, rekindled patience, understanding, money, and caving into a child's wants and demands. They hardly if ever, say no and have trouble disciplining them, if at all. They give and spoil their grandkids far too much. This is the age, which develops and elaborates on the *"Over Spoiling the Child, Effect."* But I mean really? Who'd ever think to argue with God's creation?

In addition, by law, in small text written right there in the Bible, (page 587, or okay, probably not) these grandparents have the unquestionable right to overindulge their grandchild in anything they want, need, or desire. It's their God-given biblical, holy right. Believe me, they use it lavishly. No religiously! Parents, while truly frustrated, are hard-pressed to take away, abolish, or unimaginably criticize the grandparental rights. These stoic saviors of grandchildren do a lot of winking, shushing, sneaking, and giving behind parents' backs. They often say things like, "Here... But don't tell your mother or father!"

Grandparents have an innate way of dreaming up exotic surprises, fun places to go, exciting things to do, and extraordinary gifts to buy their grandkids. Of course, the children marvel at their creative innovations for bringing, taking, spending, and buying.

GOD'S SPLENDID CREATION... GRANDPARENTS!

Allow me to state further, Myles or Beth, that grandmothers and grandfathers (AKA, grandma and grandpa, or whatever you decide to call them when you begin to speak) can magically turn average days into miraculous days of memorable adventures.

You'll see what I mean one day. You have 4 *fantastical* grandparents waiting for you. Since they already love you, they're conjuring up all kinds of spectacular riches for your future. Mommy wishes and hopes a college trust fund, and grad school is among them!

Despite all mommy and daddy's help and support, there will be times when no matter what, nothing will seem to work out right for you. Still, when all else fails, your grandparents will come to your rescue. They shall effortlessly offer you a final ray of hope, the delight of a second chance (or 50 second chances), and the excitement of a different, unique, creative idea. They supernaturally find a guaranteed way to bring your world bits of fantasy and nirvana. God's brilliant *"Grandparent Creation"* is astonishing.

How blessed children are to enjoy yet another amazing source of love in their lives? Not to mention, the never-ending blissful adoration grandparents bring to triumphs, celebrations, and successes. These angels will dry your tears, prompt a big smile, cuddle, and protect you with a huge hug. Luckily, they have no responsibilities that would cause you to be upset by punishing, reprimanding, or saying *no* to anything. I'd love that gig.

"A Few Things To Know About Grandparents:"

- Baby Sabrina or Pip, they tell great, gallant stories and tales. Some of them are even true!
- They never worry about acting silly and they love showering you with immense pleasure.

- They will play with you all day long or until they say, "I'm too tired now. Go watch TV."
- Grandparents like slipping you candy, money, or whatnot when mommy's not looking.
- They enjoy buying you things, especially when mommy and daddy say, "Absolutely no!"
- They will be your best audience, laughing and praising every single solitary thing you do.
- They love to travel and may take you with them. *You:* "Can I go?" *Mommy:* "We'll see!"
- They always have yummy sweets and foods to offer you that you'll rarely get at home.
- They know more than Google about lots of things. They're super-duper knowledgeable.
- They always bring you toys and take you to fun places. Again, it's their God-given right!
- Everything you do makes them happy. They are so proud of you and will let you know it.
- They make really good friends. You can tell them anything in confidence. They'll listen.
- Just hearing your voice on the phone brings them pure delight, laughter, and pleasure.
- Grandparents can teach you endlessly. They're very wise and will offer you great advice.
- You can do no wrong by them, even if you do wrong. They'll protect you no matter what.
- They believe in you and will faithfully be there to inspire, encourage, and cheer you on.

GOD'S SPLENDID CREATION... GRANDPARENTS!

- Grandparents are loyal, will love you unconditionally, and never cease to support you.
- They have cool sleepovers. You'll bake cookies, enjoy fun foods and watch lots of movies.
- They adore holidays, making them all over-the-top, and more special than special can be.
- Their loving smiles alone will bring you pride, self-esteem, confidence, and reassurance.
- Grand's come with an infinite supply of mushy hugs, messy kisses and skintight embraces.
- They will tell you all about their fascinating lives and family history. LISTEN to them!
- They'll always and forever be there for you, making you feel special and loved entirely.
- When babysitting, they often fall asleep. Then you can get away with almost anything.
- Grandparents will persistently come to your rescue. They are the true cherubs in your life.

This grandma, grandpa special miracle arrives from God, bursting with affection. They never run out of compassion, devotion, care, praise, excitement, sweet tenderness, faith, and genuine overflowing love for you. That is all just a part of what God puts into the grandparent mixture, and what they enthusiastically bring to their grandchildren.

Oh, How Splendid, The Creation Of Grandparents! And, God Was Pleased...

CHAPTER 34

About Maternity Clothes...

Baby, we apparently need to talk! To be candid, I genuinely don't mean to sound bitter. I don't. Like at all, I promise. Complaining again is actually the furthest thing from my mind! But, Baby Boo... Really?

Sure, I can survive relentless nausea, hot flashes, fatigue, pimples, backaches, swollen breasts, and to quote the Dr.'s (*hold please*) office nurse, "The water retention." I've coped with weight gain (badly perhaps, but I coped, nevertheless), endured a painful, itchy baby bump, boredom, feeling blue, and crying tears equal to the Trevi Fountain. And need I remind you baby of the wicked, deadly *Stretch Marks?* I stuck it out like a champ with hemorrhoids, endless bathroom trips, and heartburn. Those are but a few of the dramas I've triumphed, conquered and won. Yet all the while, I have not been bitchy, emotional, or jealous. I boldly discern I've been as resilient and robust as a brave trooper. But alas, the final straw befell upon mommy. *The Camel and His Back are Now, Broken!*

Maternity clothes far exceeded mommy's breaking point...

After desperate months of improvising and reinventing outfits in my closet using my brilliant fashionista skills (amid dismal results), I sadly threw in the skinny-*girl* towel. I finally went in search of maternity outfits. Let me say, these bizarre clothes are uncalled for and beyond what women should have to bear. Realistically, I didn't expect to dress like Princess Kate Middleton, a runway model, or a famous super-star, while being pregnant. But, come on, this horrible fashion situation went past my capability to cope? Aren't we pregnant women going through enough already? I'm only asking for a few super cute outfits here! Why hasn't the world of haute couture caught up to the modern day pregnant women's hopes to look awesome with her bump? Must we look like Betty-Boop, Minnie Mouse, an old-fashioned 1960s sit-com mom, or worse, a 1959 ultra-dated Barbie Doll?

ABOUT MATERNITY CLOTHES...

For starters, I have a mountain of whys? *Why*, I beseech, does every outfit have huge, ridiculous bows on them? I don't need to dress in micro-trends like goth or other alternative fashions such as ghetto, emo, cutesters, yuccie, grunge, punk, or any modes like that. Conversely, *why* do all the dresses look like the ones I wore when I was 5 years old? *Why* do they all fit and look exactly like the dresses my grandma still wears while sitting on her plastic-covered couch? Why are the maternity designers trying so hard to accentuate the negative? *Why* is everything so huge, baggy, shapeless, and loose fitting? More unflattering, *why* are the stripes going the wrong way? *Why* do all the clothes have polka dots, checkers, or big, bright, awful designs on them? *Why* can't they make pretty and attractive clothing? How difficult can it be anyway, dammit? Just design a normal lovely outfit and simply make it bigger in the butt, tummy, boobs, and hips. OK, fine, whatever... bigger all over! For goodness' sake, fashion people, this isn't rocket science!

My personal unforgivable, nasty, tacky favorite is the tasteless shirt with the word *"Baby"* printed on it with an *arrow pointing down?* In all honesty, is this absolutely necessary? What is wrong with people? Consequently, in my sheer desperation, I tried on one ugly dress. It looked like it had an enormous test pattern on it, right across my cutesy bump. I swear it looked like a chemistry project gone wrong, or a dartboard displaying a weird optical illusion. Visibly hopeless, I tried on another bump-frump-frock. It had so many humongous flowers on it I literally had a flashback of sitting on my Great Aunt Mildred's ancient, red velvet rocking chair. Which, BTW smelled like a football player's locker-room. Disheartened and fiercely discouraged, the next dress I put on had ladybugs, circles, butterflies, and of course, bows. Yep, sporting all 4 in one hideous dress. Like we preggers need more reasons to make us vomit? The pregnancy market is a floral-infested, polyester fashion wasteland of dreadfully ugly, unattractive garments... on steroids. They are so atrocious, I wouldn't dare take out the garbage, or walk the dog wearing any of these outfits. And so you know, I don't have a dog! Frankly, why does it have to be this way? Adding insult to injury, they're not only appalling but also outrageously expensive.

"In a nutshell, maternity clothes are "fuggo as hell." After several hopeless shopping sprees resulting in not a single purchase, for the first time, I was somewhat relieved I had been fired. I couldn't show up at the studio wearing any of those dresses I tried on. I may be expecting a baby, and my body is different, but I'm still Leona, and I want to resemble myself. The brutal waistbands, ghastly styles, the ruching effect hiding nothing, and the embarrassing way they fit a pregnant body send chills down my bump.

If everyday maternity clothes weren't shambolic enough, and holy crap they are, (See how I refrained from saying holy shit there, little one!), mommy will never forget the, Oh My God wistful emotions I suffered seeing myself in the mirror, pregnant in a bathing suit for the first time. Speaking of instant ego bombs and humongous self-esteem wrecking balls? All the summer fun, the exciting beach and pool parties with the gang, were now equal to going to the dentist for a seriously infected root canal surgery. Maybe it's just me, but I blame this predicament entirely on that damn water weight gain!

Back on topic, for the life of me, I can't understand why in every maternity department, there always seems to be a sweet,

ABOUT MATERNITY CLOTHES...

but nosey, grey-haired, little old lady crunching on rock candy and asking way too many personal questions? Rude, intrusive, none of your business questions, such as *"Are you having twins, you certainly look like it?" "You are quite big for your stage of pregnancy, aren't you dear?" "With your dairy-farm boobs you are going to breastfeed, of course, right?"* Making matters even more uncomfortable, those old infuriating ladies never have a sense of humor. When she asked whether I wanted a boy or a girl, I answered, "Neither. I want an Extraterrestrial!" She gasped snidely with, "My word," and ran off in a huff. Well, at least it made me laugh and another pregnant woman in the dressing room next to mine. I hope the big-stripped, orange and green shirt, with the long hanging bow the old lady took away, didn't hit her in the ass as she flew away. She could have at least offered me a piece of her rock candy!

It doesn't end there. Like I (or any normal woman) need additional anguish in pursuit of maternity clothes? You see, these stores have the nerve to provide expectant moms with a cute pillow that ties around the tummy. This way, a mom-to-be can envision what she'll look like even bigger and more pregnant, enabling her to buy ahead of time. The only good thing about that is not returning to a pregnancy boutique ever again. I wonder if other ladies enjoyed looking fatter and bigger with that pillow as much as I did! Just swell. Oh boy, I now felt like an 80-year-old elephant sporting my dairy-farm boobs.

Before I became pregnant, I never even contemplated maternity clothes being an issue, until my zippers no longer zipped. I naturally assumed fabulous maternity styles were prominent, and wouldn't be a problem to find. I thought maternity clothes were just something that inherently came with the world of having a baby, like food cravings, or the need to pee every 4.8 seconds. How they failed so horribly making stunning, stylishly fashionable clothes was beyond my comprehension? I feel like I should've been warned! As a stylish, natural-born Quaintrelle, I was woefully disillusioned and left feeling like a fashion victim! I assumed, if all today's stars, singers, rich and famous elites all looked adorable and exquisite pregnant, I could too. I anticipated the clothes would be amazing. Then I discovered the famous people had their flawless, perfectly fitting, voguishly styled, maternity clothes created by famous, de la mode, guru designers. Those rich, lucky, elite bitches! And no... I'm pregnant, moody, and I will not apologize for that remark! It's a vast market out there. Women are always having babies, and we are not all famous superstars. Note to self... "After the baby arrives, immediately become a rich and famous superstar." Oh, how I miss my wine. I kinda like to imagine, wine misses me too.

Don't misunderstand. While I'm super excited about you, my beloved baby alien who is growing within my bump, I still desire the opportunity to dress for a body that is somewhat like the one I've enjoyed for 28 years. I'm not asking for fashion-show-worthy pregnancy couture. Still, I'd love some cute, pretty, well-made, comfortable clothes that show off my newly acquired, braggadocios-worthy curves. I'd adore showing up to yoga, a movie, night out with daddy, or a girlfriend's dinner party looking impossibly flawless and totally put together. Yes, I'm expecting, but I still want to look classy and chic enough to make other moms-to-be, jealous and enviously want to claw my blue eyes out.

Whilst I think of it, so what? Who the hell cares if I haven't seen my feet since the President's last State of the Union address? We can all clearly see that I'm pregnant with a huge belly and

ABOUT MATERNITY CLOTHES...

exhibiting hairier legs than a, "best in show," Shih Tzu! Yet, on top of this humiliation, is it absolutely necessary to be forced into buying stupid, ugly, T-shirts that advertise for the entire world to see, (those who are oblivious and impossibly missing my huge belly) *"There's a baby on board?"* Really designers? I say "shame on all your couture houses. And shame upon your hideous fashions. You can't do better than this?"

Honestly, all I wish to do is rock a wonderfully dazzling pregnant silhouette. I want to look ridiculously hot as hell. I want daddy to feel proud of the way you and mommy are showing. I shouldn't be made to feel as though I have to apologize for the "baby on board," or the dreadful shirt spelling it out. I'm thrilled to be a pregnant woman, who, yes, may or may not weigh 350 pounds. However, I can still stand up tall and proud without toppling over. And if I do topple, I sure as hell want to look adorable doing so!

Also, there is an unfair misconception that pregnant women are hormone-driven, enormous-bodied creatures that aren't sexy, no longer feel sexy, or desire sex. I'm here to counterattack. This is utter nonsense and shamefully untrue. Most of the time anyway...

Consequently, after all was said and done, I took charge and confronted the despicable clothes battle, head-on. I humbly surrendered and gave up on the whole notion of buying maternity outfits now, or anytime in the future. In simpler terms... Never try again! Therefore, mommy decided to buy regular, charming, awesome clothes, at my favorite stores, only in bigger sizes. It worked out splendidly. Jayden or Colton, I'm so happy and overly excited seeing *"me"* again. I found the prettiest outfits that fit perfectly and were just snug enough to proudly show off you and me, and our magnificent baby bump. I do declare with a bit of sassy attitude, we look emphatically adorable and totally, *'fashion us, lovely.'* I dare say we nipped that maternity fashion crap right in its ugly ass.

We are back! Mommy looks like mommy again, only bigger, and it's thoroughly wonderful. Baby Lemony or Ozair, you should know I've also gotten used to the naked pregnant belly situation. I love our enchanting, cute as a button, darling baby bump.

Like many of life's problems, I took a seemingly negative situation and tweaked my mindset to a positive one. As usual, it paid off. I was left feeling giddy and *pregnantly* beautiful. These days, I joyfully and proudly smile, looking in the mirror. Yes, indeed I do, Colette! Ultimately, having conquered the maternity look, I was now rather pleased and self-assured. Staring into the mirror with my original fashion plate designer Leona look, I was delighted with my reflection. It felt jovial, seeing me, the news reporter, looking fantastic and like my old confident self again. More importantly, daddy thinks I look captivating and stunning, and that is all that matters to me. And, of course, his mom!

Whether you are a boy or a girl, I know for certain you will be a sensitive child. So, I am confident when you are older, you'll want to see photos of us pregnant together. Knowing this, I've decided to take lots of belly selfies, posing like a professional Vogue model. Though knowing me, I will want to remember, *'You and I,'* like this, forever.

Meanwhile, thanks for listening my little Dior, Gucci, Givenchy, Chanel, Valentino, Oscar de le Renta, Vera, McCartney, Cavalli, Cabbana, or little Ferragamo!

ABOUT MATERNITY CLOTHES...

Instantaneously, at that very Prada, Dolce, Versace moment, a light switch went off in my head with a genius thought. After you're born and mommy becomes a rich and famous superstar, I'm going to design extraordinary, chic, stylish high fashion-forward, bewitching pregnancy couture. I'll become a world-renowned, celebrated maternity Fashionmonger. I will become a trend-setting designer and I shall name it...

"*The House of Leona... The Fashion Creator For Stylish Pregnant Women.*"

Gee honey, doesn't that sound so altogether amazing, and such a thrilling Aha moment?

Hmmm, but on second thought, yeah, no, probably not... Perhaps I should turn that light switch off. Being realistic, I am a successful, experienced journalist and I'm for sure not about to go back to a trade school. Darn it, though... Mommy really does love the thrill and excitement of Paris, Italy, and fashion runways! So you'll be my thrill instead.

In closing, my sweetheart... Our open and honest, "Heart-to-bump conversation" this evening should clarify any ambiguity regarding my views on all maternity clothes. Clearly, someone has to step up and put an end to this travesty... Case closed!

Goodnight and sleep tight, mommy's little Betsey Johnson or Louis Vuitton!

Hey, beloved baby Donna Karan or Tom Ford, would you like some rock candy?

CHAPTER 35

Just so you know little one, a Mother is:

Mother/Hood

"A noun... originating from Old English, with various meanings."

"Mother, formerly the Latin Mater and Anglo-Saxon Head. Later, changed to hood."

Also, see crazy, and/or, a remarkable, amazing person...

ROBIN ROTH

The True Meanings behind being a mother are virtually endless. A mother works tirelessly to ensure that her child is equipped with experience, knowledge, abilities, and all the skills necessary to succeed as a competent, well-rounded human being. A mother continuously worries and cares for her child 24/7, throughout all the days of her life, until she leaves this earth. Most probably, thereafter, as well!

Little Quinn or Serenity, since I'm bringing you into a world (which is so unknown to you), it's only fair that I achieve everything in my power to become an extraordinary mommy for you. I don't want to miss a single opportunity to help you thrive and bring you happiness. You deserve that, at least, if nothing else. Therefore, I have spent endless hours hoping to establish what it really means to become (in every way), *"a perfect mommy."* Amidst my robust quest and need for motherhood knowledge and understanding, I'm constantly pondering this notion. So, I combined my very best attributes with my mom, grandma, friends, their moms, the mom yelling at her kid in the mall and counting to 10, and my mom-in-law. I became so anal and obsessed with my desire to be that *perfect mom*, I even turned to famous television and movie moms. Scary!

As a result of my unyielding efforts, I developed a greater appreciation for motherhood. And, you know what Joey or Yolanda, it's not as easy as it looks. It's not at all like photos you might see in a book, happy family commercials on TV, or those Botox flawless mothers in the movies. Allow me to explain what I've learned, so you know, too.

JUST SO YOU KNOW LITTLE ONE, A MOTHER IS:

A mommy is: an entirely selfless human being. She happily gives her time and love endlessly without ever being asked to. A mom's job never ends, and through it all she, *(I need to buy lots of adjectives, Mr. Sajak)* loves, worries, cares, shares, buys, takes, brings, teaches, holds, encourages, roots you on, reassures, supports, calms, feeds, helps, motivates, uplifts, enriches, inspires, adores, fixes all problems, humors, shields, protects, defends, cherishes, treasures, finds, shelters, and mends everything from a torn sock, hurt feelings, a bloody knee, to a broken heart. She aspires to make all your dreams come true and does it all with pizazz, style, sparkle, ease, enthusiasm, passion, excitement, and her very own mystical, enchanting flair. Baby, in college you'd get an "F" for that paragraph. And I do believe I literally treated myself to every adjective in the entire dictionary.

A mommy understands you and all your needs. She'll always put your desires far above her own. She relentlessly and unconditionally loves her child with all of her heart, no matter what, for all the days of her life. Being a mother means being a fearless pit bull if necessary, a positive role model, and a raving cheerleader for every minute milestone.

Motherhood involves infinite sleepless nights, laughter and tears, hamsters on the dining room table, finger-painting on all the furniture, permanent markers on the walls, ruined family treasures, spilled drinks that stain, smashed toys, stubbed toes, broken and sprained whatever, and cockroach/rat science projects. It's also being the child's hero and refuge. AKA, "An *emotional blankie.*" A mom is the steadfast safety zone that her child runs to snuggle with at night from bad dreams, sprints to when hurt, and stands behind for protection in all scary and difficult circumstances. As if no one can see them behind her! Regardless, though it all, a mother would never think to say to her child, "You owe me."

A mother is the person who makes a boo-boo all better with two kisses, a big hug, a colorful Band-Aid, and all with very little *ouch*. She can make sad, peek-a-boo tears vanish with her tender, sympathetic, "I know sweetheart" and a few, "My poor little baby," words of compassion. She can make you forget a bad day at school with her smile and a big home-baked chocolate chip cookie. A mommy can erase the sorrow from your broken favorite toy with her tender innovative words, "Hey, I've got a great idea!" She will forever keep your security blanket or stuffed animals mended with her meticulous, loving, toy surgeries. No matter how many times it falls apart, she'll bring it back to life.

Little Tori or Sherlock, a mother, suffers twice as much as you when you're upset or hurt. She is far sadder when you are sad, and even more unhappy and disappointed when you are. Her heart aches completely with excruciating pain when you are bullied, left out of something you wanted, made fun of by other kids, failed at a goal, or hurt by a friend or anyone else, for that matter. A mommy will forever be your biggest fan, the proudest of you, and the happiest for you. She is unconditionally your very *best friend forever* and ever in the entire universe, come what may! The BFF axiom was named after her.

It's always mommy who instantaneously appears like a fairy godmother in a fairytale, right by your side, as if by magic the very moment you need her. Voilà! So very "Abracadabra!" She's with you

JUST SO YOU KNOW LITTLE ONE, A MOTHER IS:

for your hundreds of firsts. Sometimes, mommy doesn't let you know she's right there watching. Oh, but she is! She's watching your first steps, first disappointments, first accomplishments big and small, to your paramount successes.

A mommy can essentially take her mystical wand of love, and presto... make all the terrifying, unpleasant, unhappy, sad times disappear right before your tear-filled eyes. There will never be a monster under your bed, an alien lurking in your closet, or a demon scaring you in bad dreams! That's a guarantee. She is a ferocious *demon* and *ghost* buster bodyguard. Mommy is a beguiling magician who'll keep you balanced, centered, and safe.

A mother is the one who stays up all night at the edge of your bed worrying when you are sick. Even with little sniffles, and whether you have a fever or not. Amazingly, she never complains about being peed, pooped, sneezed, or vomited on. And, no matter what, she keeps her sense of humor. Not an easy feat to master when lavishly puked on.

She'll protect you fearlessly from all harm. Unquestionably, she would gladly take your pain herself, including (Big breath, for another run-on sentence) your shots, falls, bruises, stitches, scratches, ouches, breaks, sprains, or anyone that hurts your feelings, if it were only possible. If only, for there are no limitations that would dare to confront, hinder, or challenge a mother's devotion or love for her child. She gives her child her entire heart,

And yet, she asks nothing in return...

A mommy will buy you something awesome and new before ever thinking of herself. In fact, she'd feel dreadful seeing anything wonderful if you're not there to see it too. Missing out on any of your joyful expressions creates sadness. Indeed, you'll always come first. For your pleasure brings her far more gratification than anything else in the world could ever bring. You are *her person* and being with you is her happy place.

Let me tell you a little secret. A mom sees and hears everything you say, do, and think without you ever knowing or even suspecting it. See, I told you she is magical. As a result of her immense gifts and superpowers, she is forced to learn a great command of self-control and understanding. Note, however, you're not scot-free about getting to do whatever you wish. When discipline, time-out, or punishment are in order, and the last resort, of course, it is typically the mom who feels sick inside long after it's all over. A word of advice... Preying on her sympathy, a few sweet hugs, kisses, and saying, "I love you, mommy," will help you out here greatly and a possible "G*et out of jail free card.*"

A mommy will keep you warm in the snow and cool in the summer's heat. She will help you feel confident when you are insecure, strong when you are weak, and bring a smile to your face when you are not at all in the mood to do anything of the sort. You should always feel safe telling a mommy all of your emotions, good or bad. Don't worry. She won't judge you, and she's always there for you to talk to and confide in. She wants to help you, and will persistently find a way and an answer, to do just that. *"And I will!"*

Finally, although a mommy may not openly brag (for fear of creating an ego- monster) every mom sees her child as (Warning! Run-on sentence, ahead) the most gorgeous, smartest, cutest, wisest, most advanced, clever, talented, brilliant beyond their years, and most special child that ever lived in the history of the universe. If she could, she'd give you a standing ovation for

JUST SO YOU KNOW LITTLE ONE, A MOTHER IS:

everything you said and did. Trust me when I say her friends are just about sick of constantly hearing how extraordinary, and astonishing you are. She'll most likely lose a few of those friends along the way as you grow up, which is a clear result of all her boasting. (Note, a hazard of motherhood.) Meanwhile, she won't care one iota! Needless to say, I will be a total bragger and for sure lose many friends talking about how wonderful you are. I say to those fair-weather friends, "Ta-ta, 'C'est la vie,' and Hasta la vista, baby!" My fly-by-night, fickle, ex-friends won't matter. For I have true-blue friends, who no doubt, will brag about you just as much, if not more!

Baby, feel safe and trust that you can always come to mommy. You can positively count on me, to be honest, and protective...

Little Roma or London, you are free to talk about anything with me. Never be afraid to be vulnerable with mommy or daddy. We are both really good listeners.

On a scale of lots to nothing, we are way over the lots, mark. Mommy is (ok, was) a reporter, so you won't ever have to bury the lead. You can feel comfortable saying whatever's on your mind. I will be forthright and completely truthful with you. Such as...

1. "What does the sign on the candy and toy store say?"   "Closed?"
2. "Is the Tooth-Fairy real?"   "Yes?"
3. "Is Santa Claus and Hanukkah Harry real?"   "Yes?"
4. "Is the Fairy Godmother real?"   "Yes?"
5. "Is the Easter Bunny Real?"   "Yes?"

ROBIN ROTH

6. "Where do babies come from?"   "A baby factory up in heaven?"
7. "What is sex?"   "A boy or a girl?"
8. "What is thunder?"   "God is bowling?"
9. "Do noses really grow when you lie?"   "Totally and very long too?"

The older you get, the more honest and informative mommy and daddy will be. Basically, until you're about 20 years old, those will be the *honest-ish* answers you'll get.

I'm sitting here with my legs up on the (*finger-paint-free*) couch, grinning. For I already see myself looking through photos of you growing up, feeling my heart swell with pride. You're all the beauty I'll need in my life, simply by looking at your smile and into your eyes. Baby Adelina, I dream of snuggling with you, playing Barbie, dress-up, watching cartoons, and braiding your hair. If you're Josh, we'll giggle together coloring, playing video games, Lego, and yes, even Barbie, if you like. I'm excited, thinking of you crawling into our bed to cuddle early on a Sunday morning. I beam with delight, imagining how my worst day will completely change when you run into my arms for a big hug, shouting, "I love you, mommy!" That alone is enough to bring joy to any mother. Realize too, she cherishes the countless treasure-chest of memories long after her child has forgotten all about them. Hopefully, I won't make you feel too guilty on this!

Above all, a mother knows when to pick her battles by analyzing what is truly important. A sensitive mom strives to look at situations from her child's point of view.

JUST SO YOU KNOW LITTLE ONE, A MOTHER IS:

A warning though... Being a good mommy means not always letting you have your own way. Yet, even more, critical or significant is allowing you to fail. That will just kill me! The responsibility of teaching you hard lessons and tough love will tear me up inside. Though I will be inwardly crying, my love for you will keep me standing firm while maintaining a sturdy resolve. A good mommy means being strong when feeling weak, and smiling when wanting to cry. Realize Baby-Boo, throughout your many successes, mommy will be there with you crying happy tears and smiling with immense pride.

So, my beloved Serendipity or Logan, becoming your mother is a miracle, a gift, a connection that can never end, and a love that will never die. Being your mommy is by far the greatest thing I will ever do. You will be my heart, and my purest, ultimate love, along with your daddy. Unquestionably, you'll always be the very best part of being me.

Woefully, in the future, when you're all grown up and daddy and I must let you go off to college, it will be the biggest challenge of our lives. Well, that and your teen years, of course. Our love will help us to encourage and be happy for you. However, most of that happiness will be what they call *"faking it!"* Oh, my God, empty nest syndrome is brutal. It's way too hard to think about now, and more impossible to conceptualize later.

BTW, before I forget, I want to ask your forgiveness now, for all the many mistakes I will undoubtedly make later. "So, my darling Dante or Beatrice, I am very sorry!" In conclusion, I can easily sum up what I have come to learn about motherhood!

> *"A child is a mother's greatest blessing... And a mother is a child's greatest fortune!"*

CHAPTER 36

Things I Promise to try, "Never to Say to You!"

The following notoriously ludicrous parental statements of folly have been passed down through generation after generation. Parents religiously believed these were golden words of wisdom. Yet ironically, every new parent promises to never, not ever, use any of them. Truthfully, Madonna or Legacy, they all used them and they still do. Perhaps these old-world, worn-out, trivial snippets of insight and quaint mantras might profoundly and mystifyingly mean something. They must since they've continued blossoming through time. I find them rather humorous as they bring back to mind infinite memories of my own childhood. Still, someone must put an end to this madness. Thus, I swear I'll do my best not to follow in other parents' broken promises or silly footsteps.

Check out these, "Days-Of-Yore," statements:

- "Because I said so! That's why."
- "Keep making those faces and rolling your eyes at me and they will stay that way forever. Don't mess with me, kid."
- "You're gonna get it. Just you wait and see."
- "Ask your father."
- "Look at me when I'm talking to you."
- "If someone told you they were going to jump off a cliff, would you do it too?"
- "I've told you a thousand times, and the answer is still no! Stop asking me!"
- "You'll take someone's eye out with that thing. Put it down. Now!"
- "Close the door! You weren't born in a barn."
- "Turn off the light. We don't own stock in the electric company."
- "Don't sit that close to the TV. You'll hurt your eyes or go blind."
- "SHE? Who the heck is, *SHE*?"
- "You are not sick... You are going to school. End of story."
- "As long as you're under my roof, you'll live by my rules!"

THINGS I PROMISE TO TRY, "NEVER TO SAY TO YOU!"

- "Stop crying, or I will give you something to cry about."
- "We'll cross that bridge when we come to it."
- "Keep it up and I'll wash your mouth out with soap."
- "Don't blame me, you brought this on yourself."
- "If you want to act like a child, I'll treat you like a child!"
- "Talking to you is like talking to a brick wall."
- "What do you mean, I don't know? I don't know, is not an answer."
- "I'm not asking you now, I'm telling you."
- "When you pay the bills around here, you can do whatever you want."
- "You're not going anywhere until you clean up your room."
- "Get your elbows off the table. Where are your manners?"
- "You'll understand one day when you're a parent."
- "Trust me, this hurts me more than it's going to hurt you!"
- "Don't lie to me. I wasn't born yesterday, you know."
- "You darn kids will be the death of me."
- "Don't burn the candle at both ends."
- "We're not laughing at you, we're laughing with you."
- "Wipe that smile off your face before I wipe it off for you."
- "Child, don't you dare make me pull this car over!"
- "Quiet down, I can't even hear myself think."
- "I know you're angry now, but one day you'll thank me."
- "God gave you a brain, use it."
- "Get up and get it yourself. Are your legs broken?"
- ("Why Jen's mom lets her!") "Fine! Then go live with Jen's mom."
- "Your room looks like a cyclone ran through it."
- "Someone better be bleeding!"

- "Use your knife and fork... My goodness, were you raised by wolves?"
- "You better erase that smirky attitude off your face. I'm serious, kid."
- "I'm serious as a heart attack. Don't make me tell you again."
- "You march yourself right back in here, and I mean now!"
- "This is the last time I am going to tell you. Get into your bed and go to sleep."
- "Don't make me come over there or you'll be sorry."
- "Let's try not to eat off the floor, shall we?"
- "You're lucky. I'd never have gotten away with that when I was your age."
- "If you don't have anything nice to say, don't say anything at all."
- "Stop that this instant! And don't argue with me or you'll be grounded!"
- "I never acted this way. What is wrong with you?" (An oldie, but a goodie!)

The winner, most famous, classic, parent failure of all and mommy's all-time favorite...

- "I'm going to count to 10 and you better stop it! 1-2-3-4... Do you hear me? 5-6-7? Are you listening to me? 8-9-10? That's it! Do you hear me? 1-2-3-4-5-6-7-8-9-10!"

Look, Kay or Jon, I'm not promising I won't quote these ancient philosophical pearls of stupidity. I'm only promising to try not to. But come on kid? Give me a break. I mean, really? Some of them

THINGS I PROMISE TO TRY, "NEVER TO SAY TO YOU!"

are just so darn good! FYI, I actually had to endure every last one of them. Like a million times. I can't tell you how often I wanted to reply with some obnoxiously sarcastic answers. However, since mommy wanted a lot of things like clothes, a new phone, a new computer, a possible future car, or a real tiara perhaps, etc., I decided it would be more productive and prudent in the long run to remain silent. That said I could wrap my finger around your grandpa getting almost anything I wanted with my perfectly polished charm and charisma. Your daddy will be exactly the same way, so do be wise, little one. "We'll cross that bridge when we come to it!" "One day you'll thank me." "Just you wait and see." "Don't blame me, you brought this on yourself." Oops, sorry, baby Salma or Jackson. Now... Go to your *womb* and stay there!

CHAPTER 37

A Lesson from a Very Bad Dream...

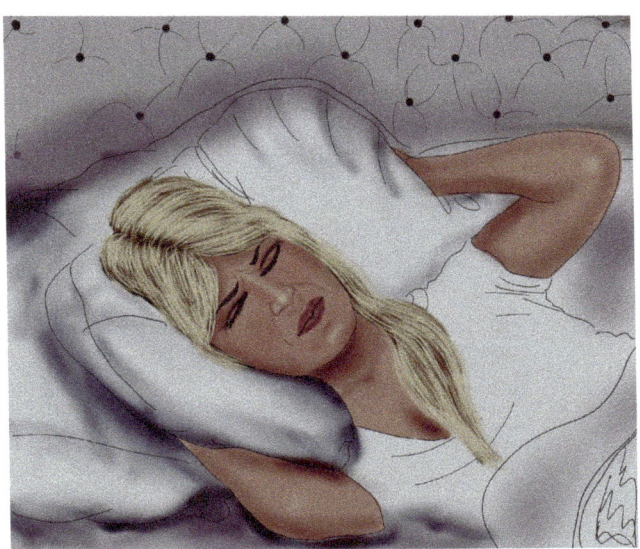

Morning, Boo! And wow, am I ever relieved it is morning! Mommy had the strangest, most awful dream last night. More like a nightmare. No, you don't have to kick me. I'll tell you all about it.

It all started out just fine, at first... We were in the present, around three months before you were born. Then, unexpectedly, with no warning and unable to control what was happening, you were born. It was as if you were growing up in fast motion. I was thrown off guard, frustrated, alarmed, and there was nothing I could do to slow down the process. Time was irrelevant. In a blink of a tear-filled eye, you weren't a baby anymore. It appeared I had been robbed and cheated out of your entire babyhood and future.

There you were, tying your sneakers by yourself. Cutting your meat without any help. Coloring in the lines, exactly as I would've taught you. Riding your bicycle with no training wheels, and putting puzzles together, solo. I don't get it? Did I lose my superhero powers overnight? Somebody, please, please wake me up from this chilling nightmare.

Alas, it only got worse. Tragically and exceedingly confused, you were waving goodbye to me as you walked by yourself into first grade! Not one tear from you and no clinging onto mommy? How did you become this independent? My eyes were so flooded with tears, I could barely find the way back to my car. How could you be in first grade? There you were with other kids laughing, reading, doing math, playing games, Legos, and trading Pokémon and Teenage Mutant Ninja Turtles cards without my help. Impossible...

I was just pregnant. My God, it was just three months before you were born?

I tossed and turned, hoping to wake up, but nothing put an end to my terrible night terror. Making this experience more horrific (as if that were possible), time flashed ahead even faster. Now, my little Cassandra or Morgan, you're going with friends to movies, enjoying birthday parties and sleepovers. What? OMG, please, oh please stop the clock.

A LESSON FROM A VERY BAD DREAM...

Do my eyes so deceive me? I'm going to be sick! There you are at teen socials, hanging with friends, driving a car, going out on dates, and dressing too provocative and mature.

Blimey, wait a minute. What is happening now? What's with all those tears I see? Why are you crying? Why are you upset? Did that *F#$*g* brat, just break your heart? Hell no! I'll kill the kid with my bare hands. Why I oughta! I stood there paralyzed, watching this hurt and pain happen to you. I had lost my *"mom powers"* and could not do a thing to help. It took laborious effort for me to witness these flashes of your unbearable sorrow. Someone make it stop. Please slow time down and end this horror. I wept to no avail.

What is this now? Is that a cap and gown? You are graduating high school with honors? I rubbed my eyes, too baffled and powerless to comprehend all that I was seeing.

Fast-forward... It can't be so? Why are you packing? You're leaving daddy and me to go off to college? Don't go! Although, what an amazing doctor you'll be, just like your dad. I felt lavish tears streaming down my cheeks, even in my sleep. Come back, Boo!

I was just pregnant. My God, it was just three months before you were born?

I tried futilely to wake up. I couldn't believe my own eyes when I blinked again. There you were walking down the aisle to be married? I tried screaming out when the official said, "Does anyone object to this marriage? If so, speak now or forever hold your peace." I know for sure I must've been screaming out loud in my sleep. "ME, ME, ME! I object." And just like that, we lost you! You're all grown up and don't need us anymore.

It was agonizing and disturbingly surreal. It wasn't like a dream at all. For it was really happening. Yet, how could this feasibly be real? I was just six months pregnant! I haven't had a chance to change a smelly blowout poo-diaper, aspirate a boogie from your nose, watch you walk, or hear your adorable voice. I never got to see any of your firsts, or even your seconds. I never got to lie to you about the tooth fairy and other parental tales.

I was just pregnant. My God, it was just three months before you were born?

Oh, no. This is too much for me to bear, as I cried, clenching my aching heart. I see a precious newborn baby? I'm looking at a tiny infant, a perfect angel. Emily or Bo, you had a baby? How can I be watching you play on the floor with a beautiful newborn? Is this *your* baby? I turned around for only two seconds, and you're a parent? I am a grandmother? Why is the clock racing time? Am I sleeping, or is this real? But how, tell me, how? *I was just pregnant. My God, it was just three months before you were born?*

Mercifully, I awoke breathless, shaking in a cold sweat with my eyes red and swollen from crying. It was horrifyingly worse than any version of a nightmare. I never want to sleep again after such a ghastly scare. *What a shocking, yet critical wake-up call?*

My little darling, mommy cannot describe the utter solace I felt when I looked down to see the funny shapes on my tummy as you moved inside of me, safe and sound. I smiled, smearing away my tears. Daddy jumped up, very concerned. I whispered gently, "Go

A LESSON FROM A VERY BAD DREAM...

back to sleep, love. Everything's fine now. It was all just a terrible, very bad dream."

"You sure sweetie?" Daddy kissed away the tears from my eyes, smiled, and fell asleep.

But, guess what, little Tia or Lincoln? Although my dream was a super intense, horrific experience, it was a genuine, *Aha* moment. I was now more grateful than ever to be pregnant with you. I vowed on the spot to relish each moment I had left. Yep, *Stretch Marks* and all. Additionally, and unapologetically corny, I realized how vital it is to appreciate each wonderful nanosecond of your childhood. No matter what! Indeed, I had learned a valuable lesson in the nick of time. My nightmare proved to be a stunning gift.

Now wide-awake and lit, I was euphorically grateful and happy to be out of that time warp and back in the real world. It was rather an epic relief to discover I was still *blissfully pregnant with you. Little one,* I love you with my entire soul, but please promise mommy you won't grow up too fast. Tonight revealed to me, I really can't deal with that.

Ya know what? I think I need to stay awake the rest of the night, for sure. Let's go ahead and make some yummy extra chocolate-chip waffles. You'll absolutely love that!

Baby Kyla or Rhodes, *thank God it's still just three months before you are born...*

CHAPTER 38

Whoo-Hoo... The Third Trimester

Sleepless Restless Nights... Pondering Random Thoughts...

Sitting here quietly, little one, in the middle of the night feeling like a pudgy half-baked soufflé, I'm giddy and proud celebrating the start of our third trimester. Yea! It's peaceful alone in the dark, gazing at a flickering gardenia-scented candle. BTW, that's mommy's favorite flower. As my mind wanders, I can't help endlessly speculating who and what you'll become one day. I could reflect upon this mystery forever. There is undeniably much to ponder. Aha, there you go, kicking me again. So it appears I'm not alone after all. I love all your gentle movements. They never seem to get old for mommy.

Baby, I just had a distasteful, passing pregnant thought. No offense intended, but I hope you will not be one of those hideous-looking babies. You know, the kind of babies that are so unattractive, people say stuff to the parents like, "Yep, that's a baby!" Or even worse, "Is that a baby?" A baby so ugly, only a mother could love. And maybe not even her? Wow, I'm deplorable. Gosh, I don't know if I'm up for the task? I'm not gonna lie, and with disturbing clarity, I believe I might be missing the "appreciation, compassion, and understanding of the ugly, gene." NO, Mommy's not shallow at all! That was merely your basic random nasty, obnoxious, paranoid, preggo response. OK, maybe mommy is a scintilla shallow. I'm only joking! Well... Sorta? Don't you worry, I'll adapt. I got this.

Jacob or Hadley, I've discovered you'll be filling a place in my heart I never knew existed. I never realized there was an empty void inside me. Well, until those *ugly baby* comments above. Eeks! I've recently learned giving birth is more than bringing you life. It is, in essence, bringing life to the universe with the promise of immeasurable new possibilities. Creating possibilities not only in our lives but in the world as well.

The gift of pregnancy is nothing short of miraculous. Think about it, it's an astonishing phenomenon. Regardless, of all I have

WHOO-HOO... THE THIRD TRIMESTER

withstood the past 6 months, I deeply adore having you grow inside me. The whole experience has been hugely extraordinary. Being pregnant and becoming a mommy has proven to me how resilient and strong I am in every way possible. I'm rather amazed and proud of my own body for allowing me the miracle of carrying a child. What an astounding machine a woman's body is, which has brought me the greatest blessing I could ever experience. Seriously, a woman's body has wondrous superpowers. Hence, I'm essentially a superhero. It boggles my mind that a human life is growing in my belly. You've made me a virtual, somewhat God-like, spiritual being. Most humbly, Leo or Ivy, I understand the beauty and meaning of life through the miracle of creating and carrying you. You're the work of God's miraculous art!

Precious, I'd like you to know before you were conceived and long before I met your daddy, I've always dreamed of you. Beguiling, for we haven't even met, and despite that, I absolutely know you. Soon you'll come down-to-earth, and already I'd die for you. This is the selfless marvel of a Mother's Love. Ugly or not! Oh, relax, I'm only kidding!

You are an angel, mommy's angel, only without the wings. Nonetheless, when I feel you fluttering, I swear I feel those wings. It's cute, because every time you kick me, I sense you're trying to give me a big hug from the inside. So telling, how I feel an endless, thrilling loop of joy washing over me with your every movement. You leave me giggling. It's cool how only you and I share this celestial, spiritual, out-of-this-world, secret bond.

To let you in on another random secret, I believe in love at first sight. Yes, that's what I found with daddy. It's quite fascinating, I've never even seen you, and yet I already love you completely. *"Love... before any sight at all."* You are the child I asked God for. The child I fantasized about and envisioned since I was a little girl playing dress-up. You are my destiny, and my world will never be the same. No matter what I accomplish, you'll forever be my greatest masterpiece. Bristol or Julian, I promise I will strive to become the perfect mommy. Though, I am not certain there is such a thing as a perfect mommy? Still, I can guarantee you that I'll go down trying with all my heart and soul. Regardless, work with me, if you will. This *mommy thing* may take me some time.

Oh, darling, it's late now and mommy is exhausted. Unfortunately, though, I find myself unable to sleep. Whatever, I'll continue talking to you and pondering silly random thoughts. Such as, I never liked the phrase, "You complete me," about love. How is that for a silly random thought? Meanwhile, as I carry you and await your birth, I've come to recognize I'm the fool. You, my baby Marie-Antoinette or Louis-Auguste, do complete me, 100% in fact! My life, which I had always thought to be perfect, was indeed nothing more than an empty shell. I was searching, along with daddy, for the ultimate fulfillment that is you. Suddenly, reality materialized. My life had no real meaning before conceiving you. While we are on random topics, in my point of view, foolish as it might be, I don't believe a man genuinely knows how to love until he becomes a father. And fortunately, fatherhood will soon become the everlasting, awesome gift you will bring to your daddy.

WHOO-HOO... THE THIRD TRIMESTER

You know, as of late, I've come to appreciate it's never really the ideal or right time to have a baby. There are always reasons, situations, problems, issues, occurrences that pop up, complications, or excuses to put it off. I've discovered you just have to go for it and blindly jump in. I was pretty unsure myself and wondered if I was ready to have a baby. Jeeze, I'm still wondering. Nevertheless, being pregnant with you is ultimately how mommy realized what was missing my entire adult life. I never comprehended nor understood the immeasurable love of a parent until becoming pregnant. On that thought, I want you to realize, having and being part of a family is not an important thing... It's fundamentally everything! Never forget this, even when you go through tough times.

It seems to me life couldn't get more heavenly than the day your daddy and I will finally get to bring you home. Nirvana, euphoria, plus lots of *"Oh shit, what the hell do I do now?" situations!* Indeed, I've often heard life changes drastically after a baby is born. Roles shift, hormones rage, chores multiply, and finances alter. A baby challenges one's sense of control, leaving parents feeling depleted and overwrought. Not to mention losing some freedoms, which can be particularly difficult for both mommies and daddies.

Parenthood, from what I can foresee, is significantly overwhelming. I imagine no mother ever thinks she has enough time, help, training, money, or emotional support. I mean, do we? I hope being a mom won't leave me feeling trapped, resentful, depressed, irritable, angry, or believing I'm a complete failure. I suppose all of these emotions are normal and to be expected. But regardless honey, of course, you are more than worth it.

I wasn't about to go into this, *having a baby thing,* blind or winging it. So, to be prepared, not caught off guard, and keeping surprises at bay, I've enthusiastically read all there is to know about having a baby. Pitifully, I watched "Nine Months," "Baby Boom," and "Knocked Up" umpteen times. I also learned all the baby cries and what they mean.

Meanwhile, according to Priscilla Dunstan, an Australian opera singer who created the *"Dunstan Baby Language,"* I learned that there are five basic sounds a baby makes just before crying. Although, I did have trouble correlating how she discovered the crying baby sounds with the opera thing. A linking hitch, all successful innovators possibly face. Regardless, Here Are The Codes:

1. Neh—Hunger
2. Eh—Upper wind (burp)
3. Eairh—Lower wind (gas)
4. Heh—Discomfort (hot, cold, wet)
5. Owh—Sleepiness

Beware, sweetie, I am counting on these 5 and these 5 alone! Don't you go inventing the 6th one, or I'll go "Mommy Dearest" on you! I'm not Aussie and I don't sing opera so, don't mess with me, kid. *"Why? Because I said so, that's why."* Oops, big slip up. Sorry!

Anyway, sweet Bogart or Bacall, you're my every desire, all the wishes in my heart, and ones I never imagined. I feel like I am waiting on the ultimate gift from dreamland. Every passing day is day closer to meeting the other love of my life... You. For now, I carry you inside me for nine months. Later, I shall carry you in my arms for three years. After that, I will carry you in my heart until the day I die, and forevermore...

My innocent yet-to-be-born baby, the sun is beginning to rise. Sorry, I've bored you terribly all night long with my odd, ridiculous

WHOO-HOO... THE THIRD TRIMESTER

mixture of babbling phrases and random thoughts. How embarrassing. No doubt, they were all textbook examples of a word salad. I suppose I've had too many random thoughts and far too much pondering for one night. Although in my defense (distinguished jury of my peers), there was an enormous, full, blood-red-moon tonight, likely contributing to my lunatic behavior. Sweetness, let's talk real soon. I'm tired, little darling. I am going to close my eyes now and dream of you.

It's funny, little Annika or Denver, much like the Grinch at the end of the story... mommy's heart feels like it has grown ten inches since discovering we were pregnant. Unexpectedly it appears the tiniest little things can take up all the space in one's heart.

A big hug and a pondering, random, third trimester, Grinchy green, mwah and kiss!

CHAPTER 39

I Mean, Like, How Can a Teeny-Weeny Little Baby Need So Much Stuff Anyway?

Miserable, feeling like the defeated Goliath, the "good grief" Charlie Brown, uncomfortable, lethargic, restless, and all the while thinking out loud, "Maybe Colette was right?" Perhaps the Dr. did mess up, and you are not alone in there. Could you actually be twins or triplets? Is it possible to be this ginormous carrying only one tiny baby? Little Scarlett or Hunter Johansson, do you each weigh 30 pounds? Please, say yes!

So I've recently discovered a fun thing? My tummy is so gigantic it can easily be used as a food tray. Because I always look on the bright side, this is considered a perk!

OK, ick, I'm barfing. Not to be rude, but for crying out loud, I wish someone had advised me, morning sickness *doesn't* only occur in the 1st trimester. Nor is it *primarily a morning thing*! Good Lord, I'm facing infinite questions, problems, worries, fears, and concerns, to say nothing of my 'to-do-list,' bursting (like my bump) with 'to-dos.' I often think how can one tiny little baby change everything. Like, altering our lives into a 360° full circle. I'm suffering intense turmoil and mayhem, all brought on by one, itsy-bitsy alien. And that's all before you even arrive? Baby Cher or Tom Hanks, I want to shout out like in an old movie, "Snap out of it" or "Houston, we have a problem!"

As I began preparing for all your insurmountable needs, I studied several lists suggesting the staggering amount of things a baby requires. I question, is it just a *"Leona thing,"* or does it seem that an infant needs more essentials and necessities than I actually do? How is this possible? And precisely why is that? Talk about high maintenance, baby?

Here's a Mind-Blowing, Heads Up, FYI, Baby List:

For starters, my needy, demanding baby, I must purchase a fine superior crib. But what if I get the wrong mattress for the crib? What if my poor decision causes you to have a bad back for the rest of your life? These endless critical decisions don't end there. Examples:

HOW CAN A BABY NEED SO MUCH STUFF ANYWAY?

- Car seat Stroller
- Bottles and cleaners
- Baby monitor
- Baby carrier
- Breast pump
- Bottle warmer
- Nursing pillow
- Burp cloths
- Nipple shield
- Nipple cream
- Changing table
- Crib
- Mobile
- Play mat
- Rocking chair glider
- Baby Rocker
- High chair
- Diapers and wipes
- 4–8 half shirts
- 4–8 Onesies
- 4 shirt and pant sets
- 4 -footed coveralls
- 1–3 seasonal dress-up outfits
- 1–2 swimsuits 1
- 5 burp cloths
- 6–8 one-piece pajamas
- 3-6 hooded towels
- Baby toys and rattles
- Ointments and creams
- Infant tub and insert
- Crib sheets
- Sling or snuggly
- Playpen
- Baby swing
- Bassinet Pack and play
- Sleep sacks or swaddling cloths
- 4–6 washcloths
- 2–4 receiving blankets
- Booties
- 2–4 no-scratch mittens
- Sun hats for summer
- Knit hats for winter babies
- Snowsuit for winter
- 1–3 winter sweaters
- Snap sleep and playsuits
- Short sleeve bodysuits
- Pajamas Side-snap tees
- Long sleeve bodysuits
- Socks
- Tights and leg warmers
- Baby booties
- Baby knee pads
- Baby beanies, caps
- Bibs
- Blankets
- Bloomers, diaper covers
- Training pants
- Underwear

Jackets, windbreakers	Shoes, sandals, boots
Special occasion outfits	Soap Baby Thermometer
Jeans and shorts	Nail clippers
Sunglasses	Bulb syringe
100 pacifiers or more (LOL)	Meds and vitamins
Pacifier clips	Diaper Genie Pail
Hair accessories if you have a girl	Infant seat

It's absurd, dear Grayson or Emma, there's so much more to buy than the list above. For instance, it's crucial I find that one essential stuffed animal, which will essentially become a part of you, like your skin. That thing you'll refuse to go to sleep without. That soft duck, cat, blankie, dog, doll, or whatever it is you will walk around with, never letting go of it. I must find this comforting thingamajig you'll become so attached to, for which you cannot live without. The all-important security object you'll secretly want to take with you to college one day. Yes, finding *this supernatural object* will create a great deal of pressure. No worries, I shall prevail. My goodness, does the list ever end? It's ludicrous, silly, outrageous, and way over the top.

Whether you are an Avi or a Sage, I still have to pick out your baby announcements.

It goes without saying, the urgency for mommy to select a trendy, stylish/chic, baby bag, which defines me. Hopefully, one that's not at all practical. Since I'll have to take it everywhere, it's exigent to make an iconic fashion statement. Yes, I'll be a new mom. Nevertheless, I won't be a fashion-deprived one! This fashionista selection might be the only one I'll have for quite a while. Gee, speaking of a bag, I almost forgot? I must pack a bag to bring to the hospital. The trick to accomplish will be getting everything I'll need in one measly little bag? I wonder what magic Mary Poppins conjured up, making it possible to live her entire life in one tiny carpetbag? I imagine that's where the "Spoon full of sugar" and the "Supercalifragilisticexpialidocious" enchantment come into play?

I've now reached the obvious conclusion that I need a baby shower and stat! So, Adrian or Parson, should mommy call Colette and take her up on her offer, or stick with daddy's mom's proposal? Oh dear, I could easily be facing a lose-lose situation on this.

Gosh, I don't want your daddy to feel left out! Hmm, huh, am I supposed to throw him a *Dadchelor* shower party? Well, if I do, those *"Woo-Hoo Dancing Girls"* won't be expected, like they were at his bachelor party. Tramps! Just saying. But, I'm not jealous! I'm not baby Envy or Malicious! I best get on that instantly. Swoosh!

"Hey, Hi Colette?"

CHAPTER 40

I Swear To God, I Feel Like a Frickin' Farmer!

Most moms-to-be are "baby curious." Hence, why we crave to know every detail about our baby. We wish we could snoop in and see everything that's going on in the womb. You know, like "In the womb where it happens!" ("Hamilton..." Oh, never mind!) We want to know how big the baby is growing each week during our pregnancy. A mom's desire to understand everything baby is pure love. So why, and I do mean why, do baby-growth-trackers have to compare a baby to us moms using fruits and vegetables? Am I a frickin' farmer? Yee-haw. Just call me Old-Mom-McDonald, wearing my soiled overalls, hair up in high pigtails, with tattered bows, singing "E-I-E-I-OOOOO!"

Sweet little Billy-Bob or Betsy-Lynn, why does mommy have to feel like a produce farmer, working out in the hot fields, while daddy comes off as a fab, super cool, fun guy. I get that mommy has to do most of the hard work and labor here. But shouldn't we catch some kind of break on this pregnancy journey? Nah-Ah pumpkin, we don't. Seriously, here's how they are essentially describing you to me each week. Allow me to show the unfair comparison of your development for mommy as opposed to your trendy daddy...

	FOR A WOMAN	FOR A MAN:
Week 4	Poppy Seed	A man's Facial Stubble
Week 5	Apple Seed or Sesame Seed	Chili Flakes or Choco. Chip
Week 6	Sweet Peas Or a Lentil	Maggot Fish Bait or an M&M
Week 7	Blueberry	5 Piece Coin or Cotton ball

I SWEAR TO GOD, I FEEL LIKE A FRICKIN' FARMER!

Week 8	Raspberry or a Kidney Bean	Peanut M&M or Jelly Bean
Week 9	Green Olive or a Grape	Thumb Nail or Gum Ball
Week 10	Kumquat	Espresso Cup or Beer Cap
Week 11	Lime or a Fig	Golf Ball or Car Shift Knob
Week 12	Plum	Right Testicle or Wine Cork
Week 13	Lemon or a Peapod	Large Boiled Egg or Post-It
Week 14	Nectarine	Rubik's Cube or Gas Cap
Week 15	Apple	Ben & Jerry's pint or baseball
Week 16	Avocado	Light Bulb or Blackberry
Week 17	Pear or a Turnip	Softball or Hamburger Patty
Week 18	Bell Pepper	iPhone 6 or Toilet paper roll
Week 19	Heirloom Tomato	Mini Rugby ball or Hotdog
Week 20	Artichoke or a banana	A pint of beer or whoopee cushion
Week 21	Carrots	Liter of Jägermeister
Week 22	Papaya or a spaghetti Squash	Bottle of Glenlivet Whisky

Week 23	Grapefruit or a large Mango	Baseball Mitt
Week 24	Ear of Corn	Car Speedometer
Week 25	Rutabaga	Left Shoe, Size 12
Week 26	Lettuce or the length of a scallion	Surface of a tennis Racket
Week 27	Cauliflower	Lunchbox
Week 28	Large Eggplant	Car Alternator
Week 29	Acorn Squash	Small Halloween Pumpkin
Week 30	Cabbage	MacBook Pro17-inch
Week 31	Coconut	Loaf of Bread or carburetor
Week 32	Jicama	Carjack
Week 33	Pineapple	Regulation Size Football
Week 34	Butternut Squash or a Cantaloupe	Ukulele or AC compressor
Week 35	Honeydew	Length of a DVD Player
Week 36	Swiss Chard or a Romaine Lettuce	Car Brake drum
Week 37	Winter Melon	Large Ruby Ball

I SWEAR TO GOD, I FEEL LIKE A FRICKIN' FARMER!

Week 38	Rhubarb or the length of a Leek	Car Muffler
Week 39	Yard-long Beans	Beach Ball
Week 40	Pumpkin	Car Air filter
Week 41	Mini Watermelon	Car Center Console
Week 43	Jackfruit	Car differential

So, little girl Violet, it's important that you recognize it's sadly still a man's world. Regardless, it's better than it has ever been before. *We can vote now!* If you're a boy, my beloved Lennon, you won't have to work as hard as women. Plus, you'll earn higher pay!

Meanwhile, my point is, why do women get farm produce and men get totally cool, awesome, fun things to describe a baby's growth? Why can't women get a weekly chart representing us more accurately? Charts showing your size in ways we relate to. Such as: (Take in a big breath) Bling high heels, Tiffany jewelry, Rolex Watches, lipstick, rings, lace bras, rhinestone picture frames, Dior sunglasses, earrings, credit cards, anti-wrinkle cream, candles, perfume, LV Purse, a Yeti tumbler, mascara, a flashy iPhone case, Uggs, glitter nail polish, concert tickets, chocolate, a Kindle, a Starbucks Caramel Café Latte, or a gift card would do the trick. All the above would perfectly represent your growth to us. Trackers, shame on all of you. We preggers deserve a prize, not an ear of corn. Milk that!

ROBIN ROTH

Ok, little Amos or Birch, Lilibeth-Sue or Blossom... Mommy has to get back to hoein' and harvestin' the vegetable and fruit crops, milkin' the cows, and gosh-golly later on, plowin' the fields. With my baby-bump growin' like a weed and all... it's darn near impossible gettin' on up into the tractor these days. With a moo-moo here and a moo-moo there, there's no end to my farmin' chores. There's enough to keep me busy till the cows come home! Or, when daddy comes rolling in with facial stubble, after a sports event, in a fancy car, with a liter of Jägermeister, a pint of Ben and Jerry's, and oh, his right testicle!

CHAPTER 41

I Promise I Will Never...

Baby Giuliana or Londyn... I hope you have some time to share one of our conversations. For various reasons, I have the sudden urge to make you a few promises for the future. If that's ok with you, honey?

Now, I love my mommy (your grandmother) with every ounce of my being. To be clear, I only hope to become half the remarkable mom to you that she is to me. There are, however, some things she, along with my friend's mothers, said and did that "I promise, I will try to *never* say, or do to you." Here, I'll show you what I mean...

I won't allow strangers, or people in general, to pinch your rosy cheeks, saying things like "Hello there, cutie, with your fat chubby cheeks!" Or "My, you are a roly-poly, aren't you?" Regardless, I will assuredly squeeze and kiss your perfect cheeks a lot. A fair warning, I'll also tenderly bite the bottom of your brand-spanking-new baby feet.

I'll never hang over your crib speaking baby talk and making goo-goo eyes at you. When you start eating foods, I'll never say, "Open the tunnel." Or, "Open wide, here comes the Choo-Choo train!" Realize your grandma will absolutely say both of um. And there isn't a thing I can do to protect you. They'll be no stopping her! I'd refuse to open the tunnel if I were you. I did! To this day, my mom's sadly still trying to tunnel-feed me.

Feel at ease, for I'll never throw away your Nu-Nu, Gee-Gee, Uff-Uff, blankie, or whatever you crush on before you are entirely ready. Even then, I wouldn't have the heart to throw it away. I'll save it forever, somewhere. I know when I threw my beloved "Old Dolly" out the car window on a trip with my parents (for the fun of seeing her fly) when they didn't turn around to go find Old Dolly, I was traumatized. Still am. Just so you know, mommy would absolutely turn around and fetch *your thing* for you. No problem.

I PROMISE I WILL NEVER...

Furthermore, when we go to the beach and you want me to take your sandy, icky wet bathing suit off because it feels cold and creepy, I'll never take your suit off and change your clothes in the middle of the beach, in front of the whole world to see. I won't embarrass the crap out of you as my mommy (whom I totally love and adore) did to me!

When you get a little older, I swear I won't make you kiss and hug everyone hello and goodbye. Nor will I humiliate you by kissing you right in front of your friends. As for myself, the kids made fun of me and mocked me all throughout elementary, from that little parental ditty. Still, I will certainly grab you, hug you, and kiss you when no one is looking. So, plan on that happening. I'll throw in a few "Why I oughta tickles," as well.

You can safely have no worries, for I will never say things such as:

"Clean your plate or there's no dessert!" *That'll never happen. Dessert's a given!*

"Why can't you be more like your nice friend, Angela?" *I would never say that! That's just entirely wrong. Besides, I just want you to be yourself. The hell with Angela!*

And, of course, the ever-fabulous classic...

"I told you so!" *Oh, pa-lease. That's just richly arrogant, overused, and cliché.*

Beloved little Chloe or Danny, I will also never say those timeless standards like:

"Money doesn't grow on trees, you know?"

Though it would be cool if it did, wouldn't it? How senseless is that statement, anyway?

Another iconic parental phrase, "I'll wash your mouth out with soap!" First of all, it doesn't clean your mouth. It's stupid, dangerous, and proves positively nothing. I remember my mom did that to me once when I said the word shit. She did, however, give me the choice of a bar of soap or liquid soap. I chose the liquid. Trust me, this was a giant mistake. I'll have that soapy taste in my mouth for eternity. FYI, choose the bar.

Or, "Wait till your father gets home, and boy, you will get it then!"

Yep, Aha right! My daddy came home, gave me a toy, a hug, a kiss, and said, go play. In reference to that classic, I won't wait for daddy. I will punish you myself, to be sure!

Then, there is the ever-annoying "What did you just say?"

Come on child, mommy has perfect hearing. I'm not 90. I heard exactly what you said.

Or, the ancient phrase as old as time "This too shall pass!"

For in reality, sometimes it doesn't! Life's not always a fairytale. Ask Princess Diana...

Or possibly, "Stop that right now. You can't always have what you want!"

Seriously, who am I to discourage you? Wowie, wow, wow. Come on, maybe you can?

There is always the nostalgic, "When I was younger!"

Unequivocally not happening. For I am still, forever, and always going to be young...

Who makes this stuff up, anyway? Of course, the "They say," people!

I will never make you eat foods that you hate. What's the purpose of that? There are undoubtedly enough healthy foods you'll

I PROMISE I WILL NEVER...

love. Hence, beets, Brussels sprouts, spinach, eggplant, runny eggs, okra, liver, and so on, are not as important as finding foods you'll enjoy eating. Power plays are so overrated and wasted on foolish nonsense. I wonder if a real historian would really know if Popeye enjoyed or even liked spinach?

Moreover, I promise to never scream into your ears asking, "Do you hear me?"

My mommy and daddy were very guilty of this darling, sentimental next one...

"We don't care if Linda's mother says she can go! We say you are not going! Done."

These typical time-honored *"mommyisms and daddyisms,"* are directly responsible for my learning the meaning of the words defiant, maverick, and rebellious.

In addition, I will never force you to take piano, ballet, karate, violin, acting, painting, ninja, gymnastics, golf, tennis, or any other lessons that don't interest you. However, I'll definitely encourage you to get involved in the arts and sports. It's my thing. I believe they are extremely essential in making you a well-rounded individual.

I also promise mommy won't spank first and ask questions later. I am not big on spanking. Though *they say* it comes in handy. Personally, I don't believe in it. The only positive is it might make me feel better. It likely won't happen often or even at all.

I won't be giving you those long, fabricated lectures on how I walked six miles to school every day in a blizzard, in 10 feet of snow. Why? Because it's the same dumb story my parents constantly told me. And also, because I grew up in Florida!

I won't burden you with my woes, or daily complaints. It's hard enough being a kid. You certainly don't need me adding any weight to your daily personal problems.

Baby Hannibal or Clarice, I won't threaten you with the notorious, nonsensical, "Go to your room and stay there!"

Clearly, mommy is not stupid. Get real? Your room has a phone, a computer, your music, your toys, cool stuff, foods you previously snuck into your drawers, and all the privacy in the world. If you need to stay anywhere, in the form of a time-out punishment, it will be 5 inches, right in front of me, wherever I am. Similarly, I will never threaten to count to 10 or any number. Hells-bells, when I say *do* something, just do it! Gee, that sounded pretty harsh, didn't it? Oh, relax. I'm so not!

You won't understand this for quite a while, but you can trust that I will never make fun of, "Your day, your music, crazy clothes, weird hairstyles, or things you and your friends enjoy doing." Well, of course, as long as it's not harmful, dangerous, or illegal! Nonetheless, don't be upset with mommy if I like some of "your-day" things and copy them. Mommy is cool, cutting edge, very progressive, and you should be aware of this fact. Yea, ok, little one, I can see you rolling your eyes already in the womb. Cut the crap. After all, I'm still looking for new, inventive ways of driving my own mom crazy. With daddy's mommy, it's obviously not at all a stretch to accomplish. But, she's great!

Now, A Cautionary Tale...

Later on, when you become a teenager, don't do what I did to my parents. I went to a big party. Then afterward, I decided to spend the night at another girlfriend's house without calling

I PROMISE I WILL NEVER...

home to let them know where I was. I mean no biggie? I wasn't doing anything wrong. Being considerate, I didn't want to wake up your grandparents-to-be. I figured they'd be sleeping, happily. So being thoughtful, I decided not to wake them up. How was I to know they were scared and waiting up for me to come home? Waiting up the entire night! Big trouble wasn't the word for what happened to me. While my parents stayed up all night hysterically worrying and crying, they called up everyone they knew. They called all the hospitals, police stations in the entire state, and humiliatingly, all my friends. Let's just say... If you ever did that to your pregnant mommy-to-be, I will find it in my heart to only punish you for 6 months instead of the overly dramatic 3 to 5 years your grandparents punished me for that little stunt I pulled. I never understood, until I grew up, why they were so damn upset. To be honest, at the time I thought, "What was the problem? I knew where I was!" Whatever? Don't do that to daddy or me. Just *call us!*

Lastly, and believe me, there are 100s more of these parental platitudes I will tell you about in time. I solemnly promise (and you have my word), I will never, not ever, no matter what you did bad or wrong, say to you, "When you have kids, I pray to God they will be just like you!" I say this because I already know you are the most amazing child that's ever been, or will ever be born. You are perfect and your kids will be too. But...?

Oh, by the way, Tess or Desmond, just in case you're thinking you've got it made and your mommy and daddy are pushovers? A warning. Don't be that foolish or cavalier. Daddy and I have a huge arsenal of tricks up our sleeves. Do appreciate we've been there, done that, and all you could ever think to do. Therefore, we have our own unique and inventive original ways of keeping you steadfast and in line. So, don't even think about it.

I close this "Heart-to-Bump Conversation" with one last, vital piece of advice. If you ever have an emergency and mommy or daddy can't be reached (which will never be the case), don't call 911. Just call for a pizza! They'll get there much faster! Big Kiss...

CHAPTER 42

All of Your Monumental Milestones and Firsts

Little one, whether your first words will be mommy, daddy, goo-goo, gaga, or whatever they are, I am confident you're going to be a brilliant wordsmith.

Cassidy or Cheyenne, I aspire to be the compassionate, warm mommy that you always run to. The one you feel safe sharing all the "good, bad, and ugly" with. A loving mommy you can trust and confide in. The one you come to for advice. The mom you enjoy hanging out and having fun with, like a friend. Daddy and I hope to be by your side for all of your wonderful firsts. We want to be present as much as humanly possible to help you unpack the endless bundle of magical life experiences. Supporting you means everything to us. You'll always come first. Nothing will make us happier than seeing your face light up, giggling with delight. Our joy is seeing your smile more radiant than the sunshine, more colorful than a rainbow, and more jubilant than any happily ever after.

These days, mommy is bursting with numerous baby-esque questions. Indeed, I do have many questions. Such as... I wonder if you'll be a security blanket, or a stuffed animal baby, who always clings to this object wherever you go? Should I make your baby food or buy it? Should we use pacifiers or pass altogether? Should we run to your rescue every time you cry or give you the opportunity to self-soothe? The list goes on and on.

Even before you are born, I can see how our time together will fly by. I woefully understand the years shall pass rapidly and we must appreciate every single second we have with you. Interesting how other women come up to me all the time and tell me just that, every single day. I smile and thank them warmly, already grasping the significance.

You should know in advance, daddy and mommy are rather spontaneous people. When we're not working (don't get me started!) we pretty much tend to *wing it*. Don't get me wrong we are big planners, too. But the fun stuff, we just like to get up and go. Be on

ALL OF YOUR MONUMENTAL MILESTONES AND FIRSTS

the alert, for you'll be going right along with our carefree approach. Our impromptu style always seems to work out better in the long run. Still, we do thoughtfully plan out all of our legendary family parties and get-togethers. Enjoyment and laughter abound, as our lineage, traditions, and customs heighten all holidays and celebrations to the max.

Meanwhile, I'm going to let you in on another little family secret. Daddy wants to sire at least 3 children. Yes, sire. His mom raised him to believe he is a king. Thank God he's humble. Hence, Victoria or Albert, thou shalt expect a fair and princely brother, and a princess sister, down the pike to share memorable fun firsts with. Hush. It's top-secret!

In case you're wondering, I've already bought the baby memory books, five in fact. I'm literally down and prepared to enter every detail and facet of your entire life into them. Naturally, I bought additional pages. As I'm sure by now you are aware, I'm quite the adjective queen. When you are born, you'll experience all the fun from a stroller's eye view or perhaps a baby carrier. I love them because they're super-cozy and cuddly.

Let talk about your firsts...

To begin, of course, there will be the first time you and I nurse. Seriously hoping this goes well. Next, there is the first time in a car as you come home from the hospital. Your first bath, which I'm sure we'll all laugh together, getting soaking wet. Your first check-up, first shots, your umbilical cord falling off (a bit ewe there), first illness, first words, favorite first toys, first chuckles, the first time you sleep through the night (thank Goodness!), the first time you roll over, sit up, and crawl. Next, your first steps, first tooth, haircut, first time climbing out of your crib, (be careful!) your first birthday, first solid foods, and the first taste of chocolate, sugar, and ice cream. Yummy-yum-yum.

As time passes, you'll experience your first time running, skipping, and dancing, and the first time you try climbing the stairs. I can hardly wait for your attempts to feed yourself. Food will be flying everywhere in your hair, nose, toes, all over the walls, the floor, and visibly all over mommy. Incidentally, go right ahead and make a big mess eating or playing. I'm fine with all of that because the memories you create can never be replaced. I can easily clean up the mess. How exciting it'll be the first time you sleep in a real bed and hopefully stay there the whole night. Another big celebration will be the first time you successfully go potty. Yea! Gosh, I dread your first punishments. They'll upset me more than you. BTW, you'll know every one of your firsts. Indeed you will, for I shall document everything with my finest photography and my ultra fancy penmanship!

Mommy moments with daughter Catalina:

- Braiding your hair... *"Ouch, stop mommy. Ouch, stop it. You're hurting me!"*
- Playing dress-up... *"Mommy, I will be the princess and you will be the old maid! OK?"*
- Your first baby doll... *"Mommy, look at me. I'm feeding my baby. I am such a good mommy, just like you!"*
- Starting your first day at pre-school... *"I don't want to go to school. Mommy, no! Put me down. I'm scared. I don't wanna go!"*

ALL OF YOUR MONUMENTAL MILESTONES AND FIRSTS

- First time taking mommy's makeup (more like stealing), and trying to put it on... *"I love the glitter, purple pencil, red lipstick, and pink stuff I took from your purse! But why can't I wear it to school? Mommy, I'm six and old enough to wear makeup now!"*
- Your first Barbie... *"I love her, mommy! Can we get more clothes, a dream house, a boat, and a dream car?"*
- Your first authentic, professional, expensive, salon gel-manicure and pedicure... *"Mommy, paint them purple, pink, orange and blue. I want to do this every week! OK?"*
- Starting to develop boobs, buying your first bra, and rolling your eyes at mommy... *"I want a big padded one! I want lots of padding. Why not, Mother? I'm 12. I want it!"*
- Getting your period. Heavens, Lord. Spare me and help me get through this drama! *"Gross, are you kidding me? How long do I have to deal with this? What? NO, no way!"*
- Your first high heels... *"I want the hot-pink, real high, 7-inch ones, OK? Why not Mother? Stop it, I won't fall!"*
- Your first time wearing mommy's tiara... *"Now you're talking! The diamonds are real though, right? Well, they better be!"*
- Piecing your ears... *"Ouch, ouch. Hey, let's do my nose and belly button next, OK? Why not, Motherrrrrrr?"*
- Your first boyfriend... *"Motherrrrr, Joe is a good kid. I'm going out with him. I love him! You can't stop me!"*
- Your first kiss... *"Mom, you said I could always come to you. I wanted to be honest and tell you that I love Joe and I kissed him. A lot. So mom, like um, what is this painful yucky sore on my lips?"*

- Your first broken heart... "Why did he break up with me, mommy? I wanna die. Why is Ringo with her? I'll never stop crying. What's wrong with me? I'll never fall in love again! Oh mommy, Boo-Hooo!"
- Turning Sweet-16! "Mother, I don't want a big, stupid party with family. I just want to be with my friends!"
- Your first Prom... "Mother, why can't I get the Vera Wang prom dress? It's only $950. All the girls will be wearing Vera. Great, I'll be the only one left out. Just forget it then! I'm not going!"
- First, sexual experience... Hell no, not in this life. You can just forget about that! "Mother, I'm not a baby. Everyone's doin' it! You can't tell me what to do. I'm doin' it!"
- Alas, your wedding day... If I survive your teens! So, Catalina, you're going to be wearing a huge, extravagant ball gown and my tiara, fit for a queen. Ya know that, right? "Mom, I love you, but this dress is way over-the-top! I'm not six anymore. Pick anything Vera Wang and I'll be happy. You do remember the Vera Prom fiasco? You so owe me!"

After pondering *all the above* (no matter how much I love you, Catalina), I *really* must review the various rearing techniques so as *not to spoil you,* creating a monstrous brat. Like the baby with the Tiffany and Company silver rattle and Waterford Crystal baby bottle.

Mommy moments with son Lenox...

- "Look at me, mommy. I'm a farting, burping, peeing champion. I'm a super-poop-hero!"
- "Look at me run, mommy. Are you looking? Are you? You're not looking! Mommy?"

ALL OF YOUR MONUMENTAL MILESTONES AND FIRSTS

- "Watch me throw the ball. Did you see how far it went? I'm an all-star athlete, mommy."
- "Look at the Lego thingy I made. Are you looking, mommy? Isn't it cool? You looking?"
- "Yes mommy, I hit him and hard too! I had to. He took my red toy truck. He's a stealer."
- "Look how yucky I got playing in the mud. Aren't you proud of me? I'm a fine mess."
- "Watch me ride on my tricycle, mommy. Oh, wait! Can you hold my frog for me?"

Then, my sweet boy, you'll grow up. Puberty arrives and your voice changes. And, the first time I catch you doing... you know what? The nasty! Gee, you were just a baby? *"Really Lenox? Well, I suppose it's totally natural. Asher, come talk to your son."*

- Lenox, soon you'll get your first facial hair and have to start shaving... *"Yes, ah-ha, that is exactly why daddy always has bits of toilet paper on his face."*
- Taking you to get your driver's license. *"So proud of you and on the first try, too. No, Lenox, we're not buying you a car!"*
- First time you lied to us about where you were all night. (And badly done, I must say.) *"Seriously, Lenox, it wasn't even a good lie, kid! Where is your imagination?"*
- Your first kiss... *"Realize your mom will see that kiss. I will totally be peeking through the window."*
- Your first girlfriend... *"I didn't like her or trust that little B... Lil brat, from the very first time I saw her."*
- The prom, the tux, the flowers, and the limo! *"You can roll your mortified eyes all you want. I'll be taking a million photos."*

- Your first broken heart... *"As your mom, I'll totally want to kill the bitch. And boy, does she have it comin!"*
- First time you got busted sneaking out of the house. *"How noisy can you be? What a disgraceful, sneaking-out attempt. Try harder!"*
- First time you got caught with condoms. (Still, glad you took our advice and wore them!) *"Come on! You put your jeans in the washer and the condoms were still in them!"*
- First time you got caught Goggling porn. *"Seriously, Lenox, the house isn't soundproof? Asher, come and talk to your son!"*
- First time you tried to smoke weed or cigarettes. *"Just wait till your father gets home! Yes, I'm aware I promised never to say that."*
- First time you got caught drinking or sneaking your dad's, Don Julio 1942 Tequila. *"Big mistake, Butch Cassidy. You know daddy marks the bottles! A shameful, pitiful blunder! Dude, you really suck at being a bad kid! You need to watch more old movies."*
- First time graduating anything. *"Lenox, daddy and I will be a hot mess and as proud as can be! You are so dope!"*
- Your wedding! *"Can't even go there! I'll say this. She sure as hell better be good enough for you!"*

Little Harper or Oliver, there will be endless amazing and fantastical things ahead of you, and so many first experiences in your life, which you will remember forever:

- First time tying your shoelaces
- First time chewing gum and probably having it end up in your hair

ALL OF YOUR MONUMENTAL MILESTONES AND FIRSTS

- First time pretending to smoke, when it's cold outside
- First time learning the ABC's, reading, writing, math, history, and science
- OMG, First Halloween… To be honest, all of them are amazing
- First Hanukkah or Christmas
- First time doing arts and crafts
- First holiday dinners
- First lemonade stand
- First time blowing out the candles on a birthday cake and having your wish come true
- First time learning to ride a real bike without training wheels
- First time climbing a tree and not falling out
- First time flying a kite and really getting it up in the air
- First time in a pool and swimming lessons
- First time swinging on a rope
- First time blowing bubbles, playing hopscotch, marbles, Monopoly, jacks, hula-hoop, jump rope, rock paper scissors, video games, and lots more
- First time playing with friends in a Blanket-Fort
- First time putting on a puppet show
- First picnic
- First good or bad report card
- First dentist appointments, cavities, getting braces put on, and getting them off
- First acts of kindness, learning to share and volunteering your time for a cause
- First time at sleep-away camp
- First pet (You better take care of it, little Sami)

- First time doing gymnastics or karate
- First time doing ballet, hip-hop, or Ninja
- First time seeing and playing in the snow, making snowmen, snow angels, and snowballs
- First trophy, ribbons, and awards
- First time performing in a school play
- First time on a Ferris wheel and other scary, fun rides
- First Tea Party
- First time running away from home
- First time baking anything
- First time going to the beach, making sandcastles, and burying someone in the sand
- First time having fun with music, dancing, singing, and laughing
- First Broadway show
- First Fourth of July and New Year's Eve fireworks
- First live concert
- First slumber party
- First dance party
- First sleepover
- First big failure, then courageously getting up and trying again
- First real success and staying humble
- Learning how to say you're sorry, and really mean it
- First time really appreciating a sunrise and sunset
- First time on a bus, train, boat, or a plane
- First time ice-skating, snow skiing, roller-skating, and bowling
- Making your first tie

ALL OF YOUR MONUMENTAL MILESTONES AND FIRSTS

- First time getting pocket money or allowance
- First time going out with your friends, *without parents*
- First time sneaking into an R-rated movie (I'm watching you!)
- First time going to Disneyland and other theme parks
- First real job and opening up your first bank account
- First crush
- First time sneaking into mommy and daddy's drawers, finding stuff, and not getting caught
- First time camping out in the wild, making a tent, starting a fire, and eating S'mores
- First time happily running around in the rain
- First time rafting, kayaking, or canoeing
- First time going fishing and actually catching a fish
- First time playing miniature golf, real golf, and playing tennis
- First county fair (oh my... the cotton candy, caramel apples, fudge, and taffy.)
- First experience horseback riding

Here are more firsts, both good and bad you'll always remember

- Having a no-reason at all, "Ferris Bueller's Day Off." AKA... skipping school!
- Trick-or-treating for the first time as a teen, no parents, just your friends. Or so you say.
- Breaking a bone. (Oh, please try not to!)
- Getting involved in a charitable organization. (You'll get more out of it than you'll give!)
- Making your own videos, just like Spielberg... (clean ones, please)

- Attending a big parade, especially a Thanksgiving Day Parade.
- Watching any overrated classic movie, like *Gone with the Wind* or *Casablanca*.
- Visiting a science center. (Other than our house, that is!)
- Getting a taste of history, art appreciation, and the creation of man. Fueling your insight into humanity such as religion, happiness, sadness, anger, joy, love, hate, and or politics.
- Research your family lineage, history, and heritage. (Awesome and valuable.)
- Learning how to let go of things. (Really, letting go.)
- Trying a daredevil stunt like free fall, skydiving, zip-lining, or bungee jumping. ("You know what, on second thought... ABSOLUTELY NOT! I forbid it!"
- Playing all out and really having fun, fully, unfettered, and as freely as you possibly can.
- Learning how to give and receive constructive criticism. (Not as easy as it sounds.)
- Trying new things. (Please try to be careful, though!)
- Going with friends to a rock concert.
- Exploring nature, hiding in a cave, hiking, and climbing up a mountain.
- Learning to give. (The "better to give than receive," thing? Turns out, it's actually true.)
- Give up something you really love for a week. (*Hey, your mommy had to do that for nine months being pregnant with you....* Guilt, guilt, guilt!) (And, more guilt!)
- Working to earn enough money to buy something you want, instead of being given it.

ALL OF YOUR MONUMENTAL MILESTONES AND FIRSTS

- Learning to drive a stick shift.
- Taking a trip on a train for several days and enjoying the journey.
- Visiting the miraculous Grand Canyon, especially on a rafting trip.
- Traveling to Europe and all around the world. It is so vital to learn about other cultures.
- Doing something where you will be treated like royalty. Something you will never forget.
- Learning to play guitar all by yourself. It's easy. Then, go write a song.
- Experiencing a power outage during a thunderstorm. Or, heck, just go to Florida instead!
- Writing a story, a poem, or a creative idea. (No, it is not stupid. Try it.)
- Check out what it would be like to have an unplugged weekend. No cell phones, video games, or TV. See if you can survive. I'll bet you won't have much success with this one.
- Learning how to be part of a team, whether it is sports or another activity.
- Blowing something up in a science experiment. (At school!)
- Stay up all night, laughing with a friend. Then, go make breakfast and watch the sunrise.
- Seeing your first Picasso, Van Gogh, Da Vinci, Klimt, Michelangelo, or Chagall. It's amazing walking around an art gallery seeing history through a master's brilliant images.

You should know, being your mommy, I will worry terribly about the mean kids hurting your feelings. I fear all those bullies terrifying you and picking on you in school, the playground, the Internet, or anywhere else. Realize, whether you want me to or not, like it or not, I swear to God, I will take their little obnoxious, asses down. Downtown, down! I know you'll hate this, be embarrassed, and get mad at me. Clearly, I won't blame you, for I'll surely be making matters far worse in the end. Sorry, but it's going to happen. I'm a mother lion. I am fierce, and I won't let anyone mess with my cub. Therefore, before you are born, I am warning you and truly apologize in advance.

Yet, through it all, there will be endless jubilant moments, happy laughter, and enormous smiles as daddy and I watch you grow up and achieve all that you deserve.

It will never get old for us. Meanwhile, I imagine mommy's heartstrings will be pulling, tugging, and aching for you to succeed and attain all that you hope for and dream of.

Sweet Angie or Ben, we won't want to miss any of your firsts. The reality, though, is nobody's lucky enough to do everything together. Wow, my heart just began to race as I realized celebrating, *a first*, often means it is followed by, *a last*. Missing any lasts will be so painful, yet inevitable. It will naturally be impossible to witness all the amazing things you will do. But destiny and fate will take you by the hand and guide you as you mature and succeed. *"This empty-nest syndrome thing"* people talk about? It will be hell!

Lastly, whether you are born a Leon or Corrine, a Hannah or a Collin, I believe children should be able to cross gender lines on

ALL OF YOUR MONUMENTAL MILESTONES AND FIRSTS

any activity or interest they so choose. If you, little Alexei, want to fix cars, and you, baby Levi, want to play Barbie, then I say, have at it. Be true to yourself, be yourself, always live your truth, and feel comfortable in your own skin. I want you to explore and become the best, happiest, "*youie-est*-you," you can, want, or hope to be. While we're on that, don't let anyone ever tell you differently.

Palmer or Callie, there are a ginormous amount of firsts waiting for you to discover, learn, enjoy, or conquer. Mommy is baby-curious... Will you play an instrument, be a chef, a realtor, an astronaut, or become an entrepreneur? Will you be an artist, a scientist, an athlete, or an author? Will you become an actor, musician, doctor, lawyer, tattoo artist, reporter, singer, a cowboy, or an Indian Chief? I can hardly wait to see how your life unfolds. No matter what, "*Be a good person.*" Regardless of who you become, daddy and I will love you unconditionally and support you tirelessly, from your very first, "*First!*"

Your birth, baby Cassian or Poppy, will produce so many brilliant colors that will glow brightly through the years. The creative strokes of your life's paintbrush will bring us indescribable, fulfilling bliss, and pride. Our hearts feel like an ocean, overflowing with powerful waves of love for you. They say (whoever, "*they* are") the definition of true love is... "To love purely with all of one's heart while expecting nothing in return." And, that is precisely what it means to be a parent. We know this already.

Above all, throughout your childhood as well as your entire life, I hope you feel secure knowing your daddy and I will protect you with reckless abandon, wild passion, and immense love, throwing all caution to the wind. (Which reminds me, don't litter.)

Although, do look out for our tickle-war attacks! We are kind of relentless about them.

Hey, Catalina, put mommy's tiara back. Now! Yo Lenox, dude, put daddy's tequila back. I mean right now! *"Egads, King Asher, come here right now and talk to your kids."*

My angel, this was another lovely, Heart-to-Bump Conversation. Let's talk soon!

CHAPTER 43

Natural Childbirth And Other Classes...

Angel baby... time is closing in as we await your arrival. Daddy and I are counting the months, weeks, days, and seconds with great exhilaration. Consequently, it was necessary and time to choose our birth plan. Despite daddy's mom strongly warning me not to, I've decided after months of serious consideration what "I" wanted to do. I came to the conclusion that absolutely, without a shadow of a doubt, natural childbirth is the only way to go! Positively! *I think? Maybe? Right? Huh?*

Thus, Anastasia or Jamison, daddy and mommy are starting our first natural childbirth class. Your dad's ultra, sweeping patience with this entire process is amazing. He's surprisingly excited and into the whole birthing shebang. I just love that about him.

Since we arrived earlier than the other couples, daddy and I sat alone talking and bursting with enthusiasm. While waiting in the classroom, chitchatting about you, we saw 3 other pregnant couples that appeared to be friends entering the class. I couldn't help but laugh at the 3 cute preggers, trying to squeeze through the doors at the same time. It made everyone laugh, putting all in attendance at ease. Truthfully, I was a tad nervous about signing up for this class. But with daddy's loving support, it turned out to be pretty fun. The evening was sprinkled with a warm, friendly atmosphere and lovely people. *At first!*

At the outset, Ms. Dankworth, the teacher, was kind, knowledgeable, friendly, and intelligent. Unfortunately, she was also a stunning siren redhead. Clearly, the big negative for mommy (currently looking like a hormonal Mack Truck) was Dankworth's perfectly flawless beauty and her 105-pound body to match. When she left for the restroom, we pregnant women reluctantly voted 9-1 to keep her on. Well, Elliot or Bristol, I'm sorry! I don't appreciate siren redheaded, gorgeous, natural childbirth instructors. I never have and I never will. Especially when mommy's carrying you, unable to compete with daddy staring at her impeccably magnificent splendor. I also didn't appreciate the way she was flirting inappropriately with your father. *My husband!* I was *not jealous*, but looking

NATURAL CHILDBIRTH AND OTHER CLASSES...

across the room, I felt comforted knowing I wasn't alone with my cold resting-bitch face and angst emotions. I was consoled by the revelation of seeing other worried, nervous pregnant women waddling around the room. Apparently, they should've voted with me!

Anyway, daddy and I learned all about breathing techniques, imagery, and visualizations, positions, gentle touch, and massage therapy, concentrating methods to lessen labor pains, and the whole general process of labor and birth. The gorgeous siren redheaded bitch, (sorry, was that my outside voice?) I mean coach, explained that the act of masturbation was also quite a good option. Seriously masturbating in agony? And that is when mommy started getting up to leave. Daddy stopped me, saying it would be rude. To which I retorted caustically, "Really Asher? So I'm the crazy one? Well, suggesting masturbation, suffering horrendous pain, while people watch, sounds pretty rude and crazy to me." Err, I stayed, as did everyone else. She continued on about hard labor, breech babies, forceps, stillborn births, excess bleeding, vaginal tearing, umbilical cord issues, slow labor, slow dilation, and cesarean births. Plus, the much dreaded 24-hour back labor.

Of course, fearing we would all get up to leave, she went on to discuss the easy, painless, perfect, no complications, quickie births, like mommy is going to have! Right?

Oh, darling Chandra or Myles, sitting on the floor next to daddy, I straightaway felt terrible for those poor, poor, other moms-to-be. I only pray they won't suffer as much as Ms. Dankworth described, bringing the whole class into a frightful panic. None of us were happy by a hair's breadth, with her heartless, insensitive, worst-case scenarios! The tactless beauty closed, explaining it was imperative to follow her directions entirely. Man, I'd say she was barking up the wrong mothers-to-be with far too much harsh info.

Low and behold, thankfully daddy gave me free rein to make all the birth plan decisions. Wise man, that daddy of yours is, my darling Achilles or Vampiress.

Being levelheaded, mommy quickly nipped it in the bud and firmly decided *not to decide.*

I'd go with the flow (See what I did there!) for now and make my final verdict later on as to the natural childbirth painful choice versus an epidural with no pain. Being a highly educated woman, I quickly considered that my choice was, in actuality, a no-brainer!

So, without making any rash decisions for the moment, mommy stood proud and confident, with my newfound, foolproof, 50/50 unwavering, absolutely safe indecision.

On a similar note, I pondered... Hmm, maybe we could find another instructor as well? One who wasn't so damn stunning! In addition, one who didn't literally enjoy scaring all us preggers to death on the whole birthing thing and all its alarming dangers and pitfalls.

Then, I contemplated further, wondering... "What would I look like as a siren, redhead?" I mused, "Should I stay a natural blonde or become a natural siren, redhead?" Nevertheless, that really wasn't the unresolved question here. I was still stuck agonizing over "To natural childbirth or not to natural childbirth? That is the question," Sir Hamlet!

Dammit, daddy's mother might well have been right, after all. I completely *hate* and *loathe* when that happens! Ugh, it's Ok baby. She's lovely, and you will love her.

NATURAL CHILDBIRTH AND OTHER CLASSES...

Little Wilson or Katerina, time is quickly nearing the moment we will hold you in our arms with immeasurable love. I want you to feel at ease knowing that when it's time, you'll be brought into this new world (one way or another) with tenderness, joy, bundles of affection, and evidently many unknowns. So, whether I'm your blonde or redheaded mommy, whenever you're ready, we'll be ready for you. You will be ready on time, yes? Won't you, honey? Please? Pretty please? Huh, I could also go for pink hair? Hmm?

By the way, I have a feeling I'll be doing a good amount of screaming at your birth, and possibly some directed at daddy. Don't fret. This screaming is nothing more than unbearable pain, according to the redheaded siren. It's not your fault, Luv. Well, maybe a touch. Wow, that was totally packed with major guilt! Oh, I thought you should know. I wholeheartedly promise I won't be masturbating! Mwah and hugs! Talk soon...

CHAPTER 44

Leighton or Sierra, meeting your daddy with his debonair, rakish, savoir-faire, panache, and exquisite looks made me weak in the knees. Our meet-cute was kismet. From the very moment our eyes met, there was an extraordinary electric synergy between us. So baby, for this Heart to Bump Conversation, I would like to tell you all about "daddies." There are oh so many fantastical, awe-inspiring, extraordinary, warm-and-fuzzy things to tell you on the daddy topic. Like mommies, of course, daddies are an astonishing species. Whether you are Berkley, a boy, or McKinley, a baby girl, a daddy is the man you'll share the closest male relationship with throughout your life. In other words, a daddy is essentially your hero, oracle, best friend, and God's miracle.

Little girls always seem to form a special, never-ending, unique love relationship with their daddies. I can assure you (as did I), you will reserve a huge portion of your heart only for him. Yes, even after you are married. He will unquestionably reserve more than a huge portion of his heart for you. This irreplaceable bond of love lasts beyond this earth and forevermore. His relentless love for you will be nothing short of the greatest love a man or child could ever know. You'll always be his perfect little girl and forever cherished princess. You must understand, this fact remains no matter how old you get.

Until you are around ten years old, you'll probably sit on daddy's lap more than in mud, your highchair, a pile of toys, the couch, the big armchair, your bed, or any other place. Your daddy's lap will bring you all the refuge, love, security, and well-being you will ever need. At this sweet age, you might even wish you could be surgically attached to his hip for all eternity. Being with daddy provides the tender, comforting place where all your joys, sorrows, tears, giggles, fears, stories, conversations, lessons, dreams, and tomorrow's fondest memories of your childhood are shared. One day, you'll come to appreciate what I mean. Mommy knows about this

ABOUT DADDIES...

all too well through the infinite, amazing times shared with my daddy. Goodness, I still run to sit on his lap. I realize I shouldn't be telling you all of my secrets and experiences of how I wrapped my beloved daddy around my finger. But you should have a head start on this. Allow me to elaborate.

Daddy will find you irresistibly charming beyond any fairytale character ever written. All his "happily ever after" stories combined, places you in the very center. Through his adoring eyes, you'll far surpass "The fairest of them all," and he won't need that "mirror, mirror on the wall," to know this fact. You'll see and feel his explosion of enormous love for you each time your eyes meet. You will own his heart without trying. One little girl kiss and hug for daddy pretty much guarantees any new toy your tiny heart desires and more. Adding a couple of affectionate, sweet, gushes of "I love you, daddy" can just about buy you the world. I suggest a diamond bracelet, and then work your way towards a Porsche. Kidding! Spending the day with daddy basically promises a shopping spree, tickets to any show or concert, the zoo, park, fair, theme parks, movies, game places, way too much junk food, and sometimes all the above in one day. Keep in mind an innocent, coy, puppy dog look of love aimed at daddy will get you out of any trouble you might be in with mommy. Or not! You might even get an actual puppy dog, to boot.

Little girls also tend to play a lot of flirtatious, captivating, feminine tricks on daddies. No doubt, you will work this strategy perfectly and to the hilt. My, how your charisma will leave him helpless like Kryptonite is to *Superman*. All of your little girl charms would make "*Daddy-Thor*," lose both his strength and his hammer. You'd cause "Spiderman-*Daddy*," to become fragile, clumsy, snarling, and tangling up amidst his web from your precious feminine wiles. *"Captain America-Daddy,"* being controlled by your coquettish ways, would instantly lose his strength and disregard his shield. *"Hulk-Dad,"* would theoretically drown underwater from your adorableness. Your girlish innocence would knock *"Iron Man-Daddy"* senseless, forcing his armor suits into peril, unable to fly. Furthermore, for sure, *"Iceman-Daddy"* would theoretically melt to the ground and disappear. And, poor *"Darth Vader-Daddy?"* For you, baby girl would effortlessly turn him into the kindhearted, gentle, anti-evil daddy, compelling him to leave the dark side and the force behind. His menacing villain days would be completely over. He'd trade his eerie hiss and mechanical helmet in for voice lessons and a trendy couture haircut. Your girly-girl superpowers will leave daddy helpless, falling prey to your emotional, mystical allure. Keeping it real, none of that will work with Wonder-Women Mommy. Understand I got your number, kid. To be fair, I know all the little girl's tricks. Been there. Done that!

Realize, baby January, daddy is a *pushover*, not an *idiot*. He may go along with all your charades and tricks, but keep in mind he knows *at all times* exactly what you are doing. Still, he will eat it up and enjoy it all the same. I'll love watching the whole show.

Then, when daddy's little girl grows up, with his vast experience, he'll teach you everything about boys, their artillery of games, schemes, tactics, and ploys. He'll help you with your many countless girl-crushes. He'll do this, despite the fact he'll want to beat the crap out of these guys if they make one wrong move. Daddy will be watching and he'll have a tough time holding back his Wolverine anger if some dude dares to hurt you. No fear. He'll catch the scoundrel. Don't poo-poo daddy's guidance on boys. Listen

ABOUT DADDIES...

up, because *he knows* all too well about this topic! You see, daddy played his fair share of dating games and all the shenanigans that go along with it. Yes, he tried with mommy! Sensibly, I wasn't fooled by his lame trickery or foolish pranks that he deftly attempted. Remember, sweet Pippa, I had a daddy looking out for me, too! So, keep your ears open!

Now, if you are Yale, my little boy, pay attention. You're exceptionally lucky and blessed, for you've got yourself one big pal, buddy, Bff, and teacher in your daddy. He's definitely your *go-to* if you want to learn everything about *"Mansplaining."* I think he invented it, in fact. From the moment you are able to move your arm, or your hand in any way at all (either one or both), good ole dad will be throwing a ball right into it. A Wilson NFL football, basketball, soccer ball, baseball, tennis ball, beach ball, Ping-Pong ball, golf ball, volleyball, or whatever object he can grab immediately. I have to tell you, he has already bought a closet full, teeming with these balls, whether you are a boy or a girl, for that matter. If there is no ball in sight, he'll throw a Twinkie at you and yell, "Catch!"

You'll be the only boy on the block with a completely assembled antique train set that daddy's been dying to set it up again since he was a boy. Additionally, you will have every Lego set, model plane set, boat set, Pokémon everything, Laser Tag, Nintendo and Genesis games *he could... Oops...* I mean, *you could* want. He'll teach you every board game, from chess to checkers, and every card game you'll ever need to know for the rest of your life. I mean it, he'll teach you card games you'll recall when you are an old man in a nursing home. Beware... he'll never just let you win for your ego. You must earn it.

You'll feel special and really enjoy yourself whenever you are with him, whether in or out of public. He's simply the kind of guy everyone wants to hang with. He'll love taking you to arcades, ball games, sports events of all kinds, as well as Comic-Con and Star Trek Conventions. He'll be giddy taking you to concerts, movies, and Broadway shows.

I must give you a heads-up. Daddy is the most super cool, *funtastic*, exciting man I have ever known. You're one lucky boy. You'll understand one day what I'm telling you now.

Later on, when daddy thinks you're all grown up, around age four, regardless of mommy's great opposition, you will be jogging, riding a bike, playing poker on Monday nights, bowling on Wednesdays, and rooting for all the football pro and college games at home, or sports bars right by his side. All other sports are a given, too. Mommy won't think of interfering with daddy's game plans as long as you're happy and safe. But, no smoking of any kind is allowed at poker night. He can have a beer or two, but *you can't!*

As the years pass, and it's time for you to become a man, your dad will teach you the entire testosterone encyclopedia on what it means to be a manly man in every way. Trust him and learn. He'll educate you about the vast world of manhood, from how to make a tie, how to dress, how to speak, shave, drive, flirt, dance, excel, how to treat a woman, and how to study and learn well. He'll help you to understand all types of cultures and religions. He'll train you to possess genuine honor and integrity in business.

Dad will enlighten you on the importance of family, as well as ethics, morals, honesty, decency, how to love, care, be

ABOUT DADDIES...

compassionate, sympathetic, charitable, and considerate. He will tutor you to be kind, humble, and to help others. Daddy will teach you how to do just about anything and everything. Moreover, what a man needs to know and understand to become successful and achieve great happiness in all walks of life. He'll show you real fun, how to develop a sense of humor, and all the fundamentals a good man should know.

Baby Winston or Andrea, Here Are A Few Things To Know About Your Daddy:

- Daddy wants to be a dad more than anything else in this whole world.
- Daddy is cool and super hard to gross out or freak out! This is an amusing plus.
- Daddy is "au courant" and talented at so many things. He'll razzle-dazzle you.
- Daddy is smart. Insanely so. With his help, you'll totally ace math and science!
- Daddy is a wonderful teacher and coach. It's disturbing how serene and calm he is.
- Daddy is patient and has no problem listening and seeing your point of view.
- Daddy has no difficulty saying, "I love you." One of mommy's favorite things.
- Daddy can teach you how to fix anything and everything. Yeah, don't come to me!
- Daddy is the *king of kid-land.* Proudly, he hasn't lost the child within. Major perk!

- Daddy is fair, nonjudgmental, objective and open-minded. What? I'm workin' on it!
- Daddy will love hanging out with you, or chill doing nothing at all. He's easy.
- Daddy may throw a video game box controller across the room if he doesn't win.
- Daddy is seriously funny. Like an HBO Special, Stand-Up Comedian, funny!
- Daddy will know from a mile away if you're lying. Be careful there. It's uncanny.
- Daddy is the most remarkable man on the planet. Even your friends will love him.
- Daddy will never let you down and will faithfully be there for you.
- Daddy can be an unapologetic, silly goofball, and a joker. You'll love that.
- Daddy will never say he doesn't have time for you. He'll always have your back.
- He might drag you outside to talk stars and galaxies on a clear night. Deal with it!
- Daddy is in touch with his inner dork, geek and nerd side. Even that is cool on him.
- Daddy's not ashamed of his Star Wars, Superheroes, and Transformers obsession.
- Daddy will polish his little girl's toes, play Barbie, dress-up, and happily wear the tiara, tutus, and all the rest of it. He'll even take you for a proper English high tea.
- Daddy is Guinness-worthy, father-material. He'll be a victorious, blue-ribbon dad.

ABOUT DADDIES...

- Your Daddy will be your greatest role model. There's no better man to learn from.

Advance notice! Mommy loves daddy with all of her heart and daddy loves mommy equally. Daddy is the mirror that reflected all of my dreams and greatest desires. Since we couldn't contain all of our immense love for each other, we realized we had to make you to share this immeasurable abundance of love with us. You can gag now. It's OK!

Here are a few things daddy taught mommy:

- When things aren't working out as planned... Break from it, breathe, and push forward.
- Never give up hope. Daddy believes that when God said, "There shall be light," he was referring to the light that comes from hope. Daddy trusts that hope keeps you on track towards your dreams. Hope is the core of our strength, power, and our reason to dream.
- Never, ever allow anyone to make you feel small or less than you are.
- Don't frown (causes wrinkles) when you can smile. Don't smile when you can laugh.
- Don't hate anyone. It will only hurt you in the end. Forgiveness is the best revenge.

Baby Aspen or Phoenix, heed and remember every single lesson daddy teaches you because you'll never know a finer man. Even though at times during your life, your daddy may appear a tad preoccupied or too busy for you, I promise he is not. He'll always be there for you, so go to him for anything you need. Your father, the loving, precious soul, might display a mysterious exterior at times, but it's only a façade... He's simply trying to protect you from all negativity by acting strong and fearless. He will do anything to keep you from being scared or worried about anything.

Daddy is mommy's tall, dark, and handsome, real-life champion. It's as if he was carved out of some very-hot, man stone. He looks like an exquisite character from a romantic novel or the prince from any fairytale. He is my biggest fan, always supporting and encouraging me. He makes me laugh, wipes away my tears, and is like a Band-Aid for all my sorrows. Being with daddy helps me strive to be a more righteous person. My darling Gwyneth or Skylar... Daddy is our foundation, our protector, our anchor, and our north. He will forever keep us on the right path. I hope you realize that you've received an extraordinary gift from above in the daddy you were blessed with. We both got lucky.

With those *very precise daddy thoughts*, The Lord Smiled and Was Extremely Jubilant!

> *God was proud of the whole daddy concept! And so, it was written..........*

CHAPTER 45

Let's Talk Cravings...

Hello, it's mommy, again... You know, baby, from everything I've read and personally experienced on the subject of cravings, I feel this phenomenon is overwhelmingly miscalculated, underrated, and a very misjudged dilemma. With all due respect to medical journals, books on having a baby, magazine articles, and pamphlets on pregnancy, it appears they all seem to glide by this serious predicament, quite briskly. Why do they obliviously dismiss it, making light of this problem we expectant mothers have to endure? In addition, it's rather unfair to those pregnant women's husbands, partners, or whoever has to run out in the middle of the night scrounging up their outlandish cravings. Stat! Surely, this is a challenging situation, which needs far more attention and consideration than it's getting or has ever received.

Baby Boo, can you hold on for a few minutes? Mommy needs to run out and buy a gallon of Häagen-Dazs, whatever flavor. Oh gosh, and the double-dipped, in imported Belgium dark chocolate, caramel bars too. Yum, be back soon, baby Cherry or Sprinkles.

Okay, I'm back! Now, where was I? Ah yes, the dreaded 24/7 cravings. As I was saying, once you get a craving in your head, there's no letting go of it. The experts say, "Try to defy your yearnings and allow your mind to push away those menacing desires. Don't give in to them. Resist and change what you are doing. Perhaps, go eat an apple."

Really? Ok then? Eat an apple? Clearly, the genius recommending an apple has never been pregnant. Push them away? Impossible! Furthermore, resisting doesn't work at all. It's like the domino effect. One craving leads to another till the dominos, dominos, dominos, fall down. Or in my case, gets eaten. Perfect. Just what I was craving, a pizza! I need a Domino's Pizza. Yes, pizza smothered with triple-triple everything on it.

More precisely, there's no amount of willpower that could minimize these intense cravings and my uncontrollable food desires. Seriously, baby Candy, Whip Cream, or Coco, I feel as though

LET'S TALK CRAVINGS...

hungry aliens are invading my body. They are demanding I eat nonstop, all kinds of weird mixtures, enabling them to taste every food known to man on Planet Earth. On that cosmic notion, sweet Asteroid or Comet, the most agonizing sting is watching food commercials on TV and knowing whatever they are advertising *is closed.* Hearing words like, "Delicious, delectable, tasty, rich and zesty, thick and juicy, tangy, scrumptious and dripping with flavor, is more than any pregger should have to tolerate. There needs to be a pregnant women's union to protect us from this unjust sort of thing!

Note to self... First thing Monday morning, start a "Pregnant Women's Union."

It makes me wonder, "Are there commercials like this on Mars, also meant to annoy and tempt expectant mothers?" Ah yes, Mars? Mars candy and Mars ice cream bars! Yum! Do you feel my frustration, babykins? What am I to do, baby Saturn or Pluto? Baby? Yes, I need a tasty Baby Ruth peanut and caramel candy bar with Sriracha sauce.

My cravings never seem to end. I want chocolate, any kind of chocolate. I need fries dipped in fudge pops. I want Beets wrapped in clams. I must have a double quarter pounder with extra cheese and pickles. I desire double chocolate waffles with powdered sugar and syrup. I dream of melted-cheese, dripping over chili peppers. I crave spaghetti with Vermont syrup and sugar like in the movie, "Elf." I want barbecue potato chips with tons of melted marshmallows. I crave ice cream with sour pickles smothered all over with bacon and shrimp. I want oranges and Tabasco sauce. I seek sweet potatoes trickling with chocolate fudge caramel. I need mac-and-cheese with spicy as hell taco sauce and snails. Pulled pork or ribs with vanilla sauce seeping with pecan fudge. I demand chocolate-chip icing oozing over lemons and tomatoes. Give me bananas with meat sauce on top. I need chocolate, baked over salami. I crave Froyo, the size of a wrestler's waist with every flavor and double toppings. I want to eat spoons of peanut butter just like Brad Pitt ate in, "Meet Joe Black" with whatever I can find to put on top. Including Brad! I beg for broken pieces of double stuffed Oreo Cookies over sizzling pork-fried rice. I want 3 types of sugary cereal with eggnog, candy canes, and gingerbread, though Christmas is nowhere around. I need watermelon and anchovies. I want cheesecake without any cheese with avocado and chili-ketchup. I want a taffy, cotton candy, jellybean and popcorn soufflé. Give me double-fried chicken without the chicken, and Nutella dripping over pork ribs.

 I do hope I put that into visuals you can understand and throw up, thinking about? This is getting too bizarre. I must get hold of myself. "Resist and defy, indeed?" Amid my stressful ordeal, I considered opening a restaurant called "Crazy Concoctions!" Sorta!

 And while we are on this topic, how is it possible for a woman to go through nine months of being pregnant and not know it? Forget the huge baby bump, the cravings alone scream, "I am pregnant!" I don't want to be a mean, doubting, distrustful person... But honestly, how could these women *not know*? The baby is moving all the time. How do they explain that away? There was actually a TV show called, "I didn't know I was pregnant." Please girl, really? They claimed they had a tummy-ache and when they went to the toilet, a baby popped out to their utter surprise! Moms, I'm not irrational? If you're pregnant, honey, you know it! For heaven's sake, I knew I was pregnant even before the *"Hold Please!" So,* hand over the Milk-Duds, chips, and anchovies, and no one gets hurt!

LET'S TALK CRAVINGS...

All righty, I got that off my chest, baby Ginger or Cinnamon, so I'm good now. I'm fine and in control. I have no desire for any food whatsoever. I can *roll* out all of my food thoughts from my craving mind. Roll? Hmm, roll? A delectable egg roll, a gooey-sticky caramel roll, a California roll, a delicious Tootsie Roll, or, for sure, a cheese roll? Damn, I *do not* want to think of food or cravings anymore! *I do not*! I do not... Do-nots? Doughnuts! Krispy Kreme Doughnuts... I'm talking all of them, every darn Krispy one of them. Oh Lord, I can't stop! Oh, Gee wiz! Hmm? Cheez Whiz over Nachos! And...

Leona, girl, stop egging yourself on! Ah yes, egg omelets with meat, cheese, and onions. I guess it's true... "You can't have your cake and eat it too!" But gosh, why not? Why must I resist all my pregnant cravings? I say yes, to double fudge butter-cream cake, strawberry shortcake, and carrot cake. Yes, to short ribs over pie with hot sauce. Yes, to melted chocolate over pizza with peanut butter and steak very rare with broken cookies and pudding on top. It's so hard to decide. Huh, maybe oysters with Fritos? Baby Hummus or Chip, mommy has to run to the store. We'll finish our Heart to Bump Conversation later!

CHAPTER 46

What's in a Name?

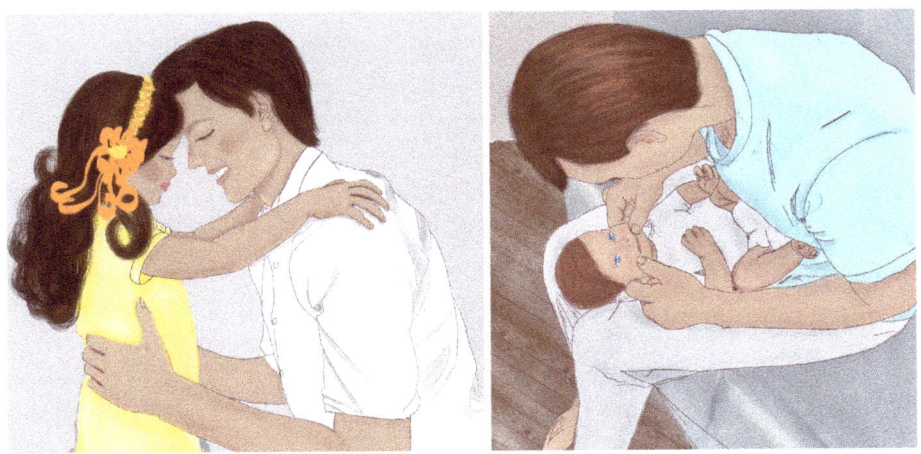

Guess Who? It 'tis mommy! We seriously need to talk about baby names today. Theoretically, one might ask, what's in a name? Is a name really important? Does it matter that much or at all what your name is? A name is essentially everything. It is who you are and who you will become. You're your name. Quoting the master William *Shakespeare,* "That which we call a rose by any other *name* would smell as sweet!" Trust this to your core. Even the oldie-but-goodie hit "The Name Game" explains this theory. *"Taylor, Taylor, Bo-Baylor, Banana-Fana Fo-Faylor, Fee-Fi-Mo-Maylor, Taylor!"*

As your birth is fast approaching, daddy and I have been spending our nights at home just hanging out. In my condition, far be it from daddy to complain. As a result, we have become TV junkies. We've binge-watched Netflix, Prime, Hulu, Apple Plus (See, I had an apple!), and every cable station we are overpaying for. After depleting those, daddy and I have been viewing all the bake-off programs, golf and tennis matches, and infinite game shows. We've played scrabble, Monopoly, cards, chess, and pool. We have also competed in Cards Against Humanity and Trivial Pursuit... the genius editions. We've become game experts waiting for you. Lots of empty hours will do that. No guilt!

Moreover, we've been spending an endless amount of time fulfilling our first major responsibility as parents. We have spent hours searching for the perfect name for you, little Frankie or Johnny. Sure, I understand we've had months and months to figure this out and come to a decision. You're probably getting rather concerned and nervous by now. You may question, "What's the big deal? What's so hard?" Well, in a word, plenty!

You see, a name not only stays with you for the rest of your life, but a name must also fit and describe perfectly who you are, as well as who you will become. Just imagine going through life with the name Seymour or Sheldon, when you are more like a Rylan or Alexander? Suppose we named you Ralph, Milton, Sam, or Harvey, when you should actually be a Hayden, Reagan, Merlin, or Jayde. How can daddy and I name you Sue, Jane, Sally, or Betty, when you more accurately should be a Harmony, Chloe, Jillian, or Zara? It could be tragic naming you Don rather than Remington,

WHAT'S IN A NAME?

Joe instead of Ensley, or Karen when you are more of a Nadia or Demi. It could be a true disaster. This could ruin your entire life, your confidence, self-esteem, and accepting who you really are. You understand? We can't blow this. It's imperative for daddy and I to nail this name thing.

Another big thing to consider, we are going to be saying your name a million times a day. So, we better really love it. I mean, Zelda, Zelda, Zelda? "Yes, Zelda! Stop it, Zelda! Let's go, Zelda! Murray, yes! Murray, be quiet! Murray, I said no! Murray, go to your room." If I'm constantly calling your name, it better make me smile. Just saying!

What about Mary or Jane, when you seem more like a Raquel? Or, perhaps Rick, when you resemble a movie star, looking like a Channing? Heavens, the wrong name can destroy you. It could alter your destiny. It could scar you for your entire life. No, this name has to fit and portray you. You should also be happy about the name. I'd never forgive my parents if they named me Krystal Ball, Robin Bird, Rapunzel, Paige Turner, Dick Perv, Joy Cox, Sam Sung, or Sally Farts. FYI, I knew some of these people, for real.

The other day, mommy came up with the most perfect girl and boy names for you, Valentina, Jazlynn, Donasia, Hailee, Alianna, Bailey, Arizona, Antonella, and Gia. If you are a boy, then Aubrey, Taylor, Parker, Carter, Francesco, Othello, Jackson, and Emery. Still unconvinced, daddy swiftly shot them all down with one flying bullet.

Ultimately, I decided on Lindsey, regardless of your sex. That didn't go down well either when daddy roared out, "Absolutely not! I knew a mean, ugly bully of a kid named Lindsey who was so awful to everyone in Jr. High. No one could stand the kid. I'm not going to think of that brat every time I say my son's or daughter's name." I got his point, for I had a similar situation with a girl named Cybil. So, we kept on searching.

Weeks later, daddy came up with the boy/girl name, Charleigh, spelled just that way. I almost threw a fit myself, because I once dated a guy name Charleigh who was an egotistical, obnoxious, cruel, creepazoid. "Forget it, Asher! No Charleigh, Charlie, Charlee, Charley, or Charles, for my kid!" He agreed, and so we continued on hunting.

We progressed on to television, Broadway, and the movies for help with names. Take in a big breath here for a world-class, run-on sentence. Baby, I could do this all day! Allie and Noah, Barbie and Ken, Vivian and Edward, Harry and Meghan, William and Kate, Sandy and Danny, Scarlett and Rhett, Sally and Harry, Katie and Hubbell, Rose and Jack, Annie and Alvy, Leia and Hans Solo, Adrian and Rocky, Baby and Johnny, Carrie and Mr. Big, Andie and Ben, Anna and William, Frances and Marcello, Holly and Gerry, Monica and Chandler, Lucky and Ricky, Olivia and Fitz, Doug and Carol, Jack and Kate, Meredith and Derick. Ilsa and Rick, Milo and Mandy, Edward and Bella, Bridget and Mark Darcy, Toula and Ian, Cosette and Marius, Elphaba and Fiyero, Tevye and Golde, Angel and Collins, Christine and The Phantom, Hamilton and Reynolds, Shrek and Fiona, Donna and Sam. Agreeing they were all a big no, we kept searching.

Desperate, we went to famous stars, Tom and Rita, Brad, Jen, and Angelina, Paul and Joanne, Beyoncé and Jay Z, and on and on. Again, we were left with a resounding, NOPE!

Honestly, honey, a bad name or a wrong name could lead to harsh criticism from classmates and bullies. A strange, nerdy, different,

WHAT'S IN A NAME?

or hard to pronounce name could keep you forever out of the cool groups. Not that Jennifer or Robert will open the doors, but it could help. I don't want your name keeping you from the success that you will no doubt deserve. Apart from the fact, your daddy was starting to get frustrated... we kept looking.

That's it. Laurence for a boy, Heather for a girl... easy, simple, refined, and done!

Daddy was happy. But no, it was just not you! Your name should be more classic and not that simple. Your name should stand out and impress people enough to remember you.

All right then... How about Mercedes or Porsche for a girl and Calvin or Levi for a boy?

Daddy was happy again. Heck, no. Nix, nada, nope! That is altogether not you, either.

When you walk into a room, people will expect a flashy car or a pair of designer jeans?

Back to the chessboard, Apple Plus, and Netflix, little one. Wait a second, Chess, Apple, or Netflix? Is that too weird? Don't worry. We have plenty of time left. We'll try again later. Oh damn, golly gosh, Ugh! I almost forgot? What about your middle name?

CHAPTER 47

Selecting the Perfect Pediatrician?

Good Evening, little Anne Boleyn or Henry VIII. Yep, we've finally narrowed it down to those names. Oh, chillax, mommy is teasing. My beloved Peter Pan or Wendy, I only wanted to see if you were paying attention. But, for real, it's Maybelline, Clinique, or Zanzibar!

Kidding! Mommy's an epic jokester. However, child, don't get an attitude with us. We haven't deleted any of those names yet!

What an exhausting day I had. Mommy spent the entire day in the 100-degree weather, plus humidity, running around interviewing pediatricians for you. (Bit of guilt there!) A pediatrician is a doctor with a high level of patience who never enjoys a full night's sleep, sometimes skates around their office, and specializes in children. They can also be a tad crazy or childlike, which are occupational hazards and possibly a necessity. It takes a fun, caring, sensitive person to become and love being a pediatrician. Since all children essentially hate going to the dr. (can't blame them, shots and all) it's imperative for mommy to choose a special one for you, my precious Cinderella or Aphrodite, Dick Tracy or Tess. I had no clue how complex the pediatrician decision would turn out to be.

First, there was Dr. Strange. I mean, *Dr. Stringe*. Which basically turned out to be the same thing. Picture if you will, a 6'4," 41-year-old doctor with a Mohawk, a gold loop earring in one ear, and a tunnel earring with a huge hole in the other, sporting lots of tattoos everywhere. He wore a fluorescent, multi-colored doctor's robe, straight out of the 60s. He was in no way your average Harvard, Yale, or Princeton graduate type. He spoke with an accent that I couldn't recognize nor distinguish. What made matters worse was I didn't understand most of what he was saying during the entire interview. Yet, I did hear him say loud and clear, "Infant schedules are worthless, I believe in drugs, I don't have much faith in vaccinations, breastfeeding is overrated and unnecessary, most babies are bad babies, let your baby cry for hours, it's foolish to worry

SELECTING THE PERFECT PEDIATRICIAN?

about the baby so much, and by the way, we don't have a well-side waiting room." As mommy panicked and looked for an exit sign, Dr. Stinge/Strange didn't stop there. He went on further to state, "I do believe it is crucial to hit or smack your kid when necessary. After all, it has worked for thousands of years. Lastly, Mrs. Robins, please don't call the office all the time for every little thing that pops up, unless you see a pool of blood or you drop the baby on its head!"

Little Samara Morgan, imagine your freaked-out mommy making a mad dash out of Dr. Strange's office. I quickly realized my first clue this Doc was a *"big no,"* were the many scary skulls sprawled about the office. Not to mention, chilling death and Satan pics everywhere, and the black and blood, red glitter seats in the waiting room. Obviously, there were no Mickey or Minnie images on the walls, nor a single superhero. Seriously, baby, I actually twisted my ankle sprinting out of his office. He lost me at, *well... Everything!*

After interviewing the next candidate, I was convinced I found your pediatrician, *Dr. Rippleoff.* He was caring, sweet, nice, and didn't rush my visit with him. Then, just as I was satisfied and ready to choose him, *Dr. 'Ripoff'* arrogantly informed me, "I keep my patients on a retainer basis. I charge every month, whether I see the child or not. Plus, I charge for all visits and all phone calls." Leaving briskly with an already sprained ankle, I was stopped abruptly and told I owed $350.00 for a *normally free* consultation. Just let him try to collect the $350.00, that's going towards our fabulous glider chair. Pah-leeze!

Next came Dr. Samuels, a real charmer. Indeed, what a lovely dear man he was. His being 84 years old, hobbling around with a walker, wearing eyeglasses flaunting ultra-thick lenses, and practicing in an antique office that smelled of mothballs and farts, didn't bother mommy one bit. That is, until he asked me a clueless question as I stood right before him, pregnant as can be, and looking as if I were now carrying those triplets Colette had referred to. Dr. Samuels smiled warmly, with his obvious false teeth, (as they were slipping off) tilted his gray head and asked, "So, Mrs. Robins... Are you adopting?"

Before limping back to Dr. Strange/*Stringe*, I had one last interview with a man named Dr. Marcus. As it turned out (which made no difference to me) *the man* turned out to be a woman. Dr. Shondra Marcus was amazing at first sight. No Mohawk, no satanic anything, picked up immediately that I was pregnant, and bills for only services rendered. Her beautiful child-friendly office smelled like cotton candy, and reassuring superheroes were decorating the entire waiting room. Although I wanted to, I didn't jump right in. I observed, looking for what all the baby books suggest you look for in a pediatrician...

1. Her credentials were great and judging by all her awards, she is very experienced.
2. I observed how kind she was with all the children, the moms, and dads, in her office.
3. She is also a mother of two, which I found very comforting.

SELECTING THE PERFECT PEDIATRICIAN?

4. The office staff was awesome and she was very respectful to them. I liked that.
5. The office had a sick and a "well side," which is a definite prerequisite for mommy.
6. She is funny, sincere, patient, and interacted warmly and playfully with the kids.
7. Her office is modern and state-of-the-art. Her practice is totally up-to-date and clean.
8. She was kind, thoughtful, and understanding with mommy. We clicked at once.
9. She answered my 500 questions with the utmost of patience. Kudos there for sure!
10. We have the same child-raising philosophies on everything. That's super reassuring.
11. Dr. Marcus seemed extremely confident, relaxed, and calming. I liked her so much.
12. She told me when in doubt, to never worry about calling the office. Always call!
13. She was cheerful, courteous, spent time with me, and didn't rush me out the door.

How about that, sweet baby Measles or Chickenpox? Dr. Marcus was even more remarkable than I had hoped for. I absolutely adored her. Mommy is extremely thrilled and excited to have found her. I left Dr. Shondra Marcus's office feeling relieved, super lucky, and displaying the biggest secure smile on my face. Congrats baby doll, you now have an amazing pediatrician. Furthermore, and happily for mommy, it's one less task to be concerned about. Hmm... Hey, what about Shondra for a girl or Marcus for a boy?

CHAPTER 48

There is So Much I Want to Teach You...

It's the wee hours of the night, and mommy is sitting on the floor in the middle of your lovely room. I do this a lot. But at my stage of pregnancy, I'm speculating how I'll get up off the floor? Managing this feat is not just a passing thought. It's now a troubling mystery. I suppose I'll have to wake up poor daddy.

ROBIN ROTH

As absurd and ridiculous as it sounds, I can actually sense your divine aurora and presence in your nursery. It's an enchanting room and I know you'll love it too. It tickles me pink and blue hanging out in here. Somehow, I feel closer to you, more peaceful, and connected. Still, on my next visit, I trust it is best to sit my butt down on the $350 glider-rocking chair *Dr. Ripoff* is still billing us for. FYI, a bill I quickly throw into the trash.

There is so much about life mommy wants to teach you. There are extraordinary, astonishing miracles of awe, and fantastical mind-blowing marvels I want to share with you. Life flows with an abundance of happiness, beauty, laughter, wonder, and pure goodness. Sadly, it is also true that life has many negative problems, cruel paths, tears, difficulties, or hard times. Many of which are filled with harsh unforeseen ups and downs.

When you least expect it, suddenly a storm rolls in and washes away all the joy with it.

But know this little angel, clouds don't last forever. Amazingly, when things seem their worst, all clouded up with impossible darkness and woe, that's when a dream comes true. Yes, baby Thunder or Stormy, realize you must always have dreams to believe in, to reach for, and to accomplish. Never walk away or quit out of fear, doubts, or insecurities. Hope is your compass and your GPS. Hope and belief will turn your dreams into realities, and there is no dream too big or small to become a reality. Still, you must stay on course and work hard for them. My mantra has always been, "Nothing worthwhile in life comes easy!" The harder you have to work to reach your goals, the more you'll appreciate and be grateful for them. Follow my mantra and your own truth until your dreams materialize.

THERE IS SO MUCH I WANT TO TEACH YOU...

Never stop reaching for the moon. Never give up, give out, or give in to any of your ideas or dreams. For they are the flame, the splendor, and the sparkle in your life's very existence! They provide the glow, which makes your world special. Most people don't grasp that, *"luck doesn't just happen."* Luck comes to those who work their ass off and persevere against all the odds. And believe me, there are incalculable odds. Though it may get unbearably difficult at times not to think of throwing in the towel, that's when you must stop, reboot, and push even harder. No matter the obstacle, never quit believing in yourself, never compromise your integrity, or who and what you are. Be yourself. For if you attain success through unethical means, or by not doing the right thing, well then the reward is corrupt, cheap, and pointless. I guarantee, one day you'll realize this for yourself. Still, carrying you inside of me all of these months, I know and sense with certainty that you'll handle life ethically and morally with your whole being. I feel it.

I've always trusted in my quiet, inner secret, "There is always happiness on every road." Nevertheless, you must search and scout it out for yourself. I promise it's there.

As you grow, darling stay humble, kindhearted, and always look for the decency in mankind. Of course, we all tend to criticize and judge people unfairly. Naturally, it's far easier and more fun to find fault in others. It's human nature at its worst. Thus, try to look for the positive and the good in people. It takes a special, caring person to get past other individuals' negative traits, seeking out the real goodness and grace within them. It'll make all the difference in the world, and might often surprise the crap out of you.

So little one, I would like to spare you much time and mounds of endless hours by teaching you something I have embarrassingly just recently learned myself... Live your life as much as humanly possible to the absolute fullest degree. Discover your existence entirely to its maximum potential, without any guilt or apologies for having done so. Do be acutely aware not to hurt anyone in the process. Take advantage of every moment. I assure you, life is very short and the opportunities tend to slip away ever so quickly. You don't get many second chances in life. So, appreciate it all, and enjoy it the first time.

Before long, you'll find the years passing you by. Stop, take a big pause, and slow down. It's a warning, a lesson you're missing out on too many of the important things that matter. Ok be successful, enjoy life, travel, and make lots of money! Yet, understand, no matter how rich you are, you can't take it with you! Love, family, and friends are the keys and core to everything in life. I assure you, in the end, that's all that truly matters.

Above all, don't allow a moment to be wasted. Use today to make all of your tomorrows brighter, happier, and far more significant. Baby Harlow or Ezra, I get this all sounds complicated, confusing, and too serious for you now. It won't be later, but feel safe and secure knowing mommy and daddy will be there, having your back (And your front), every step of the way. Know also, we are your loving family who will cheer you on. You can talk to us tirelessly about anything that happens in your world. Hence, don't worry or fear being punished for sharing your innermost feelings or problems with us.

Wow, you poor darling. Just listen to mommy rambling on and on like an old mother hen. Sorry, forgive me! It's because there are so many things I want to tell you about and teach you. After you're born, you will be so darn busy growing up you might not have the time to listen. So, I thought I'd talk to you now and plant some of these seeds of knowledge. Regrettably, I can't plant all of these seeds in one "Heart to Bump Conversation," sitting uncomfortably on your floor. Love does make one do crazy things. Hopefully, I'll try to control myself in the future. Hmm, I guess probably not so much!

I can already see I'll have to learn how to give you space and allow you to make at least some of your own mistakes. Even if it kills me, and you can be sure it will. You see, I too have much to learn. It seems you and I will be learning everything together.

Gee, hon, your nursery is so dreamy and adorable. It's cool looking at your babyish storybook, innocent decor, which you'll probably want to paint all black when you're 12.

Uh, oh? Gee, mommy is in big trouble. I am noticeably in a bind and pitifully unable to get up. Poor daddy is sound asleep and couldn't hear me if I screamed my head off. Now in a panic, how will I get up myself? LOL, whatever! It's 4 A.M. I'll just sleep here on your very soft, cozy carpet for the night. Daddy will find me in the morning. I hope, I hope-a? Remember, I did warn you there'd be problems in life. Kisses and hugs!

CHAPTER 49

Another one of God's Miracles... Friends!

And, God said, "*Children will need friends!*" And so it was. And, God was satisfied...

Baby Brie or Troy, along your life's journey, something extraordinary and ever so precious could happen... *"Friendship!"* Through unselfish, sharing, and caring comes this God-given gift of friendship. And, if you're very lucky and blessed to find a *real friend*, treasure it, cherish it, and never let it go. No matter what! Undeniably, there is no wealth greater than the love of a true best friend. "*A best friend is the family you choose!*"

Through childhood friendships, you will learn to understand what others are feeling. You'll discover what you say and do can dramatically impact the confidence of others. Friendships teach empathy, compassion, sharing, patience, and how to enjoy endless fun. Making friends as a child can be as easy as running up to another kid and saying, "Let's play!" And Abracadabra, as if by magic, you're now friends forever! Well, at least for 10 minutes. Other times, you might be shunned, rejected, or ridiculed by kids. And, let's not forget learning how to cope with being bullied or being made fun of by the cool group. Nevertheless, childhood friendships overflow with emotional highs and lows.

It can be quite touch and go. However, when it clicks, there's nothing like growing up with a close childhood friend. If you're ultra fortunate, you keep them for your entire life.

What a gift to have a lifelong friend who knows everything about you. How you grew up, the experiences you've gone through together, knows all of your secrets, won't ever judge you, and still love you anyway! This ultimate friend may know your whole family (including your crazy uncle, mean sibling, whacky Aunt, and lovable grandma) all your other friends, if you cheated on a test or anything or anyone else, and is pretty aware of all there is to know about you. Everything! For instance... when you were fat or thin, when your hair was long, short, fake, or blue. All the times you loved, hated, or lied to your parents. They know it all, the good, bad, ugly, legal, and illegal. This friend always has your back and stands by you through thick and thin. "Lots of thick!" These friends will shape you more than you realize, for they were by your side from the very beginning. Pacino or Meryl, please appreciate how lucky you would be to have a lifelong friendship. Allow me to share pure wisdom. "You must never do anything to jeopardize or lose this friend." Trust me, regardless of what went down, it's never worth losing your BFF over.

Naturally, you'll always remember your first childhood friends. The ones you see every day at school. Your play-dates filled with adventure, mischief, dangerous or silly fun, giggling times, and getting into trouble. Making friends is a vital part of growing up and an essential experience for your emotional development, confidence, and self-esteem.

Sadly, along the way, your friendships might somehow lose their spark, causing you to lose touch with these good-ole friends. Regardless, years later, you might actually reconnect on a road trip visiting them at college, or a Vegas Tequila, weekend reunion. If you do, you could quickly grasp, even years later, the realization of how you ultimately helped each other to become the best versions of yourselves from that day you first met. Besides, you'll have some pretty awesome memories to reminisce about, which could, in fact, rekindle your friendship. "No, I'm not referring to the catty, Colette type of friend!"

Little one, you will make many friends along life's journey for all different reasons. There are friends for life, friends for a season, work friends, travel friends, sports friends, lighthearted friendships based on convenience, Rah-Rah university or school friends, and fair-weather friends. There will also be those friends you can't imagine life without. Though a sad awakening, sometimes even those can fizzle out.

Regardless... all your friends combined will be an important, vital part of your life. With them, you'll discuss problems, advice and opinions, enjoy hysterical laughter, share gossip, crazy fun experiences, cool events, proud moments, and help one another to grow. In the end, friendships can define who you are and who you might become. To say you have even one *great true friend* is profound, and you should consider yourself blessed.

To cite a lovely, wistful, true Nigerian proverb, *"Hold a true friend with both hands!"*

Friendships are vitally important. *They* (whoever 'they' are) have given it numerous names. Such as: Your BFF, buddy, chum, amigo, pal, bestie, best-friend-forever, my plus one, playmate, confidant, supporter, staunch friend, trusted friend, faithful friend, devoted friend, a partner in crime, wing-man, kindred spirit, soul-friend, companion, compadre, fellow conspirator, second-self, sounding board, and oftentimes your loyal accomplice.

I say, call it whatever you like since it all boils down to the same thing in the end. A real friend is the *one* person who will be there for you, with compassion, no matter what. That *one* person is more than a beloved friend. They are family! This true-blue friend will always greet you with a cocky warm smile, a big hug, and a shoulder to lean on. In fact, regardless of how much time has passed, mere words will most likely not be necessary.

Concerning this lucky treasure of having an amazing best friend for a lifetime, well, allow me to enlighten you properly. These friendships are rare and can come out of nowhere. This friend is *"your *person*" and "your *friendship-soul-mate*." Funny, you never know when one will pop up and you can't just go looking for them.

Remember and understand little Trevor or Kylie, this critical piece of advice...

"To have a good friend, you must be a good friend!" I'm very serious about this.

It's no mystery why there are so many songs, movies, TV shows, books, and poetry written about friendship. I wholeheartedly don't believe one can get through life without them. Friends are irreplaceable rare stones, rubies, pearls, and the purest gold and diamonds in our lives. Every friendship gem brings vibrant colors and sparkle into our world. Whatever, Emerald or Alexandrite, you'll quickly learn mommy loves jewelry!

Appreciating his miracle... "The Creation of Friendship," God smiled with an abundance of glee, and was gratified!

CHAPTER 50

I'm Overdue! Hello? I Said, I am Overdue!

Lazy Baby, I hate to bother you, but to be blunt, you are three days overdue! To be more precise, three days, eight hours, and fifty-two seconds. I hope you won't grow up to be one of those, "Oh, I'm sorry I'm late, the traffic was horrible," type of person. Now, in case you didn't already know, despite all my complaining, moans, and groans, I do love being pregnant. But, mommy is obviously ready, sweetheart. They say, "The world is changed by people who aren't ready." So, perhaps, that's you? I promise, Di or Bo, I'm not rushing our labor. But allow me to put things into perspective for you.

You really need to, "Come out, come out, wherever you are!" I'm not comfortable, nor happy! It's embarrassing, busting out of my clothes. I'm frustrated for I can't button-up, zip-up, cover-up, or pull-up my self-designed preggo outfits, even in extra-large sizes.

Next, the seat belt in mommy's car no longer wraps around us. And when I push my seat back far enough to enable us to fit into the car, my feet can barely reach the pedals. Do not even think of humiliating me further, forcing mommy to buy a seatbelt extender! Don't feel bad that *you're late and I'm exhausted.* Daddy loves doing a 12-hour shift at the hospital, then after work going to buy groceries and running around doing mundane errands. Just like mommy always did after work! (FYI, this is called sarcasm!)

Daddy and I've done everything the books suggest helping (*forcing!*) you to go into labor. For example, we've gone for rides in the car on very bumpy roads. Daddy was so patient when one of the roads caused 2 brand new tires to have blowouts, requiring him to change tires in the heat! Mommy drank gross castor oil, but threw it all up. Yeah, I did, and who wouldn't? Daddy and I had amazing XXX Sex. It was actually fun, so thank you for that. We progressed onward, eating spicy foods, pineapple, dates, nipple stimulation, jogged, went dancing, worked out, and drank red raspberry leaf tea. And still... *Nothing!*

I'M OVERDUE!

Oh, my little Tardy or Delayed, you should see how much fun daddy has watching mommy prepare for sleep at night. I prop 8 pillows under my tummy, 4 under my legs, and 3 under my head. Your loving daddy even bought mommy the infamous sleep pillow, the body maternity pillow, and the B.S. *"My Pillow,"* (the one with the creepy guy who does the commercials). Regardless, they all failed, so mommy's wide-awake most nights.

Hurry you up? Don't be silly! Just because I can't walk, bend, stand, sit up, lie down, sleep, or do most anything else I'd like to do is no concern of yours. (Guilt-Guilt!)

No problem here. I'm fine, even though I have downright exhausted all the "Keeping busy possibilities a woman can do while pregnant!" Honestly, mommy has seen every motion picture released, not only from this year but also for the last 50 years... and some even twice. I even went down the yellow brick road of horror films. I'm speaking of scary and chilling movies making the "Conjuring" and "The Exorcist" look like sweet Hallmark movies. Not at all the best film selections. It's no wonder I can't sleep at night?

In other breaking news, since meeting the stunning, redheaded, siren, labor coach, mommy has changed her hairstyle 4 times in the last 6 months, alone. I've enjoyed being a "Bouncy Clairol Margot Robbie Blonde, a vibrant Jessica Chastain redhead, a cutesy Jennifer Lawrence brunette, and of course, a raven black-haired Selena Gomez." I totally believe I rocked them all. I had my stylist put in a few pink and purple extensions just for some added kinky fun. However, those are all gone now. For extra, enticing amusement, I cleverly threw in several worldly accents and dialects to accentuate my new looks. Poor daddy never knew what he was coming home to. A good sport, but I don't think he's had much fun with my silly hair trials. He prefers my natural-blonde hair. What? *It is natural!*

Additionally, mommy has visited every museum and art gallery in the city. I have done lunch with everyone I know, including people I don't even like... At all! I became desperate and repeatedly went out to lunch with Colette. As you were with me, you can grasp this wasn't any fun for mommy. Luckily, nothing chocolate-fudgy desserts couldn't make better. Alas, they did give Colette some added fuel to my already blazing inner fire.

Ironically, I came to realize just how fabulously rewarding completing a colorful, 20,000-piece puzzle can actually be for one's self-confidence. An activity, along with solitaire, which basically every pregnant woman swears she won't ever be reduced to.

With all this extra time, I read my ancient, "Dear Diaries." I wrote a chapter in them every day of my life from ages 10 to 18. Revisiting my happy youth awakened and reminded me I was a fun, cool girl. Thinking of my past, I smiled, feeling, "you go me!"

Staying busy, I cleaned all the drawers, closets, and cupboards in every room in the house. It might also interest you that all our photos are now meticulously placed into lovely useless scrapbooks, which no one will ever look through. I didn't stop there. I sold things on Craigslist, eBay, and Facebook Marketplace. I've been a busy little beaver. Wow, scary... that's something my grandma would say. Oh wait, sweet pea, I forgot the best part. On a whim, I learned to needlepoint and knit. Ah-ha, you heard me correctly. You don't have to believe me. Neither does anybody else. And yet, my achievements are sprawled all over the house. Possibly my low point, and it's entirely your fault! The good news is I stopped just before making those tacky Doll, *Toilet-Paper-Roll-Covers,* seen in old people's houses. You better come soon, or I'll have to resort to that, too! This scared daddy because he grew up with them. *However, nope, mommy didn't stop there either!*

I made a cast of our baby bump. It's kind of *awe* (ish) *and* sweet, but pretty weird, as well. I've endured enough mani-pedi's to try out every color in the nail salon. Every color! I baked almost everything I had seen on Facebook. Most of the recipes should have sent these bakers to FB jail. I've read every book written on having a baby and medical journals too, which I can never unsee! I washed and put away all your adorable blue/pink clothes, dreaming of dressing you up. I've walked to every park and mall within a 150-mile radius with swollen legs! I've shopped online to the point of behaving like a lunatic, ashamed and with oodles of regret. I started writing thank-you notes for baby gifts we haven't even gotten yet. Irrational. Not knowing your birthday, I still foolishly ordered birth announcements to send out later on. Pathetic! Daddy is now begging you to, "Please come!" I came this close to starting pole-dancing exercise classes. Funny, though, daddy seemed very excited about that whole idea. But darn it, the required cute outfits didn't fit me. Hey, kid, I started writing in your baby book. Come out, so we can add all the good stuff. Baby Boo, I've practiced all the new labor relaxation techniques and the latest new age guru meditation videos. Did it help me to be serene and calm? Not one single drop!

Please, go into labor! You are now 3 days, 9 hours, and 52 (53, 54, 55, 56, 57) seconds late. What's your deal? Daddy and I are all ready to go to the hospital. Yep, all packed and excited to go. Of course, due to the *delay,* daddy and I have had so much fun packing that we've done it now 4 times. So, we're ready. Ready as in,

"*Ready, set, and go!*" Why is it the 9th month of pregnancy seems like a year, and way over 30-31 days?

So, for real, the longest pregnancy on record is 375 days? "Don't even ponder doing that to me!" My, "past your due-date baby," tomorrow's going to be such a lovely day to be born! Think about it. Daddy and I certainly will. After all, you'll be 4 days, 10 hours, 36, 37, 38, 39 seconds late. Hmm, Doll, *Toilet-Paper-Roll-Covers*? How tacky can they be? Daddy said, "Please, pretty please, come before the toilet-paper-doll invasion!"

Incidentally, sweetie, I have to ask. What the heck is going on in there with you? You are tumbling around like crazy. It feels as if there's a galactic battle going on inside of me. Are you cramped? Regrettably, there's no extra room for you to hang. I think I'd explode wide open if I grew another inch. No worries, my darling, late, tardy, lazy baby. Do what you gotta do. No rush, no stress. We're confident you know exactly what you're doing. When the time is right, you will be born! "Tick-Tock, Tick-Tick, Tock-Tick?"

Oh, hells-bells baby Jayden or Victoria. My cell's ringing clear across the room. It's utterly impossible for me to get up. Damn, I'm so tired I can't even feel my teeth. Err.

"Hell-a, Hello? Hello! Hello?"

"Hi sweetie, it's Colette!"

"Hey, Colette. Listen, don't be upset with me, but I really can't talk right now."

"Oh, sorry. Did I catch you in the middle of breastfeeding the twins?"

"Um... Well? Um... It's a... Well, actually... Um? I'm a..."

I'M OVERDUE!

"Oh, My, God? Leona, are you seriously still pregnant? Are you kidding me? I can't even! Ok, doll, since you are an ex-journalist, I'm not going to bury the lead here. Look, you can't ignore the *elephants in the womb*? It's crazy. How are you still pregnant? It's hard to even imagine. I'd be insane, jumping out of a 20-story building by now. Hey, so I meant to ask you? Did you really decide on naming the babies Azazel and Oaklynn? I hope those hideous names were just a passing fancy. You can't do that to the poor kids.

"*KID. A kid! One child, Colette! One baby! One Singular Sensation! A child!*"

"Yea, we'll see? So, what are you, like, 12 months pregnant? Good Lord, I think by now you seriously need to start charging these babies rent. I believe at this point, you can literally evict the kids. Legally! Gosh, I'm guessing you must be as big as a house!"

"CLICK!"

"Hello? Leona? Hello? Leona? Did you just hang up on me? Are you kidding? Why are you being so oversensitive? Was it something I said? Leona, are you there? Hello! Hell-O-OOO! Hello? LOL! Umph... Huh, I must have hit an overweight nerve? Whatever, Sourpuss! You need to bake some sourdough with all that sour... LMFAO!"

CHAPTER 51

The Biggest Challenge of All...

Little one, allow me to bore you and tell you some of mommy's life history. Fragments of what I've been doing before you were a mere glimmer in my eye. My career as a photo/journalist has auspiciously been remarkably fulfilling. I'm grateful to have chosen a profession I love passionately. I was excited to go to work every day.

ROBIN ROTH

Before God, daddy, and I created you, I was immensely appreciative and supremely fortunate to have been an established, well-respected reporter. Mommy worked for the biggest photo agencies in the world. I also wrote and photographed for the most popular, prestigious magazines encompassing the realm of news, politics, travel, entertainment and film. I free-lanced regularly as an anchor for two of the most distinguished and esteemed cable news networks. I particularly enjoyed covering serious, significant, and important, breaking headline world news stories. As a reporter, I believe in sticking to the facts of informative, accurate, transparent, and honest journalism. I primarily trust in the old-school philosophy of *"who, what, when, where, and why."* I don't value reporters who deliver the news in a slanted style, befitting their own political gains. Or any news reported through personal viewpoints, opinions, and spin. I prefer covering news events, unfolding in real-time. Regrettably, on occasion, I've been stuck and virtually forced to report for the gossipy, lying, scandalous, and slanderous types of news outlets.

Many of my interviewees have often, accidentally or carelessly, revealed critical state secrets or personal info. On those occasions, I was told firmly, "Understand, that is off the record, and you can't use it!" No doubt, I can't use it, for those were the authentic facts and the real truth. You have no idea little Barack, Nixon, Reagan, Biden, or Bush, the intelligence I've been privy to or discovered! Consequently, I've come to realize and truly believe there is far more smut in Washington D.C. than there is in the La-La-land of Hollywood! Though, I still find it fascinating and captivating getting to interview world figures. I'm intrigued reporting on leaders in politics, including past and current presidents, senators, congresspersons, and other principal players in the United States and abroad. Like, the late Supreme Court Justice, Ruth Bader Ginsburg, my little baby Ruth.

It's fun on occasion, interviewing and photographing the most famous and notably talented celebrities on the planet. People are forever asking me to spill secrets about famous people I interview and what they are like in person. It's ironic, oftentimes people who appear to be ultra-nice and humble, in actuality, are egocentric, holier-than-thou, and conceited. The celebs and political figures you'd imagine being reserved, arrogant, unfriendly, and pompous are often delightful, easy to talk to, kindhearted, open, and fun. It seems the old adage "the bigger they are, the more down-to-earth they are" is spot-on.

For now, I've happily decided to take my leave of absence to enjoy being your mom. Well, that... and *I was fired!* Still, you'll need me far more than anything I could ever do as a journalist. Besides, I feel my purpose and commitment to raising you is far more important. My little Anderson Cooper or Shannon Bream, the future will determine if and when I shall return to being a reporter. So for the foreseeable future, it'll simply be, "This is Leona Robins with Breaking News coming to you live from my baby's nursery!"

Just so you realize, baby Benzos, Gates, Alice Walton, Zuckerberg, or Buffet, your mommy has had many jobs in her lifetime and remarkably proved to be rather efficient at most of them. Well, okey-dokey, maybe with a few exceptions, before I zeroed in on journalism. I highly suggest you look into several careers as well. It will mold you into a polished, well-rounded person. No matter what, in the end, "you must love what you do."

ROBIN ROTH

For Instance...

At the tender age of 15, I worked in a very cool *dress boutique*. Despite my efforts, I'll never understand why I was fired? Just cause I accidentally tagged all the wrong sizes on the entire new fall collection? So what if it caused a riot in the store? I shouldn't have been fired! I thought women, *size 18*, would be thrilled fitting into a *size 4*? Picky, picky!

And how could I forget that cool job *operating the projector in a movie theatre*? That was such an awesome job, plus all the candy and popcorn I could eat. And sneak out! Actually, the way I thought about it at the time, everything should have turned out great. But, unfortunately, one night I borrowed a hit film, a projector, and took it home to watch with a select group of friends. Busted. I was so caught. Hey, I was 16 and a rebel. I might still be working there today if I only got the damn movie back to the theater in time. Fired Again! I felt it was excessively unreasonable. So unfair, I even offered to share half the profits with them. Baby, I ask you? Is there any place left for the small entrepreneurs of the world? It took a long time till I went back to eating popcorn. Seriously, like 10 days!

Continuing on, I never got why I was canned at *Burger King* for simply refusing to make it their way. I'll admit, it did sting a little when I was asked to hand in my crown.

And Oh, My, Gosh, I could never forget that job during the summer before college. It was a secretarial job working for a *music-publishing house*. They published songs written by mega rock stars, which, of course, became huge hits. But, every once in a while, when I was bored, I would peek through some of the new songs and change a few lyrics here and there. OK, maybe more than once in a

THE BIGGEST CHALLENGE OF ALL...

while, and notably more than here and there. Fine, all right, let me just say I changed words everywhere, often, and every single day. Give me a break. I made those songs so much better. Way better. So what was the big deal, anyway? Then one slow day, right in the middle of improving Katy Perry's ~ "Roar," Taylor Swift's ~ "I knew you were trouble," and John Legend's ~ "All Of Me," I was caught red-handed. Zap, pink-slipped, and fired! Seriously? My lyrics were insanely superior. My Lord, some people seem to have major egos, don't they? While those songs became iconic hits (like forever) I still chalk that fiasco up to grave professional jealousy!

Luckily, I quickly found another job for the rest of the summer. Thank goodness I did, because I needed spending money for college. I worked for a talent agency, which was one of my all-time favorite jobs. Hence, why getting fired from the agency was earth-shattering. So, I made the slightest teeny-tiny error in judgment. I accidentally sent the wrong bands to the wrong conventions and cities. I admitted my blunder. Clearly, it was my bad. Regardless, after the audiences stopped booing and throwing things at the poor band (that was not supposed to play there in the first place) everyone settled down and enjoyed the show, anyway. Umm, sorta, kinda? However, thinking back now to the angry crowd in Salt Lake City... maybe, perhaps, not so much? Yea, aha, they really weren't too pleased with the group "Punk Metal Death Band Aliens." And, I'm guessing the "Sacred Heart Boys Choir" didn't go over too well at the "Skulls and Demons Bikers Convention, either? I question, has everyone completely lost his or her sense of humor?

I still feel the talent agency could have at least given me the chance to clean out my desk. I loved those earrings in my top drawer. A few weeks later, I happily started school at the University. It all turned out in the end and I've never been fired from another job since.

Meanwhile, after many years, I'm starting an entirely brand new job and vocation. One, which I'm a bit nervous about, as I'm not sure I have the skills or experience for it.

Motherhood...

It's quite obvious motherhood is a very complex position. You can ruin an innocent child's life forever. Further daunting and concerning, this is a lifetime employment for which you really can't be fired from! You see, I really liked the "you're fired" safety net. Irrespective, the facts remain, motherhood is an extremely difficult, multi-faceted, 24/7, endless job. The position doesn't provide any medical or dental plans, no 401-K's or pensions, no bonuses, no traveling expenses, and no sick days paid or unpaid. There is no time off (ever), no lunch breaks, very little personal time if any, no keys to the executive bathrooms, no special parking spaces, no company cars, no paid vacations, no raises, no Christmas bonuses, must work all holidays, and no professional discounts or gratuities of any kind. More to the ultra preposterous point, there is no salary at all. None whatsoever.

Regardless, there is pay. Tremendous payment beyond any riches imaginable...

This job comes with infinite love and endless affection, enormous achievements, proud moments, never-ending laughter, tender, warm, beautiful times and memories, and an overabundance of joy and eternal happiness. Fundamentally, it is absolutely by far and quintessentially the most important job in the entire world. Without question, this is one position I will not now, nor ever, take lightly.

THE BIGGEST CHALLENGE OF ALL...

Naturally, there will be little practical jokes here and there, now and again, to keep us both on our toes, little Barrett or Meg.

Baby-Boo to recap, (with a few minor errors) mommy feels she was a fabulous:

Dress boutique clerk, movie projectionist, Burger King chef, publishing house secretary, and talent agent. That's why I am certain I will triumph with this motherhood gig, too. We all live and learn, so don't be worried or afraid. I totally got this. Whatever it takes, I promise you, I will be the best mommy ever. I will report all baby news as fact, dress you in all the coolest clothes and in all the right sizes, never change anything you ever write without your permission, buy movies for you and your friends to watch with lots of popcorn and candy, and get you where you are supposed to be and at all the right times, places, concerts, and events. Heck, mommy will also let you eat fast food on occasion and have them make it your way! I vow I will strive to be the coolest mommy on earth.

Baby Blair or Jackson, very soon I am going to become your mommy. Officially, the greatest, career move of my life. I'm head over heels excited, to the moon and back!

So, little one... When do I start already?

CHAPTER 52

A Huge Thank You to Daddy!

Asher my beloved husband, it's no mystery, nor a secret, why I quickly fell deeply in love with you. I became weak as I felt and heard the sound of my heart falling. Since the first day we met, you've made my life sparkle and glow with infinite happiness. You've made me feel and understand all those corny, clichéd, romantic words written by celebrated poets to be true. My darling Asher, you are the love of my life, and this love is extraordinary. My love for you is everlasting and imprinted securely within my soul. I burn for you! As if that weren't enough, you have brought to my world another great love and the most astonishing perfect gifts of awe, our child and becoming a family. This gift of a new soul defines the meaning of life. How can I possibly thank you for this heavenly wondrous majesty of birth? The miraculous royalty of life that God, you, and I together have created. We are now united for all eternity through one little person. It's astonishing how two souls became one, and as one soul we've manifested a baby, and made an "Us!"

I am pregnant bursting with emotions and feelings. Literally, bursting! Thank you, Asher, my luv, to the far corners of the universe and beyond:

- For your nonstop patience and empathy, tireless encouragement, your undying friendship, continuous perseverance, and for keeping the *"wowmance," alive and sizzling.*
- For tenderly putting up with 9 months of countless, and at times, ridiculous, pregnancy dramas. For supporting me with loving, strong shoulders and humor. You surely helped me enjoy our pregnancy. Lovely how through it all, expecting little Darious or Rowen, brought us even closer together than we already were. I appreciate and I'm quite sure (though you never once complained) there were many times when you felt as if you were on the outside looking in. Perhaps feeling denied, overlooked, or neglected. For that, my love, and

A HUGE THANK YOU TO DADDY!

for my behaving very self-absorbed through the process, I'm sorry.
- For holding my hair like a BFF as I vomited with morning-day-and-night sickness.
- For constantly making me laugh, and more crucial, making me laugh at myself.
- For rushing out, all hours of the day and night, in search of my outlandish, crazy, irrational, and ridiculous cravings without being angry or grumpy. A huge wow there!
- For lying *right to my face* that I was never bitchy, jealous, or emotional! That acting performance alone earns you a nomination for sainthood, or at least an Oscar.
- For hours massaging my feet, belly, back, while pretending to ignore my icky feet.
- For being thoughtful and involved with all the baby decisions and plans. Staying up nights talking about the baby and listening to my complaining, with sweet empathy.
- For helping me off floors, couches, chairs, beds, tying shoes, and shaving my legs.
- For putting together (by yourself) the entire nursery, and for dealing with all of the nonstop *"Just one more thing,"* extras with wit, cute sarcasm, and whimsical playfulness.
- For cooking, barbecuing, and bringing home endless dinners with a brave smile.
- For spending every pregnancy moment you could with me, creating happiness.
- For eagerly coming to all the birth and breastfeeding classes with true enthusiasm.

- For putting up with the 1000s of my messy pregnancy projects without protesting.
- For examining, contemplating, and rejecting over a million baby names together, and for understanding why we still haven't been able to pick a single one out yet. Eeks!
- For always being kindhearted, caring, and helping out without ever being asked to.
- For all of your flattery. Or shall I say *little white lies?* For telling me how beautiful I am, and how adorable my baby bump is in a sincere way, persuading me to believe you.
- For being so damn hot, overly sexy, and having the best abs and butt. Which, FYI, is entirely irrelevant. I just thought I'd see if you were paying attention. True though...
- For going out, all by yourself, to buy tons of amazing, adorable gifts for our baby.
- For being excessively happy, delighted, and utterly thrilled about having a baby.
- For spending our date nights reading baby books and watching baby videos. Even more so, because it was your idea! By the way, you never fooled me... What a guy! I saw you constantly hiding your glass of wine so as not to make me suffer from wine envy.
- For loving me, being attracted to me, and still wanting sex with me. Even, after all our pregnancy has put you through, and becoming this waddling girl you didn't marry.
- For eating my bizarre cravings right along with me. It made them taste even better.
- For being understanding, loving, and thoughtful, more than any pregnant husband has ever shown. It's remarkable how

A HUGE THANK YOU TO DADDY!

faithfully encouraging you've been, telling me such things like, *"Honey, you got this,"* whenever I was insecure about becoming a mom. For validating me... *"Honey, you must be exhausted,"* and *"I can't even imagine what you're going through."* Your inspiring words, *"Honey, you're remarkable. I'm so proud of you. I love you to pieces!"* Asher, you've been more astonishing than I ever hoped you'd be.

- Finally, for making baby and me the center of your attention and universe. Realize that I know and appreciate the millions of special things you do for me and for being you.

Sharing this experience has made me love and admire you even more if that is at all possible. Our love is now deeper and has been rekindled. Not that it needed to be. This entire journey has reminded me of what a magnificent man you are. Which, by the way, I already knew! You made being pregnant easy. Well, that's a big lie! Let's just say easier? Thank you for being excited with each baby kick and everything we jubilantly did getting ready for our baby. Thank you for your timeless love and for being an amazing husband.

It's funny, all the things we hope to achieve or attain, believing they are vital and important, like chasing dreams, being successful, affording possessions, and trying to get so much out of life, all seem rather trivial now. Soon-to-be-baby, you've taught us what is most important in this world. And that is life itself! Giving birth to you will be the most astonishing thing I will ever do. On your birthday, daddy and I will be born again as well.

ROBIN ROTH

Oh, And Asher, love of my life, father of my child, however grateful I am to you, (*And I Am!*) to be clear, "No and No again." Your wonderful mom or dad *may not* come into the labor room, call, or text during the entire birth. In addition, no coming to the hospital *at all,* until *after* baby Mozart, Celine, or Streisand is born. Period! Thanks so much for handling this sensitive dilemma. And, good luck with that, too! Love you, babe.

CHAPTER 53

What Mommy for Sure, Knows for Sure!

My Precious baby, Socrates or Simone de Beauvoir... I consider it imperative and I am compelled to make my little, "What I know for sure, for sure, bible of wisdom" as a gift to you before you arrive. However, please note, though these great pearls of knowledge are solely my truth, beliefs, thoughts, views, and sagacity of life, they don't necessarily have to be yours. Nevertheless, you won't appreciate most of them until you are much older. So hopefully, whether I am with you for many years to come, or not, I want you to know my personal philosophies about life. After all, be aware having to hear these philosophical insights at this juncture is entirely your own fault! Really, baby Aristotle, Confucius, Iris Murdoch, or Hypatia, we both know you brought this all on yourself! Since, *"You Are Overdue,"* we've got plenty of time for mommy to share with you my wisdom from my vast lifetime of experiences. I repeat, it's completely your fault and beyond my control. But you do realize you can stop all of this at any time!

So let's begin, shall we?

1. I know for sure, you must persistently and relentlessly believe in and strive to achieve whatever it is you desire, want, or need in life. Never stop reaching for your dreams, hopes, and passions. Who cares if other people may think your visions and ideas are silly delusions and fantasies. What gives them the right to judge you, anyway? Ignore them all. Listen to your gut, your inner voice, and not those clueless, green with envy people.

   Do you have any idea how many people thought Steve Jobs and Einstein were idiotic, crazy men, with their far-fetched, ridiculous ideas? Well, as it turned out, most of us are enjoying their crazy, idiotic, ridiculous ideas today! Those negative, aspiration-spoiling, individuals most likely don't have goals and dreams of their own, and are clearly jealous that you do! I say, "The hell with them. Do not give a rat's ass about what *"they* think!" Keep in mind, while reaching for your dreams, aim directly for the stars. Dream big! Think about it. By achieving great accomplishments, you're helping others who cannot do this by themselves. Remember, on your journey towards success, be kind, and don't step on or hurt others to attain your goals. You don't want to harbor regrets. So be fair, honest, compassionate, and conscientious. Moreover, stay dedicated, work hard, and carry on with the greatest of integrity and ethics. "When you believe in your goals and perform better than everyone else, you can be proud that you won fair and square!"

2. My *Cutie Patootie*, I want you to grasp the concept of, "The more you give, the more you receive." Needless to say, on the other hand, don't merely give for the sake of getting anything back in return. For, if you do, you'll miss the entire point of giving in the first place. Simply give all you can from your heart, unselfishly, and without any agenda.

3. Concerning love? Well, now here's where it gets a little sticky... or, perhaps, a lot sticky. I have for sure, come to the conclusion (which is quite hard to do) that you must continually keep an open mind and heart. Honestly, don't worry about getting hurt, because in all seriousness, you most undoubtedly, definitely, absolutely, without a doubt, *Will!* You can't always escape the blissful agony and pain of losing love. But I promise you, win or lose, the risk is well worth the joy of experiencing true love. No doubt, your heart will eventually heal. Note, I said eventually! Go for it and live in the moment.

4. Never lose faith in achieving anything in life! Realize and trust with certainty that **"There's always a way"** to attain what you want, need, and wish for. Dreams really can happen. Envision it,

imagine it, see it, feel it, taste it, believe it exists in your reality, and it shall become your reality. Be the dream! *"There's always a way" because it is true!* Understand it's the journey that makes you grow as a person. It's the journey, not the destination, which teaches us the most valuable lessons. The results make you happy, yes, but the journey makes you flourish in much-needed ways. Never forget... *"There's Always A Way!"* This piece of wis-dumb is neither vague nor open to interpretation.

5. Ultimately, you must learn to never let doubt creep inside your creativity, aspirations, goals, dreams, and so forth. Doubts will destroy your best and most inspirational thoughts and ideas. Don't invite them in, for they will rob you of your visions. Doubts, placed on your visions, are a deadly toxic poison, and a cancer that only aims to obliterate. Doubt or negativity toward anything good can become evil. Successful people, such as inventors, visionaries, scientists, doctors, creators, and artists, never permit doubt to enter through their creative locked doors. Uncertainties and insecurities create death upon imagination, goals, and ambitions. Certainly, you'd never open your doors to death. Imagine that your goals, dreams, ingenuity, and ambitions are your sails. These sails balance and push you through the rough seas of life and drift you toward the serene, calm tides of success, fulfillment, and happiness. Sure, of course, it's fine to hesitate, or have a moment of indecision on a project or an idea. In fact, it can be beneficial, helping you to tweak, and improve your discovery. I know this for sure and lived it. When doing something good, original, and creative, I have no doubts that you should... 'Not doubt!'

WHAT MOMMY FOR SURE, KNOWS FOR SURE!

6. This *Life-Changing Biggie,* I know for sure, for sure. When conflicts arise in all aspects of life (and no doubt they will, Murphy's Law and all) just keep an outlook of certainty. Don't be afraid. Instead of being afraid, tell yourself, *"I'm excited!"* That simple shift changes everything, including the chemicals and endorphins in your body, as well as your outcome. Being afraid brings failure. Being positive and being excited brings success. Tap into it. You'll see the results will astound you! "**I Am Excited!**"

7. Don't surrender to *insecure or nervous feelings*! In its place, when you're in a difficult, anxious position, tell yourself to have a full glass of some major "Attitude!" Follow that word all the way into the depths of your soul. Society admires and respects confident, secure people, even if it's only an illusion. Infusing and focusing your mind on the word *"Attitude,"* will change your whole vibe and ambiance into a confident, secure person. If you can't find a way to cop that *attitude,* of which I am speaking, then fake it till you feel it! You know, say it out loud several times… "Attitude, Attitude, Attitude!" It works!

8. On that note, Maddox or Blakely, I have learned *never* to say or think those two little words, *"I can't!"* Saying "you can't" only guarantees that you won't. Can't, is a dirty and negative word. Because, "I Can, they Can, and, dang it… So Can You!" Typically, most successful people exude confidence, high self-esteem and possess some *"major attitude,"* not insecurity! They are *"excited, not afraid."* They are filled and bursting with, *"I can!"*

9. I absolutely know for sure, for sure, never to judge anyone until you, yourself, essentially walk in his or her Jimmy Choo or Christian Louboutin shoes... Period!

10. I know for sure, for the most part, if you fall in love too hard and too quickly, it won't last! When a candle burns exceptionally bright, while it is beautiful, it will usually burn itself out. Fall in love slowly! Take your time, and no one will ever hold a candle to your love. This lesson, I know for sure, does not apply to love-at-first-sight, like with your daddy and me. As it can happen once in a bright blue comet, baby Constellation or Cosmo!

11. I have learned for sure, and mind you, it took me years to understand, that I am a girl who could never be, or should ever be, conquered, bossed around, taken for granted, or controlled! Whether you are a boy or girl, neither should you! Learn this lesson quickly!

12. Without sounding too shallow or superficial, regarding certain proverbs such as, "The grass is always greener on the other side," "All that glitters is not gold," or "Money doesn't buy happiness," well, I must say, that my "I know for sure, for sure" verdict is kinda-sorta, still out on the likes of those truisms. Right now, for me, it's a toss-up!

13. Moving back on track and what I really know for sure is... When things pile up all around us, it's human nature to get upset, stressed out, and worry from all the pressures and problems of life's daily situations. Like most people, we react, freak out, yell, and get angry at the situation or person causing the predicament. Nevertheless, at that moment, *stop*, and ask yourself this one easy

WHAT MOMMY FOR SURE, KNOWS FOR SURE!

question… "Will I even remember this issue in five years?" I know, for sure, that 99.9% of the time, you won't. So, you know what? In my best Gandhi or "Frozen" advice, "Let it go." Just… let it go!

14. When your caboose of life falls off its tracks, don't bitch and complain. Simply put your darn train-car back on its tracks, as fast as you can. Then, proceed to ring your train's whistle as loud as possible with moxie, courage, attitude, and pizazz! Like our mentors, Lauren Bacall, Nelson Mandela, Mother Teresa, Kennedy, Lincoln, Einstein, Helen Keller, Rosa Parks, Muhammad Ali, Anne Frank, Martin Luther King, and Marie Curie, would do! Fix the problem on your track and continue on. Baby Colombo or Elle Woods, this same principle goes for any decision you make in life. Fix, solve, and reboot with strength, flair, action, and whoop-de-do vigor! Stop the "shoulda, coulda, woulda?" Don't look back and do not waddle in regret. Monday morning quarterbacking is only positive if you are a football coach. If you are, then go ahead and look back all you want.

15. On the regret notion above, I have learned it's reasonable to have regrets from time to time. Moreover, it's completely natural. Yet, how you respond to them… well, that's the important factor. Pick yourself up, dust yourself off, and throw your regrets to the wind or right into the trashcan. After that, go have some fun, eat lots of carbs, drink, be merry, press on, and ride the tide. P.S. you can substitute your own personal fun choices on this!

16. I know for sure, it is crucial to your well-being to acknowledge when it's time to say: "Ta-Ta, Too-Da-Loo, or Ta-Da!" Like, *as in, "Goodbye, Ciao, and Adios."*

17. I know for sure that *amazing fun,* the fun you will remember for the rest of your life, hides deep in the heart's core of spontaneity. Fun is neither overrated nor exaggerated! My little Felicity or Jubilee, make sure you experience massive quantities of it throughout your life. You will be amazed by all the colors that will shine through within your smiles while having fun! You are born alone, and you will die alone. I say, fill all the in-between years with an overflowing abundance of fun, and lots of over-the-top fabulous!

18. It's an important time-saver to recognize and determine when the person talking to you is just serving you a big plate full of "Blah, Blah, and Blah!" Don't stay here too long! Walk away, yadda-yadda, and guilt-free.

19. I know that real growth comes from change. Step aside, get out of your comfort zone and move out of your own progressive way. "Change and grow!" Of course, it's natural and pretty scary at times, attempting to change. You are entering into unknown territory. That's precisely when you need to say out loud, *"I Am Excited and Attitude!"* Stop living in fear of change! Change brings a clean slate. Overcoming our fears makes us flourish. Quoting the wisdom of Star Trek, "Fear of death is what keeps us alive." Now get on the Enterprise and swagger off with that thought, my baby Captain Kirk or Lt. Nyota Uhura.

20. I know indisputably all of the "What if," "Maybe I should have," and "If I only," types of reservations have an ugly way of haunting us all. It's best not to second-guess or give merit to many of them. Don't permit those thoughts to linger around you for any

length of time. It will only create sadness, regret, and confusion. In the immortal words of Cher, "Snap out of it!" So, "What if," "Maybe," and "If only," you just don't go there?

21. I discern for sure, disappointment, failure, and loss are the same rocky roads that lead you right back to eternal success. Persistent sadness, negativity, gloom, and doom are your enemy, roadblocks, and a guaranteed dead end. They are wicked, negative barriers that will keep you from attaining personal joy and lasting happiness. Move on, and next.

22. I for sure know, sometimes you just have to trust in yourself, even and specifically if you don't! Jump into the deep end and take a chance. As in, risk it all. This is where all the magical, phenomenal things materialize. Embrace the unknown places where others are scared to go. Again, believe in the dazzling philosophy of *"Excited with Attitude!"*

23. I know for sure that absolute fulfillment comes from kindness, giving of oneself, sharing, helping others, *and silent charity*. Don't give with any expectations of a reward in return. Just give and be generous. These sentiments alone, baby Jax or Evie, without question, tweaked, enriched, corrected, and aligned my life with remarkable fulfillment.

24. I also know, for sure, as written previously, that friends are the most magnificent gifts in life! It is vital to appreciate that these friendships must be enormously cherished and valued! It's our loyal friends who get us through life's challenges and joys. They stand by our side, with compassion through all of our ups, downs,

laughter, tears, the good and bad times. Please do be a great friend back, Chandler, Rachel, Ross, Phoebe, Joey, or Monica.

25. I know it's imperative and crucial to become the best and the *"YOU-E-EST YOU"* that you can possibly be. Always stay true to yourself! Don't ever change who you are for anyone. Revel and celebrate, you! Recognize you're one of a kind! There is no one like you and no one can replace you! So highly appreciate, rejoice, and value yourself!

26. I know, for sure, that abstract, out-of-the-box thoughts and ideas lead to an explosion of great inventions and discoveries. Reach for them! Don't waste time! Don't wait till later. I must warn you, all the "I will do it later," "One day I'll make it happen," "Someday, when I have more time," "I will get on it tomorrow," won't ever transpire! Escalate the importance of now! *Now* is the time! For later, won't likely ever come to be.

27. I've learned you must discover and genuinely get to know yourself through introspective, wide-open eyes! When you know for sure who, that is, saturate your soul with an, "I absolutely rock attitude of self-love, self-respect, self-esteem, self-confidence, and self-importance!" (And all the other, self-type synonyms.) With humility, of course!

28. Know and grasp all that defines you. You cannot move forward without knowing this.

29. I know for sure you must never take the good times of your life for granted. Yet, however, you must learn from all the bad periods. Which ironically, will make them good as well, in the

end. Appreciate today, everything and everyone in your life! Time is not promised. Don't wait for the possibility of losing anyone to finally show your love and gratefulness. Let your friends and family feel and see how much you love, treasure, and value them! Trust me on this one, Baby-Boo!!! You won't get a do-over on this point.

30. I know and pledge, *I'll Never Grow Old Gracefully!* For that, is what old people do! It's far more fun and interesting staying youthful. Therefore, like a rebellious teen, I'll go down kicking and screaming with gusto, wearing a huge tiara when I'm 100 years young! Oh, frickin' yeah!!! That is unquestionably happening for me, and it should for you, little Katniss Everdeen or Ferris Bueller! It's quite odd how a day can seem to go on forever, but your life passes by in a minute… So, live every second with enthusiasm and passion.

31. I know for sure because of Maya Angelou, *"When someone shows you who they are, believe them the first time!"* This statement, (my favorite quote) conveys pure wisdom that you should pack into your brain and live by! Maya's brilliant insight, profound words, undeniable, life-changing truth can save you much heartache. Remember them…

32. I've always known it's more than necessary to be zany, goofy, silly, and foolish. Try completely letting loose once in a while. Maybe even more often than that! It's so very healthy and phenomenally liberating for "The child within us all." This unconventional behavior is the ground level of exhilarating delight. Be whacky! Go for it, and frequently!

33. Don't hate. If someone hurts you, you must forgive *for yourself!* Hate will only hurt, destroy, and eat *you* up inside, *not them*. I once asked an astonishing Holocaust survivor, "Why aren't you bitter and bursting with hatred? How could you forgive and move on after all of the horrible abuse and evil atrocities which you have lived through?" With a warm smile, she replied, *"My dear, if I didn't forgive, they would have won. Hate and anger would have only destroyed what was left of me, robbing me of any future happiness and accomplishment! I chose mercy and forgiveness. Without hatred in my heart, there was room for me to blossom with victory, love, joy, and bliss. So you see, my dear... I won!"*

34. Okay, for me, this philosophy is the most important lesson of all. I know for sure my soul mate wants my life to be filled with pleasure, happiness, delight, and everything wonderful. Baby Rihanna, Common, Charlize, or Tyler, your daddy is entirely amazing, gentle, and kind. Your mate should be the same and never try to dominate, bully, abuse, control, or rule over you! Even if you learn nothing else from me, please remember, trust, and heed this advice. This is incredibly essential information! There is *no* second option.

35. This is one of my favorites... I know absolutely for sure, to live life completely while you're young, and to live it even grander when you're old! Strive to live to a ripe old age, but die young at heart. This wis-dumb leads to the core of life, and the essence of living life euphorically. Waldo or Salma, life flies by ever so quickly. So, "La dolce vita, baby!"

36. In a relationship, if you don't truly *"Like"* someone, then love is completely worthless, and will never sustain your relationship. "Friendship is the seed level of love."

37. Failure doesn't mean you are broken, and it doesn't indicate a lack of achievement. Failure merely cleanses us and provides another chance to start over and succeed!

38. I have learned, "Saying I'm sorry" doesn't necessarily mean I am wrong. So don't be terrified of saying it! It could end a fight or erase the stress and tension from an argument. Cast your bitter baggage of anger to the wind with a simple, "I'm sorry." *It won't kill you.*

39. Most of all, I know for sure, in the end, you must love yourself and your life as well.

40. I know absolutely for sure, the old adage, "Don't put off till tomorrow what you can do today," is accurate. It's more than an old saying, for later never seems to transpire. It seems every single day life piles more "To-Do things" on our plate. There is always new stuff to do as soon as you catch up with the old stuff! It appears that a permanent, never-ending, "To-Do List" plagues our lives daily! If you have something to do, do it already!

41. I know you will never find love if your heart is closed. "Hoo-ah" that, Mr. Pacino!

42. I know for sure and can guarantee that rushing will always slow you down. If you are late, just continue on as if you weren't. Rushing creates mistakes and winds up taking you more time in the end. Hurrying makes you drop things, neglect

responsibilities, and mess up the work you are doing. Being hasty promotes forgetting something, or worse, God forbid, getting into an accident, that was virtually unnecessary! I often feel the universe intervenes, causing something to happen which makes us late or early, avoiding a potential catastrophe. Alec or Lizbeth, here's an idea... just set 2 or 3 alarms to be safe.

43. I've come to realize, it's better to make the best out of the worst situation, rather than complain about it! Who knows, sometimes the worst situation can turn out to be the best thing that could ever happen. Somehow and in some mystical way, mommy feels like we are all being guided. *"You don't live life... Life lives you!"* You can trust me on that.

44. I know for sure, and it's not just a hunch. From watching everyone around me for many years, I have discovered "Love isn't blind, Trust is!" And isn't *trust* everything?

45. Little Ariel or Prince Eric, appreciate you are special just by simply being you. If the people in your life don't see that, well, then the heck with them. It's their loss. Period!

46. I know the purpose and total summation of a person's life, and how successful they were in living it, is undoubtedly measured by the love of the people they have left behind.

47. I know love doesn't hurt! I repeat, *"Love does not* hurt!" If someone is treating you badly, abusing, hurting, making you unhappy, and when you explain it to him or her, they don't stop this abuse? Trust me, they don't love you. You need to walk away. No... run!

48. I used to believe my fears of getting older derived from pure ego and vanity. Later, when I became an adult, I realized my fears came from losing older people who I loved.

49. I know for sure, little James Bond or Dana Scully, that no one completes you. I reiterate, *"No One Completes, You!"* That is all such mumbo-jumbo Hollywood lingo.
    "You Complete You!" You need to love yourself first. Then, and only then, will you have that romantic, balanced, authentic, secure, swoon-worthy, healthy relationship! Remember, *you* create the music of your life. You are the architect and conductor of your world. Design and orchestrate your opus well, with immeasurable loving symphonic care!

50. It is genuinely impossible to love someone you can't laugh or cry with. True that! Burping, farting, or watching you on the toilet... Well, that's a whole other story!

51. As I previously mentioned, the most insightful, profound fact that I have ever learned in my entire life is... *"Nothing worthwhile in life comes easy!"* This statement is truer than true! Sweet baby Finn or Gemma, most of the struggles you may endure for the sake of great achievements make the rewards of glory all the more special. This is one of the most valuable philosophies I can share with you! It comes to mind, comforts, and helps me through the conflicts that typically arise during anything important I hope to achieve.

52. The one thing I know without any exception is... "The biggest love-hate relationship in life is the dreaded scale!" On that point, why does food have to have calories, anyway?

53. Yes, for sure, we all know that disappointments arise from our failures. Paradoxically, there are those other times when the gift of victory rises through our failures. Just think about all the scientific and medical discoveries that have resulted from failed efforts. Surprisingly, look how they turned out to be the breakthrough and missing link for other cures, inventions, and theories. Thus, embrace your failures and turn them around to your advantage. The moral here, as I have said before, "Don't ever give up!" Ride the wave.

54. I have come to realize, by the time you confidently feel you have finally figured out and mastered life, the rules all change! Life is constantly and relentlessly shifting, and you must keep up and evolve with it. Yes, it's true sometimes life isn't fair. Aha, lots of times, in fact. So what? Don't shrug your shoulders and accept it. Change it. Go make it fair! All the while appreciating, that right is always right, and wrong is always wrong.

55. I know for sure... Not to be jealous or resentful of others. We all have our own paths to follow. Live and be happy with your own life. Honestly, no one has it as great as you think they do! Really, they don't. What I'm saying here is, "Live the best life you can!" Although it is a most difficult thing to do, don't be preoccupied with comparing or judging your life by what others do or have.

56. Keep moving forward. There is no potential in the past or you would still be there! Don't look back. You've obviously learned there is no future in it! Onward soldier!

WHAT MOMMY FOR SURE, KNOWS FOR SURE!

57. I know positively, saying to a loved one, "I trust you," is sometimes a far greater compliment and means more than, "I love you!" Trust encompasses enormous meaning.

58. Baby Hudson or Phoebe, I know beyond a morsel of a doubt that, "Doing the Hokey Pokey and Turning Yourself Around" is not, in any way, what it's all about! Like, in any way at all! Not even one hokey-pokey drop! But still... keep dancing!

59. Don't just reach for the moon... Grab it fiercely until it's yours!

60. I know and I promise you, when you pick your nose in a car, somebody always sees you and says, "Ick, Ewe, Gross, that's disgusting!" You'll always get caught! You're not invisible like you thought when you were 5? So, that's a snotty, helpful, nosey, heads-up.

61. I know that people who constantly look and act abundantly happy, or appear to have it all together, in reality, aren't as happy or together as they seem to be. Don't be envious.

62. I know without hesitation if you judge or gossip about others, for sure others will judge and gossip even worse about you. That's the law of the universe and the 11th commandment. In the end, it seems karma is alive, well, and the biggest bitch of all!

63. If you find yourself facing dark clouds, hit them head-on till they burst and float away!

64. I know from experience, being kind and thoughtful to a person you like is lovely. But to be caring or compassionate to a person you don't like, or one who has really done you wrong, well, that's goodness. Those extreme, selfless struggles of forgiveness

count more than you know. They shift the earth towards grace, light, and a benevolent splash, more...

65. I know realistically, there aren't just two sides to every story. Unquestionably, there is your side and their side. Oh, yes, and the people's side who overheard you, while impolitely, eavesdropping. Let's not forget the friends you discussed matters with. It's vital to realize it's best to be discrete, keeping personal affairs private and to yourself.

66. You genuinely don't know a person until you see them react while angry or upset!

67. I rightly know from past experience, one should not be small-minded and only pay attention to hearsay, rumors, and gossip. In other words, don't rush to conclusions and be so quick to assume or judge wrongly. Find out the real facts and details. "You cannot make an omelet without breaking a few eggs." Realize that you can't create a long-lasting, happy relationship without the truth! The whole truth and nothing but...

68. Try not to foster racist, homophobic behaviors, and ignorant narrow-minded thinking! My point, grow and be more accepting! That goes for hate, prejudice, and bigotry of any kind! God loves *everyone,* or he wouldn't have made us. We are all unique and special.

69. Life is short, maybe shorter than you expect. So use your words. Tell your friends and family how much you love and appreciate them. Better yet, show and remind them often.

70. I know for sure in life, you will sometimes get stuck for answers. You might hit the wall and have trouble deciding what to do or lack fresh ideas. It's normal, and no matter what the situation is, don't worry about doing the wrong thing. The only thing wrong is not doing anything. The bottom line is, "If you don't try new things in life, well gosh, then, you haven't lived your life!" According to Einstein, "A person who never made a mistake never tried anything new!" Sweet baby Nolan or Penelope, don't be that person!

71. If a person treats you wickedly, unkindly, abusively, cruelly, disrespectfully, rudely, harshly, or Yakety, yakety, yakety... Hmm, that is unacceptably not at all acceptable. Opt for door number four and leave. Indeed, don't put up with their snarky, nasty meanness!

72. Don't poo-poo infatuation, puppy love, enrapture, enchantment, smitten, love-struck, or a crush. It's a fabulous start, even if these feelings are fleeting and not "your forever!" If nothing else, it's a magnificent sensation, making you feel blissfully alive while it lasts.

73. I know you must never zone out of your life! It is fundamental to live, control, and guide your existence wholeheartedly. Consume your life with a tank filled with self-love and nurturing warm compassion. Zoning out, no matter how bad things appear, is never the answer. If so, you'll find yourself driving your *"Road Trip Of Life"* (Without Oreos or any snacks) towards a negative dead-end to nowhere. What a big waste of mileage and gas!

74. Try not to scrunch up your forehead or squint your eyes all the time! This will give you wrinkles and lines. FYI, Botox, fillers, etc. hurts like hell. (From what I've heard!) Geez, little Bennett or Tess, pay attention. I'm teaching you *critical* life lessons here!

75. I know it gets pretty damn cold and lonely up there on the moral high ground. Bend a little. Always needing to be right can also be wrong. It's not so fun being cold and lonely.

76. I have come to learn a thing or two about the following phrase... *"That which does not kill us makes us stronger."* Sadly, little one, as ridiculous as that sounds, and as much as I fully hate to admit it, those words of wisdom happen to be true!

77. Here's what I know about rainbows... Don't just look at a colorful rainbow's beauty. Climb it all the way up to the top and over to the other side. Dorothy did and arrived in Oz!

78. When you meet someone you really like, don't pretend to be something you are not. "Be you, completely, from hello!" Otherwise, eventually, you'll grow tired of pretending to be the person you've portrayed yourself to be. Since that make-believe person is not you at all, most likely it will cause this fictitious relationship to fail, anyway. Don't do it.

79. I know positively you should strive to be happy all the time. Even when you're not! If you can't find the *happy within you,* then be an actor and pretend you are happy (AKA, faking it) until you finally believe and feel it yourself! The results are quite astonishing!

80. Don't harp on, talking about your past mistakes. Honestly, nobody wants to hear you complain. Realize it's all your screw-ups and mess-ups that actually make you successful and interesting. They also provide you with a wellspring of fascinating and funny tales to tell at dinner parties. Embrace them. Besides, it's quite healthy to laugh at yourself. Shhh!

81. Little one, too much of anything, whether it's good or bad, is not really a good thing. Balance is the key to life. Have your occasional zeros and tens, but seek a balance. Your highs and lows should balance out at around five. This applies to every circumstance or occasion through all of life's situations, from diet to exercise, work to partying, earning money to spending it, love, anger, all your emotions, and beyond. Just, *"Give Me Five!"*

82. If you love someone, love them well! Love completely, with all of your heart. Don't hold back for fear of getting hurt. Seriously, you most likely *will*. But, gee it's so worth it.

83. Life is bursting and abundant with never-ending good, bad, amazing, and sad periods. Throughout your life, it'll feel as though you're overflowing with nonstop ups and downs. Try to ride the waves instead of fighting them. This will make the ride easier to endure. But never allow anybody to boss you around, push you around, or control you in any way. To ensure happiness, you must stay true to yourself. This advice will never fail you!

84. Change is the only constant in life. So get used to it! To move forward and grow, you might have to break from the past. You needn't forget the past, just move on to the future.

85. Not all heroes wear capes. There are angels among us! And thank God for them!

86. It's significant to understand that some people get angry or belligerent because they didn't get the things they thought they deserved in life. Open your heart to them, too.

87. One last thing I surely do know, and can I get a drum roll, please? Be the author of your life, your experiences, and your future. Your emotions will subtly guide you through your journey, and your perceptions will gently paint your reality. Keep your mind open!

In conclusion, little Kimmie or Jake, I categorically know for sure that mommy totally loves you so big, and will for all eternity. But, your having to suffer through all of this "What I know for sure, stuff" is your own fault! Past-due baby, you had it coming! I'm guessing I've bored you enough by now. Save yourself and simply go into labor. OK?

AND THAT'S WHAT MOMMY KNOWS FOR SURE, FOR SURE...

CHAPTER 54

Another Call from Daddy's Mommy...

"*Hello, Leona dear. My goodness...* we haven't spoken for ages! How's my beloved Asher? Sorry. And how are you feeling?"

"Mom, we spoke three days ago. Everything is perfectly great and on schedule."

"Well, you know me. I never like to meddle. We all understand, it's not my style! I prefer to stay out of things. Regardless, dear, you're awfully late. Aren't you worried?"

"I'm not unusually late, mom. Actually, my doctor says all is fine and dandy."

"Well, I am not so sure I'm comfortable with his dandy judgment. In my opinion, dear, this is exactly what happens when you just lie around all day doing nothing. When expecting in my day, I was constantly busy, moving, and working. The proof, my dear is, Asher was ten days early. Whatever! Surely you know what's best? BTW, aren't you the least bit nervous about becoming a mom? It's not so easy, you know. I hope you're doing major intense research? Oh, one final thing before we hang. Leona, I've decided to cook fresh, healthy meals daily. This way, I'll be prepared to bring food to the hospital when you *finally do decide to go into labor*. Ash works so darn hard, and whenever you're ultimately ready to deliver, he'll be starving. At least he'll have my food to eat. Oh, and if you want to eat too, I suppose they'll be some left over? Leona dear, I don't want you to feel left out. I'll be there throughout your entire labor. I'll hold your hands, support your legs in the stirrups, help you breathe, wipe your forehead, or whatever you need. I'll even cut the cord. You can rest assured and relax, for your devoted mom-in-law will be right by your side, and Asher's. It'll be a fun birthday celebration. I also meant to tell you, your mom and dad don't need to be at the birth. It's unnecessary. I got your back. And, of course, grandpa-to-be will be taking photos and videos, taping the whole thing live. Hey, you'll feel like a working news reporter again! How exciting for you! Leona, there's no cause to be shy about videotaping the birth. You've got nothing Asher's dad hasn't seen before.

ANOTHER CALL FROM DADDY'S MOMMY...

Besides, dear, we all know you aren't modest or bashful. After all, remember, I was at your bachelorette party as you and your friends so masterfully performed and danced on that stripper pole. I do trust that's what they call that contraption these days? Is it not?"

"Um, Mom! Listen, mom, about you guys coming.... Mom, wait! Hello, mom?"

"Whoops-a-daisy, nonsense dear. You don't have to thank us. We're thrilled to be there. Costly flights, cars, and hotels, it's what we're here for. We'll be at all your births! Great, then, it's settled. Hurry up, get busy, and have my grandson already. Bye, tootles!"

"MOM... WAIT!! MOM? MOM? MOM! MOM? MOM! MOMM! MOOOOOM! Ugh!"

Baby Ian or Mia, please feel confident knowing that your mommy is not nervous or worried in the least about becoming a mom. I will reign victorious.

Meanwhile, I'm gonna kill your father. I'll give him 24-hours to fix this mess!

CHAPTER 55

Another Call from Mommy's Mommy...

"*Hello darling, how are you feeling?* You must be exhausted! I'm so worried about you. Tell me your husband, **Ashes,** is helping out with everything?"

"***Asher*** is great, mom. He's a prince among men and my devoted prince charming."

"Yes, and that's exactly what I'm afraid of. Has he been waiting on you, hand and foot? I don't care about the glass slipper details. Is he taking care of you and the baby?"

"Mommy, he is amazing. He has done everything humanly possible throughout my entire pregnancy. For the record, we are happier and closer than ever. To be perfectly honest, mom, I could never have done this without him. I love him with all of my heart."

"Well, good. I'm delighted to hear it. Gosh, you're going to be the best mom in the world. I'm so excited and thrilled for you. Because of who you are, being a mom will be a piece of cake. You were destined for motherhood and will love every sweet mommy moment. So darling, by my calculations, you should be going into labor anytime now."

"Yes, essentially, I should be. Unfortunately, however, I am now a few days late."

"Oh, stop, you are barely even late at all. Leona, you were actually 2 weeks late. Though I confess, I loved having you inside of me for that little extra time. Ya can't rush these things. Just enjoy, stay off your feet with your legs up, and rest. Remember, when the time comes, don't eat anything. It will only make things harder for you during labor.

Regarding your delivery, honey... Daddy and I don't want to interfere or intrude whatsoever, nor get in Prince Charming's way, or yours. This delivery is your miracle day. So, we were thinking, have ***Armando*** call us when you go into labor, just to let us know what's going on. We were also going to suggest that your dad and I should just stay at home and come after your precious baby is born. But, regardless, sweetie, if you would prefer me to be with you, and that is what you want, I would love to be there in the labor room with you. However, we imagine you'd rather be alone with your prince. Whatever you decide is *perfectly, perfect* for us. We'll do whatever you both want. You know that."

"Mom, I love you guys so much. Thank you for understanding. Please, realize this is a very special moment in our lives. So *Asher* and I would really prefer to be alone. You always know what I am feeling. However, the next baby, unequivocally, you are there!"

"Love it. You got yourself a deal, beautiful daughter. Did you pick a name yet?"

"What's the rush? Hah... Nope. Let's talk soon. Promise to keep you in the loop."

"Good luck Leona. You won't need it, for this is your fairytale dream come true!"

"Sweet, you remember. Love you, mommy. Please give my love to daddy, too."

"Will do. We love you more. Now, stay off your feet. Let **Aston** do everything."

"***Asher*** mom. Once and for all, his name is **ASHER**! You're so stubborn. LOL!"

CHAPTER 56

OMG... OMG... Are We in Labor?

Ow, Ow, Ow, Owza, OUCH! We Are!
Owie-Ow, Oh Lord... You're Coming!

"**Asher! OH, MY, GOD! Sweetie!!!!** Asher! Do you hear me? Honey, my water just broke! This is it! Call the doctor and hurry. Let's go! Now! Now! NOW!"

My darling Quinton or Sofia, my thoughts driving to the hospital, have gone wild. When daddy cuts our umbilical cord, and you take your very first breath, know that it will also take mommy's breath away. I used to believe giving birth was my biggest fear. Now, I have come to understand that it is my greatest achievement. I will savor every second of your birth. Well, after the epidural, that is! For goodness' sake and mine, regardless of the redheaded siren coach's doom-and-gloom scenario, labor will be so easy-peasy-breezy!

"Come on, Asher! Drive faster! You're driving like a little old lady. Dammit, Step on it!"

"Baby, you do realize I'm driving precious cargo? But, regardless... Yes, dear!"

"You have such a wise daddy, Ayden, Remington, Landon, Julieta, Madison, Lily, or Alexandra! He totally knows when to shut the F@#!$%and up! I love that about him. For all eternity, I will always reflect that the most magical day of my life is today. The day you are born. Holding you in my arms for the first time in person, as your mommy, will be heavenly beyond my wildest imagination. Wow, imagine that? I'm going to be a mommy!*

"OOOOHHHHH! Asher, are you timing my contractions? Asherrrrr! Are you?"

"Yes, angel. You're doing so great. You're awesome and mighty! You're powerful!"

"SHUT UP! OOOOOUUUUUCHHHH! WTandF%@#*! Shit! Sorry Ash, but it hurts!"

"Of course, darling, as you wish. Love you honey, and I won't say another word."

Milan or Carrington, today, your birthday, the moment you are born, I will also be born! For I've never truly, in the most esoteric sense, existed before your creation. I mean, the woman I am existed, but the mother in me, never before. A mother is something absolutely divine and a blessing to behold. Moving forward, I'll be an entirely different person. Continuing on the topic of mothers, you should know statics confirm, somewhere in the world, every 10 seconds, a woman is giving birth. It's crazy to comprehend how women are responsible for bringing every human being that ever existed into the world. Women created all human life that walks our planet. Think about it for a second? It's astounding! We are all here because of a woman. It's mind-blowing. Not to get political at this agonizing moment, but why again do women earn less pay than men? Just sayin!

Anyway, my sweet angel, my Baby Boo, I have cherished each day and every moment we've been together as one. There isn't a more miraculous feeling in the world than feeling your life within me. I only wish daddy could've experienced this wonder. I giggled all the time while loving every single movement you made. The most rewarding, beautiful feelings I've ever known have come from carrying you. Giving birth, I can only imagine will be my supreme blessing and the purest, most perfect form of falling in love.

"OUCHHHH! Dammit, Asher, just run the frickin' lights and the stupid stop signs, already! Need I remind you, sir... you did this to me! This is all your damn fault. Ouch! Seriously man, drive faster! I can't take it anymore! Like what are you doing, 25 mph?"

"Leona, relax, Luv. We're almost there! Breathe, doin' terrific, you're so amazing!"

Napoleon or Josephine, I can't even begin to imagine the extraordinary euphoria your daddy and I will feel when we meet, and you inexplicably recognize us and our voices in person. Hopefully, you'll be filled with warmth knowing you belong to us.

"Asher, *pluck a duck!* I knew we should've called an Uber. At least they know how to drive. Go faster. With any luck, a cop will stop us and escort us to the hospital!"

"Luv, we're very close now. Only a few minutes away! Umm, Pluck a Duck? Lol?"

Baby Piper or Stephano, I pray your birth won't be too traumatic, scary, or painful.

In closing (and because daddy drives like a turtle) I have 1000 extra hours to tell you one last thing. I pray you'll find love in your life wherever you go, and in everything you do! I cannot wait for you to experience all of life's beauty to the fullest! I want your days to be filled with (no correction), overflowing with laughter, peace, and happy memories to cherish forever! "OUCHHHHH!" *With each day that passes, daddy and I will love you more. No pressure, but you're now our reason and purpose for living. Don't grow up too fast. Indeed, you'll outgrow our laps, but don't ever outgrow our hearts and love for you. No matter how old you get, you'll always be our baby. I fathom this will get very old for you rather quickly. Even though you'll roll your eyes a lot, I promise you'll get used to it.*

"Damn, Asher! Good Lord Almighty, aren't we there yet? Really? Move it. Drive!"

"Flying darling, pussycat, angel face, gorgeous, mighty powerful wife! I love you!"

"Asher, I want you to call the hospital right now! Call them at once. I want you to demand that they bring the epidural outside to the parking lot. Immediately and STAT!"

"But of course, sweetheart! I do believe that is standard epidural procedure and protocol? I will do everything in my power. You're doing incredibly amazing. Breathe."

OMG... OMG... ARE WE IN LABOR?

"Don't make me laugh, Asher, and don't patronize me, either. OUCHH. Oh, Lord!"

Oh, little baby Amber or Kensley, you'll soon be born, and we'll meet face to face for the very first time. Then, they will place your naked body on mommy so we can bond, skin-to-skin. This is the most glorious expression of love, mind, body, and soul that we will ever share, and it is our first. I am drowning in tears, and my heart is beating rapidly with anticipation, just imagining the excitement and pure paradise we will soon experience.

"OUCH! OMG! WTF? Lord almighty, for God's sake Asher, aren't we there yet? Are you kidding me? Give it some gas, rapido, faster. OUCHHH! F@#!$%and*! WTF?"

"We are here sweetie-cakes, snookums, angel face. It's all good now. We're here!"

"No? Then where the hell is my epidural? We're in the parking lot. So where is it?"

"Giving birth is the most spiritual, serene relationship between God and Woman. Together as partners, they bring into the world the stunning miracle of life."

"Hey Jude or Amy, trust me... When you have a baby, don't let your mate drive to the hospital. Call an Uber! The fire department! The police! An ambulance! A pizza, even!"

CHAPTER 57

It's Time!!!!

O-M-Gosh baby, it's time and we still don't have a name for you yet.

Alas, after what seemed like a ten-hour drive, we arrived safely at the hospital. As planned, we finally made it into the home-style birthing room. It's pretty incredible, too. But why is it so bright in here? Are we putting on a show? OUCH! What's going on? I'm soaking wet? How is my water still breaking? So awkward, I'm leaking like a running faucet. "Nurse? Nurse!" Where the heck is she, and more to the point, where the hell is my epidural? OUCH! I've been here now for 10 minutes, so plug me in, Nurse Ratched!

"You're fine, honey. I'm Britney, your nurse. Yes, that's your water breaking and your bloody show, as well! We're going to take phenomenal care of you, so don't worry about a thing. Now, change into this clean, dry gown, opening in the back. OK, honey?"

"Where's my epidural, Britney? You were supposed to meet me in the parking lot!"

"Honey, we don't do epidurals in parking lots. LOL! Who told you we do, honey?"

Baby Boo, in my inside voice, I'm angry and thinking, "Owe, don't *honey me,* lady!"

"Mrs. Robins, your baby's heartbeat is perfect. Everything is going wonderfully.

"It's Leona. Like, great and all, Britney, but where is my damn epidural already?"

"Leona, my darling, my love, sweetheart, they're working on it! It'll be here soon."

Little baby, whatever your name is, if there were ever a time I wanted to claw daddy's sparkling blue eyes out, this would be the time. And, as you can hear, we decided against natural childbirth. I mean, why should we both be in agonizing pain? Mommy ultimately decided to enjoy your birth with daddy, minus the unnecessary pain and stress.

"Asher, dammit, where is Dr. Myers already? Didn't you call him? Where is he?"

IT'S TIME!!!!

"Yes, babe, I did. The Dr. said labor would take quite a while yet. He suggested we go on to the hospital, and when we got settled, to call him. So, Nurse Britney, please call Dr. Myers at once. As you can see, Leona would *really* like to get that epidural, ASAP!"

"Of course, will do, *Mr. Robins*. Regardless, she is only dilated 1 cm right now. So I'm guessing the Dr. might not order it yet. Be patient. Leona, relax if you can, honey!"

"Relax, really? FYI, Asher's a *Dr.*, not *a Mr. and,* stop calling me honey. Order it!"

"Hello, Dr. Myers office. Hold please! ... ... Thank you for holding. Go ahead."

"Yes, hi, this is nurse Britney, over at the hospital in maternity. I'm calling for Dr. Myers on behalf of Leona Robins. She is in labor and strongly requests that the doctor come at once. Mrs. Robins is in a lot of pain. She is upset, and demanding her epidural."

"Hold Please!"

Wow, mommy was pissed. Hold please, again, and twice? Seriously? Is this a prank? Not funny! And just like that, daddy massaged mommy, and for the moment, I calmed down.

This is it, little Amelia or Sanjay. Mommy is in labor for real. You are on your way, and only 8 days, 4 hours and 28 (29, 30, 31) seconds overdue. But who is counting? It is time and I can hardly believe it. Ok, I've got to relax. (Breathe, Leona.) To be fair, how can I relax? We're about to meet you at last. "OUCH! Keep rubbing, Asher. Don't stop."

Listen, Di or Kit, if you're not ready, mommy will understand. There is no rush. It's rather cool you can still hear me and talk to me. I will miss our "Heart to Bump Conversations," greatly. The nine-month mystery of you is going to unfold. Within a few hours (mommy hopes that's all it will be), we will know who and what you are. I can barely control my exhilaration. OUCH! Our beautiful child, we are about to touch you, and see you before our very eyes. It's happening. You're coming. Gee, how I desperately want to kiss you and hold you. To speak to you face to face, to listen to you cry and coo. I'm certain I won't be able to take my eyes off of you. I long to stare into your vulnerable baby eyes, count your fingers and toes, and cradle your tiny hand inside mine. It's all so surreal. I'm anxious to feel your newborn soft skin against mine, to smell your sweet, baby scent, and explain to you tenderly, "Yo, hey kid, I'm your old lady, and I got this!"

OUCH! The realization that you are ready has somehow eased my anxiety and fears of your imminent birth. Mommy is prepared, calm, serene, and relaxed. Little Nora or Legend, that's what's known as, Fake News. "#OUCH! F#%!@K. #EPIDURALME!"

My nameless baby, you're not even here, and yet I'm unable to imagine my life without you. Silly how I can't stop crying and wiping away an ocean of happy, joyous tears of wonder. Looking up, I saw tears raining down your sweet daddy's face, too. He spoke...

"Leona, it's insane how much I love you. You are miraculous for having our baby."

"I Love you more! Asher, you look nervous and pale? You're scaring me. You OK?"

"My angel, don't you dare think of me? It's all about you and the baby. I just hate seeing you suffer. I wish I could take the pain for you. Oh, no! Oh! No! Dammit, to hell!"

"Oh no! Oh, No! Dammit to hell, what... Asher? Tell me. What's wrong?"

IT'S TIME!!!!

"Um, um. Nothing sweetie. Everything's good. It's all fine and dandy. I got this!"

"Don't even think about messing with me right now, dude! You got this... what?"

"Ok, fine... Don't get upset. Stay calm, all right? My mother and father are here."

"Asher, no way! Get um out. I am not kidding! WTF, I thought you already settled this matter. You promised me. Didn't you already explain everything to them? OUCH!"

"I most certainly did. No worries, this is so done. I will be back instantaneously."

"Nurse Britney? *Dammit, girrrrrrrl,* I need my epidural! Hello? You there, Brit?"

"Yes, honey. I'll call one more time. OOPS, I did it again. I honey-ed you... LOL."

"Not funny, nurse Britney Spears. Whatever. Stop, honeying me, and epidural me!"

"OK, my love. (Asher rushes in huffing and puffing) I'm back. It's all taken care of."

"It's all taken care of, what, Asher? God in heaven, please tell me they've left."

"They are *far* gone. No problem Leona. In fact, they may not ever return after what I just did. We actually may never see, nor hear from them again, evermore. I basically banished them. On the plus side, though, they left the video camera. LOL."

"Ha, thank you. I love you. OUCH! OUCH! EPIDURAL, NOW! Nurse Britney!"

"Coming, Mrs. Robins, honey."

"Mrs. Robins is my mother-in-law! I'm Leona, and stop calling me honey! Geez..."

And with that, daddy gave mommy his hand and blurted out... "Hold, Please!"

Together, we laughed. Love that man! "OUCH! Epidural me, Nurse Ratched, Honey!"

CHAPTER 58

Our Very Last Conversation Till We Meet...

My beloved, nameless baby, poor daddy hasn't eaten all day. Darn, his mom was entirely right about this one. I hate when that happens.

"Asher, sweetheart, please go down to the cafeteria and bring something back up here to eat. You are famished. Go, babe, I'll be fine. I mean it. OUCHIE-OUCH! Go on."

"Leona, I'm good. It's all right. You can't be here by yourself. Not for one second."

"Please, honey, it's cool. You have to eat. You'll only be gone for a few minutes."

"You sure? My angel, are you sure? I hate leaving you here alone like this."

"I'm absolutely fine. Just come back quickly, and not like you drove here! Ha-ha."

"Very funny! You're such a funny girl. OK, then. I'll run fast and be right back."

Baby Boo... I purposely sent daddy away because I wanted us to have our very last mommy and baby, "Heart to Bump Conversation," in private and out loud, as usual.

It's Time!

Thrilling to fathom that it is time for real. Well, if the good Lord cares anything about my sanity, that is. It's odd, though. I still feel like a kid, myself, and yet I will be responsible to you forever. No offense, but deep down, the thought of that scares me to my core. Still, life with you will be far more exciting, wonderful, complete, and fulfilling.

It's Time!

OUR VERY LAST CONVERSATION TILL WE MEET...

To think of me giggling as I dress you up in your tiny, blue, baby boy clothes. Or washing your adorable kid jeans, only to find two rocks, four marbles, and a very dried-up frog, jumping out at me. When you're older, driving you and a bunch of boys to a little league game. On the other girly-girl hand, buying pink ruffled dresses and bows, smiling with delight. Imagine taking you to your BFF to have fun playing dolls and dress-up. Later on, for sure, I'll yell at you to "Stop wearing mommy's high-heels and lipstick."

It's Time!

I'm not sure if you've noticed, little Cameron or Micah, mommy hasn't slept very well during the past few months. Because I haven't discovered that cozy, comfortable sleeping position I hoped to find, haunting emotions and feelings of inadequacy have made it quite impossible to sleep. I know it's crazy silly, but I ponder, thinking, what if every time I put your diapers on, they fall off completely? Or, when you cry, will I know how to comfort you and make you happy? Will I be strong enough to nurse you back to health when you get sick without freaking out or panicking? I muse when they say all of this comes very naturally to women. Believe me, baby, no doubt, I am so counting on that to be true, more than you know. If not, I'll seriously need to find out who and where "they" are so "they" can come over and help me. Not the best time to lose confidence in myself.

It's Time!

OMG! I wonder, am I ready? Am I properly prepared? Did I buy enough bottles, toys, pacifiers, burp cloths, blankets, diapers, and unquestionably everything else you'll need? Did I read enough baby books? Did I get qualified baby advice and ask all the right questions? Did I pick the right pediatrician? Did I find the most experienced child care?

Well, as they say, "Ready or not, here you come." You'll be placed in my arms any time now. We'll be clinging tightly to each other for dear life any minute. You'll hear mommy's voice, and soon be able to see my eyes, and hear my heartbeat as you sleep on my chest. How strange this will all feel to you. Warning: When you come out, everything might appear a little bright, too cold, and very noisy. Don't be afraid. Daddy and I will be by your side protecting you and fixing everything so you feel safe. After you're born, you won't have to hear mommy screaming in pain anymore. (Guilt, guilt!) Relief for us both.

It's Time!

After *Nurse Ratched-Honey* calls for an epidural, it will only be a few quick, painless, easy hours, until you arrive. Right, Kermit, Amiyah, Wiley, or Roxie? In case you're wondering, we still don't have a name for you yet. I think we want to see you first to get a better idea. No worries though, we have many names in our "possibilities" file.

It's Time!

As this is our last *"Heart to Bump Conversation," alone together*, I want to thank you from the depths of my heart and soul. Thank you for preparing me for motherhood each day throughout our pregnancy and for your endless patience. For growing without developing any real problems, or scares other than stretch marks and maternity clothes. Thank you for sharing your hiccups, kicks, and reassuring me that your heart was always beating strong within me. All your love, together with mine, has bonded us for life. Sure, I admit, I complained entirely too much. Looking back, I deeply regret that, because the truth is, I loved every second of carrying you. It was a beautiful miracle feeling your life inside mine. Thank you, baby, for our endless, special, fulfilling tête-à-têtes over the past 9 months. You delivered to mommy every single day and night, the heavenly marvels, lessons, wisdom, teachings, guidance, info, and vital knowledge you received from God.

It's Time!

I'd like you to know, I shall profoundly miss our extraordinary, "Heart-to-bump conversations." Of course, we'll continue them in person, but this beautiful gift of ours has been breathtaking and uniquely spiritual. Very otherworldly and magnificent, don't you agree? So baby Reese or Paxton, I will love you today, tomorrow, and till the end of time. No need for any Nostradamus quatrains or secrets to predict this prophecy for you.

It's Time!

And not a minute too soon, may I add! My darling child, this lightning rod of a moment is mesmerizing, and I am trembling with spellbinding, entrancing awe.

"Baby Kafi or Galena, *Shhhhhh! H*ere comes daddy! Lickety-split, see you soon!"

CHAPTER 59

They Don't Call It That For Nothing

Labor:
The process by which a baby is prepared for delivery from the uterus, along with other products of conception... the surrounding bag of

water, the membranes, and the afterbirth (placenta). Additionally, also known as childbirth, or the process of delivering a baby and umbilical cord from the uterus, to the vagina, to the world. During the first stage of labor, which is called dilation (AKA "Are you kidding me? I can't do this!"), the cervix fully dilates to a diameter of about 10 cm - 2 inches. Or big enough to fit a huge watermelon!

Also, See... Pain!

Pain: is defined as an *"unpleasant feeling"* conveyed to the brain by sensory neurons. Or, in *mommy's* more accurate definition, "Make it stop! *Fand*%#$*! Ouch! Help, get it out!"

Substantially absurd and not a drop of truth regarding that, *"Unpleasant feeling"* lie. Not to sound judgmental, but how full of crap can a definition be? Wow, such a web of lies. There isn't an ounce of room left for spiders to fit in. Mommy would define pain with tear-filled eyes, shrieking... "OUCH, there is no way I can do this. I'm suffering from untold anguish, torture, and a resounding WTF!" More to the point... Where the hell is my epidural? *"Ooops, you* didn't *do it again, Britney! You joking? Call my doctor, now!"*

So then, baby Owie or Owza, let's talk more in-depth about labor. *Labor* is a cute little word used to describe... going to work, the act of working, or the notorious act of childbirth. This is also quite feasibly the most ridiculous, laughable understatement ever written or expressed in any modern language. Who, I dare beg the question with great animosity and hostility, (And I hate begging anything, let alone a question, so thank you for that scribe-person) came up with the definition for this miraculous act, this undisputed miracle, and the pièce de résistance of unbearable agony, to officially be called "labor?" Evidently, no one who's endured the enchanting, barbaric, agonizing pain of childbirth.

LABOR?

You can be sure this has nothing to do with 9 to 5, lunch, coffee breaks, or being made to sit on the boss's lap of bribes and harassment. Even Google's synonyms are more honest.

LABOR?

What I'm trying to say... this isn't a realistic description of the labor experience. It's kind of like expecting to get your teeth cleaned and ending up with 10 badly impacted root canals. Or, an associate asks you to watch her huge dog for a few days, and after a week, you find out she's left town. Or, being told you're required to babysit, and you end up watching the total high school population for a month. This definition is false advertising!

Baby Boo, I don't want to scare nor burden you, but there are many more precise and up-front ways to describe or define *labor* properly. As in and for example:

Brutal, arduous, difficult, grueling, conflict, battle, or struggle? Or Paul McCartney's song, "Birthday" but with the added screaming, "Ow-Owie-Ow." And also, like Linda Ronstadt's very oldie-goldie, "Hurt So Bad." Ixnay on the word, labor. Just call it, *PAIN!*

"Dr. Smith, Dr. Smith, the expectant mother, has arrived. She's dilated 6 cm, and contractions are 4 minutes apart. She's yelling lots of 4-letter-words in filthy formations."

"Fine Nurse Hazel, prepare her for... *PAIN.*" See? Simple, direct and to the point!

Keep in mind there are many descriptions and various types of pain...

There is the "Yowch! I cut my finger, opening the coffee can," pain.

There is the "Ouch, ekes! I slit my tongue, licking some envelopes," pain.

There is the "Wowza, crap, F@#%and^$)@*C, I think I broke my leg," pain.

There's the "My sleeve got caught in the bakery bread slicer, and cut my arm off," pain.

There is the "Oh My God, after surgery pain," requiring vital opioid assistance.

There is also the annoying "Oh, dammit, I cut my legs shaving. I'm bleeding and I should have used the expensive, new improved, razor and shaving cream set," pain.

(Sidebar: to be straightforward, I haven't been able to shave my legs for over 5 months.) Note, these pain examples can often be difficult to tell apart. Of course, childbirth pain is a whole different ball game, hitting the Ouch-ball way out of the labor and delivery park.

It's odd, because mommy is in so much pain (*an unpleasant feeling!*) during this so-called process of labor, that I have the urgent, unimaginable desire to scream mean things at daddy. Such shocking, awful, terrible things I've never imagined saying to him since the day we met. I wanted to, no I needed to, yell things at daddy using dreadful bad language, and wicked curse word combinations. Combinations so obscene, I have never created or even thought of in my life, let alone screaming them at poor daddy, of all people. (Reflecting back, I may have created a few of them in the far corners of my mind towards my demon brother Jeff and catty Colette.) I'm

LABOR

sure that you can hear me now, hollering X-rated, erotic, horrible, dirty, nasty words at daddy. Porn-ish words I've never spoken. Well, out loud anyway. Although I'll admit some of those nasty words, I did actually enjoy very much *doing* with daddy. Of course, and needless to say, got me in this 'pre*dick*ament' to begin with! I'll explain this in more detail when you're around 40.

When I calmed down and returned to the reality happening before me, I heard (and maybe you heard too) your sweet, loving daddy saying cute things to mommy...

"Keep breathing honey, Hee-Hee-Hee-Whoo. Don't stop, angel. You're a labor Rock-Star! Hee-Hee-Hee-Whoo. Doing great. I love you, Leona. Hee-Hee-Hee-Whoo!"

To my now struggling, torture-ridden, Raggedy Ann body, daddy's voice was like hearing the sound of sharp, pointy porcelain nails clawing slowly down on a chalkboard.

That was when mommy, again and once and for all, sweetly talked to daddy.

"Ash, I swear to God, if you don't, #@#$^andand^@*)+$@%#, fricking' get me my epidural right this second, I want a divorce. Dial my lawyer or get the epidural Dr. now!"

I never saw daddy sprint that quickly before. I actually didn't realize he could run that fast. I do believe he clocked and beat an Olympic record. Good for him, I'm proud.

When daddy returned to our room, tiptoeing on fragile eggshells, and gasping for breath, he spoke timidly, "Ok, babe, the Dr. is coming in *any second* with the epidural."

Waiting for that, *any second and* begging between contractions (another inadequate term), the only comments I managed to stammer out at daddy, using no profanity, were...

"Why did you do this to me?"

"I want my lawyer!"

"You'll never be allowed to touch me again! Anywhere on my body! Like, ever."

"Keep that damn, dangerous thing away from me, from now till the end of days?"

"I thought you loved me. You caused all of this!"

"Next kid, pal, you're having it! Pregnancy, stretch marks, labor, pain, and all!"

"I want a vacation! As in the entire European Continent, Africa, Tahiti, and Egypt, too!"

"Stop looking at me! Why are you staring at me that way? Stop gawking at me."

"Hee-Hee-Whoo, nothing. I want drugs. Now! Now! Now!"

"Quit saying I'm beautiful. Don't you see my eyes bulging out of their sockets?"

"So you know, Asher, that *any second* response time of yours, well it's way past up!"

And just like that, the epidural cavalry, my epidural doctor, my new god, and hero entered the room. As he approached, it was as though the heavens opened up. The room glowed brightly. I heard angels flapping their wings, cherubs singing, golden harps and all.

To my utter surprise, befell a brilliant miracle. The epidural was astonishing and took away my pain dramatically. I don't know how it worked so fast, but I was a grateful, happy mom-to-be. The pain now was a breeze in comparison. Mortified and ashamed, I realized everyone was gazing at me with disgust. Good news, though, the devil-incarnate I was temporarily housing, flowed out from my body. Labor had become a fun, beautiful birthing experience. It makes no sense why any woman would refuse an epidural? Damn, daddy's mom was right, again. I'll have to admit that to her, too. Ugh, it will never end!

It suddenly dawned upon me at this pain-relieved moment that perhaps a befitting and humongous apology was required for all I had disgracefully screamed at your daddy.

"Asher sweetheart, my Boop-De-Doop... Um, honey-cakes... My hero, I'm, a..."

"Leona, get real. You don't have to say a word. Stop, I totally get it. I love you!"

"Ash, you realize I didn't mean a single word of it, right? It was the pain talking."

"Of course, Luv. However, some of it was downright naughty, very erotic, and sexually tempting. Seriously, we must try some of it in the future. Most of it, in fact!"

Together, we spontaneously roared with thunderous laughter. Even Nurse Ratched, honey, giggled. Daddy is such a forgiving person. As for me, I'd still be fuming. I mean it. Pain or no pain, I don't believe a meek "I'm sorry" would work here had daddy talked to me that way. This would surely warrant a, LV-type purse, an 18-karat gold necklace, bracelet, or ring type of trinket, my dilating baby Stone, Sapphire, or Emerald.

Little one, mommy was forewarned and learned rather quickly that all modesty goes right out the window during labor. I'm saying all humility and shyness. Ok, there are crowds of people running in-and-out of the room. All the while my pregnant breasts, stretch marks, and private parts were on stage, completely exposed for all to see. On stage, like at a sold-out concert. I felt like a naked giant float in a parade. The mortification and indignity didn't just end there. There was poop, vomit, farts, blood, and amniotic fluid gushing out of me. Nurse Britney Ratched, honey chimed in, trying to comfort me with her nursing-101 bedside manner, and kindness classes. "It's quite normal, Leona, honey. Don't be embarrassed or uncomfortable. It's all a part of this glorious birth progression."

By now, mommy didn't care anymore. I was out of unbearable pain, and that was all that mattered. However, I felt awful for daddy having to witness all the horrible yuck!

I totally wouldn't blame him baby, Blueblood or Fartacus, if you never have a brother or sister. What a remarkable man, smiling away, pretending not to notice all the grossness.

While daddy and I watched the heart and contraction monitors, focusing on each contraction, I couldn't imagine going through this without an epidural. At that moment, I immediately thought about our childbirth classes, and couldn't help but wonder how all the other women were doing with their deliveries? I hope they opted for the no-brainer, easier epidural and not the "natural childbirth, Hee-Hee-Hee-Whoo," ridiculousness that didn't work at all. It made all the difference in the world. It turned your birthday journey from a nightmare to such magnificent joy, which we will remember and cherish always.

Between contractions, I touted (in a bitchy tone) "Asher, I knew something was fishy about that Siren, redheaded teacher. Obviously,

LABOR

she didn't explain labor correctly. Not one iota. We were very ill-prepared for all of this. I had her number from the moment I laid eyes on her. *So Hee-Hee-Whoo, you, lady!* Asher, I'm not jealous (as you clearly know) but thinking about it, our birthing bitch, I mean coach, (or whatever her name is) wasn't really pretty or gorgeous at all. Right, Asher? Asher. ASHER! Did you hear me?"

"Um, no. No, honestly, she wasn't at all beautiful, my darling? She pales to your beauty on your worst day. You are, without a doubt, the most gorgeous woman in the world!" Evidently, little one, daddy was full of S#@!and%*T. But, come on, the man is no dummy. Still, he looked exponentially relieved, having given the correct *mansplaining* answer. I simply laughed adoringly at his perfectly suave, polished cleverness. Although, when Nurse Ratched, honey laughed, I sent her one of my perfected, snarling, dirty looks.

In fact, my very best, well-practiced, resting bitch face. Naturally, I followed that up with a wink, a smile, and a "Thank you, Britney." At this point, I owed her that much, at least.

Little one, I believe you can still hear me. Not certain, but I will continue talking to you, anyway. So even after 10 hours of labor, daddy, you, and I are surprisingly having the best time. I hope you hear us laughing and happily telling you stories while we are enjoying the whole birthing process, without most of the pain. Don't get me wrong. It's not a walk in the park, but substantially an easier stroll with anesthesia. This is such an amazing, thrilling celebration of birth, more fabulous or memorable than we hoped for.

Baby Cassidy, Shane, Dillon, Blaine, Robin, Dorothy, Blair, Cosimo, Lavender, Asia, Sacha, Tamar, or maybe, Willow... I think we are getting really close to you being born because everyone's telling mommy to push now. It probably sounds like a lot of people shouting at me, from your perspective. Blimey, a woman's work is never done?

I only wish you could see your daddy's beaming face right now. He is currently the first-string, birthing cheerleader with his angelic smile and sparkling dreamy, ocean-blue eyes, which I could swim in forever. I know, gag me! Goodness, what a profoundly exquisite man he is. What makes him further desirable and wonderful is how he shines without any egotistical, sanctimonious attitude. Seeing him, watching you come into the world with love and excitement in his heart, inspired and motivated me to push. With his enchanting oasis of tranquility, he stood in all his glory, cheering me on...

"Great Leona, push, push harder. Harder, don't stop. You're doing great! Oh my God, I see the baby's head. The baby is crowning, babe. This is the coolest thing in the world, ever. Like ever!"

It's rather funny because all the cheering that mommy heard was far different from what you might've heard, little Whoopi, Triumph, Spirit, Cheerio, or baby Hooray.

"Give me a P. Give me a U. Give me an S, and an H... Push um out, waaaaay out!"

"Be aggressive, B-E aggressive! B-E-A-G-G-R-E-S-S-I-V-E... Be aggressive!"

"Big G Little O... Go, Go, Go! Big G Little O... Go, Go, Go!"

"V-I-C-T-O-R-Y... Victory, Victory, Vic-tory!"

LABOR

With daddy's satin voice and his symphony of expressions, he praised me with boundless encouragement, "Great honey, keep pushing! Push harder. Bear down. Don't stop. You're doing amazing. I am so proud of you! God, I love you. Our baby is coming." As I bellowed a cacophony of horrible sounds, piercing from my throat, your sweet daddy wiped the sweat from my brow, swept his finger across my lips, gently stroked my head, and then gave me the most loving kiss I had ever known in my entire life. "Push Leona, sweetheart, keep going, push hard! Push, push, push, my Luv!"

Then, sweet daddy tenderly kissed away from my eyes, the happy, excited, overflowing tears of birth. And at that intense, overwhelming moment, I took a long pregnant pause...

So, I thought... Hmm? He wants me to push, does he? Well, all right then. I couldn't think of a better time or a more perfect opportunity that I would ever have again, to ask my beloved for the princess-cut diamond ring and the Porsche Targa sports car I've always dreamed of! And, before I could demand my obnoxious, foolish request...

"OM... OMG... OMG... OMG.. OMG... OMG... OMG.. Oh, My Godddddd!

OK, my angel here goes... Whether Pink *or* blue, we love you! #HeartToBumpforever!

Have a smooth trip baby Princess, Porsha, or Avi. Your ETA is now. See you in a sec!"

CHAPTER 60

I Made a Wish... and You Were Born!

Nurse Britney Ratched, honey, who stayed by our side throughout the entire birth, excitedly screamed, shouting at the top of her lungs...

"Oh My Goodness, your precious bundle of joy is gorgeous! Absolutely perfect!"

But then... came utter silence for what seemed to be forever. Frightened to death, I questioned, crying uncontrollably... *"What's wrong? Dr. Myers, I beg you! Talk to me!"*

"Nurse Britney, why isn't my baby crying?" I pleaded frantically, "Asher, why is our baby totally silent? What's the matter?" Nurse, our baby is not crying. Tell me what's happening?" Paralyzed, unable to breathe, my heart stopped beating. It felt like hours had passed as I waited for answers. What is wrong? Someone explain! What's going on? Oh, God. NO! No! No, God! Weeping wildly, "Asher, the baby is quiet. Is our baby? Gone?"

And just like that... came the most luminous sounds I will ever hear in my life! "Waaaah! Whaaaaah! Waaaaah! Whaaaa! Whaaaaa! Waaaaah! Whaaaa! Whaaaaa!"

"Leona, the baby is 100% fine and healthy. Our nameless angel is crying and bellowing like an opera singer." With happiness and grateful joy, daddy gave *us* a big hug and kiss.

"Oh, thank you, God!" My tears of relief and bliss had cleansed my soul for all eternity.

Nurse Britney immediately carried you over to mommy and gently placed you in my arms, skin-to-skin, enthusiastically and sarcastically stated, giggling, "Hold, Please!"

Daddy and I cried with grateful laughter as we saw your angelic, beautiful, innocent baby face for the first time. We were bedazzled by your perfection, and we simply could not take our eyes off of you and your magnificent splendor. As you lay on mommy's diminishing bump, daddy lovingly held your tiny hands while uncontrollable tears ran down his cheeks. We were in such awe we actually forgot to ask if you are a boy or a girl.

And then, Doctor Myers spoke extremely excited with glee!

"It's a... ... ...

It's a... ... ...

It's a... ... ...

Congratulations, you two!

You are the proud parents of a beautiful baby... ... ..."

www.ingramcontent.com/pod-product-compliance
Lightning Source LLC
Chambersburg PA
CBHW041436060526
44119CB00108B/483/J